THE GREAT ORATORS OF THE REFORMATION ERA

LUTHER · CALVIN
KNOX · LATIMER
ZWINGLI · FENÉLON

GH
www.gideonhousebooks.com

The Great Orators of the Reformation Era

Martin Luther, John Knox, Hugh Latimer, John Calvin, Francois Fénelon

Published by:

Gideon House Books
2137 Ash Grove Way
Dallas, TX 75228
ISBN-13: 978-1-943133-62-8

Also from Gideon House Books

Missionary Methods: St. Paul's or Ours? by Roland Allen

Humility: The Beauty of Holiness by Andrew Murray

The Essentials of Prayer by E.M. Bounds

Till He Come by C.H. Spurgeon

Sovereign Grace by D.L. Moody

God's Light in Dark Clouds by Theodore Cuyler

A Church in the House by Matthew Henry

Indwelling Sin in Believers by John Owen

Secret Power by D.L. Moody

Thoughts for Young Men by J.C. Ryle

The Divine Liturgy of St. John Chrysostom

A Study on Dispensationalism by A.W. Pink

Prevailing Prayer: What Hinders It by D.L. Moody

The Duty of Pastors by John Owen

The Expulsive Power of a New Affection by Thomas Chalmers

According to Promise by Charles Spurgeon

The Resurrection: A Symposium by Charles Spurgeon

The Acceptable Sacrifice by John Bunyan

Find these titles and more at

www.gideonhousebooks.com

Contents

PREFACE

THIS volume, as was its predecessor in the World's Orators Series, is devoted to the oratory of the pulpit. The exclusion of secular oratory results from necessity, for during one thousand years the World's Orators were, with rare exception, ecclesiastics.

The term "Reformation Era" is construed in its broadest meaning, and the volume begins with Wyclif and ends with the famous Court Preachers of Louis XIV. This extension of the scope of the volume is justified by the arrangement of the remainder of the series.

The Editor-in-Chief acknowledges his indebtedness to the learning of the Associate-Editor in this volume, Joseph Cullen Ayer, B.D., Ph.D., who has, in addition to valuable general assistance, contributed several important translations.

The Editors call attention to the portraits accompanying the text. The illustrations, except those especially noted, are authenticated portraits of the great orators whose names they bear.

HISTORICAL DEPARTMENT,
JOHNS HOPKINS UNIVERSITY,
JULY, 1899.

THE SERMONS OF THE REFORMATION ERA

ST. FRANCIS DE SALES points out, in one of his sermons on the gift of the Holy Ghost at Pentecost, the significance of the fact that the visible manifestation of the Spirit's presence took the form of fiery tongues. He sees therein an indication of the large part that the tongue would take in the work of the Christian Church. The idea, however far-fetched and fanciful it may appear at first sight, is highly suggestive. The power of the Christian Church has always been that of persuasion, and its moments of weakness have been those unhappy times when it has been tempted to abandon the method given at Pentecost and has proved itself unable to resist the temptation. The Church grew and attained its position of authority in the Roman world solely by the power of the spoken word. It was the greatest triumph of oratory that the world has ever seen, however far that oratory may have departed in form from the oratory of the schools.

The Protestant Reformation is the second great triumph of the spoken word in the history of the Christian religion, and this can be said without reference to the truth or falsity of the multitude of conflicting doctrines that were preached by the various parties of the Reformation. Men will always differ as to the justification for the schism from the ancient Church, as to the abuses which have been alleged as the cause of the movement, and as to the validity of the claim made of restoring a purer and more evangelical form of Christianity. In the history of oratory, nevertheless, the Reformation remains the greatest event since the days of the Fathers.

In studying the preachers of the Reformation period, it is impossible either to understand their work or to recognize their comparative merits without viewing them in connection with the people among whom they worked and the great movement in which they took part. For the preacher and the people are bound up together most intimately, so that there is no more accurate test of the depth of the religious life of a community or an era than the sermons that are delivered in public worship. The preacher may indeed be the prophet, but he is still more. There is a certain priestly function which he is called upon to exercise: he represents the people in their worship. He is an indication of the depth of the religious culture of the people who assemble week after week to listen to him, not merely because in many cases he is the only religious instructor they have, but also because his message is to a very marked degree influenced and shaped by the influences that affect his auditors. That which they feel imperfectly, he feels in fuller force. He may be at times a leader; he may be able to mould the minds of his hearers; but he is rarely able to rise far above those to whom he ministers.

These considerations hold good in respect to the great preachers of the Reformation. Some of them have been able to take a position of leadership so pronounced that the movements with which their names have been associated have seemed to be their own creation, and the power whereby they produced their great effects to be their unaided eloquence. There have been at all times men of commanding genius who have been associated with the revolutions in the history of the world. There has been at the same time, however, a long preparation, not clearly seen, that not only produced those men but also formed those circumstances that made their work possible. In the story of great discoverers Columbus enjoys a well deserved preeminence. But the discovery of America was by no means dependent upon the happy inspiration of his genius. In the great convulsions of religious thought that filled the sixteenth century the names of Luther and Calvin stand forth as leaders and even as originators. But a more careful examination of the history of the times shows a large number of men, independent of one another yet all bent on much the same task. Everywhere forces were at work producing approximately the same results. These considerations must be borne in mind in estimating the preachers of the Reformation period. They have attained in the popular imagination a prominence that disguises their real position and does injustice to their work. For they were great preachers, not so much in that they were orators or disciples of Chrysostom or Gregory, but in that they were able to give expression to the thought that lay in men's breasts, and to arouse to consciousness the spirit that was as yet dormant.

In studying the eloquence of the Reformation it is necessary first of all to note those causes which produced that great revolution in thought. There were in general three causes which gave opportunity to the orator to appeal to deep feeling. These were: the consciousness of nationality; the moral revulsion from the unsettled and degraded state of the Church; and a quickened religious feeling. These causes were not confined to any one part of Europe, they did not of necessity lead to any schism in the Church, still less did they tend to bring about a revision of the theological systems. These results were dependent upon circumstances which were for the most part local, and were particularly influenced by the difficulty under which men of all parties labored, whether in dealing with opposition to an established order or with criticism of official acts.

And here it is well to add that men are not for long successful in inculcating the principles of religion and virtue when they themselves are not sincere. The advocate may for a while conceal his sentiments in a case, but he cannot do so for a lifetime. Men may have their personal failings and act from mixed motives and often fall before temptation; but the first qualification for continuous success in pulpit oratory is probity of character. Then again it is not natural for men to listen to appeals to the deepest sentiments of religion for any great length of time unless there is some response in their hearts. They may have very erroneous conceptions of religion and imperfect understanding of the dogmas on which their religion is based, but there is quite enough of interest in the world to render tiresome and ineffective the continual religious appeal that awakens no response. Again, the divine authority of the Church, and even the strongest claims as to the necessity of belonging to the visible Church, are by no means dependent upon the entire freedom of the Church from abuse in every age. The recognition of failings on the part of those who in times past have been concerned in the unhappy religious difficulties that have rent the seamless robe, is one of the unpleasant and even painful duties of the historical student.

The various reforming movements that at last culminated in the upheaval of the sixteenth century were not in the first instance attempts to alter the theology of the Church, but were parts of that great development of the consciousness of nationality and race that was connected with the breaking up of the mediaeval theory of the Holy Roman Empire. In the days when that dream of a united Christendom held the States of Europe loosely bound together, and the united action of Western Europe made that union of nationalities seem a reality, the conception of a Church that was as widespread as that Empire was not only easy to accept, but was the only natural conception of the Church. Where men held to that thought of the political union of Christendom, there they had no difficulty as to the union of the Church. Their thought was moulded so as to accept it. But with the rise of a distinct national consciousness,—such as can be traced in England earlier perhaps than elsewhere, partly on account of its early consolidation and isolation,—there came a restlessness and opposition to the Roman system, which was not understood or judiciously treated by the ecclesiastical officials. Theology might point out with convincing clearness the necessity of submission to the universal pontiff, but there was always present a negation to the conclusions of that theology. A correct understanding of the relations of the national consciousness to the Church need not have led to hostility, but in an actual fact it did so lead. This was the basis of the Wyclifite revolt from the Church; the breach with the traditional system did not necessarily involve a breach with the theology, but as an actual consequence the theology was in many essential points rejected. The same course can be traced in the other attempts at reformation which were undertaken with more or less apparent justification.

When the reforming movement began to take form on the continent under Huss, the same appeal to the instinct and consciousness of nationality was made, and a hundred years later the German Reformation under Luther became a national movement because it appealed to the sentiment that was awakening: Germanic nationality as opposed to Italian domination.

This appeal to a deeply rooted instinct is one explanation of the marvellous effect of the preaching of the reformers. They could never have gained an audience if they had done nothing more than propound a variation of the doctrines of Justification by Faith or Predestination. In later stages of the transformation that was taking place, the minutest points of difference, as between the Infralapsarians and the Supralapsarians, were made essential points of issue between great parties. But before the new ecclesiastical spirit and the pride in the new work could gain force, there must have existed the strong feeling that the nation was an independent body and the desire to realize that independence in every way. This gave force to the oratory of the reformers, and bound their work into a whole. It was Germany against Italy, the German people against the Italian officials; and in the crisis that was before the Church, the Church saw nothing of the real cause for unrest and dissatisfaction, and could do nothing to restore quiet. Luther's first important writings, in which he gave form and direction to the Reformation in North Germany, are concerned with these points, and found a ready response in the minds of those who had no interest in his theology. Of these works one was an *Address to the Nobility of the German Nation*, and the other, *On the Babylonish Captivity of the Church*. The force of the German movement gave strength to the Swiss Reformation, which was the more distinctly theological in spirit. The English position, in spite of personal complications, was distinctly national. When therefore the preachers denounced some abuse or attacked some perversion of doctrine that had attained common acceptance they were able to obtain a favorable hearing, for the attack was an attack upon what was thought to be opposed to the national feeling.

The second cause that brought about the Reformation is to be found in the confusion and corruption prevalent in many parts of Europe. The corruptions in the Church were consequences, not of the Church's system or theology, but of the changes that had taken place in the common life of society. These faults in ecclesiastical administration were freely recognized, and an attempt to correct them was made at the Council of Trent, which devoted a large part of its time to the elimination of patent abuses. But the causes of the abuses and corruptions, which were very real and glaring, apart from the infirmities of human nature and natural depravity, belonged to that revolution in thought and feeling which was connected with the revival of arts and letters, the recent geographical discoveries, with all the new thought that they aroused, and the upheaval of the older standards of value and modes of living. This change in thought and feeling produced on the one hand an indifference to the traditional faith and customs. Religion lost its hold upon many, and the opportunities of gain irresistibly tempted many to traffic in the holiest things. But on the other hand there was dissatisfaction with the existing order because it did not seem to conform to an ideal system. The defects in personal administration were attributed to the institution, and the Church was thus made a party to the misdoings of its officials. The tendency to revolt from the institution on account of defects in administration had been fostered for a long time, and the constant appeal to a general council, a council superior to the Pope,—an appeal that played so large a part in the politics of the day,—was the legitimate offspring of the reforming councils of Constance and Basle a hundred years before. Men were, accordingly, neither unused to the idea of a reform, nor without occasion to feel that a reform was necessary. But the sense that there was a wrong to right and that .the interest of the Church and morality demanded some reform, was enough to render effective any preaching that sought these ends. No great oratorical art was needed to point out the wrongs; they were evident. Men were not sufficiently interested in the Church to distinguish between the Church and the faults of the individuals in the Church. Both were the object of denunciation, and both were attacked with the same vehemence. But in this attack there was not a mere spirit of rebellion against the existing order. It was animated by a high and moral principle, however mistaken it may appear to many. Even the crudest vagaries of the sectaries, the wildest iconoclasm, had a certain moral basis. In this respect the French Revolution is a parallel instance. No one would defend the excesses of that tremendous social upheaval; yet in the careers of some of the most bloodthirsty there was a generous and patriotic feeling and a moral impulse in spite of the most immoral acts. This revolution was the parent of the greatest oratory that has appeared in France. But the spirit that animates that oratory is moral, and it appeals to moral instincts.

A third cause of the Reformation is to be found in the deepened religious spirit that had risen in conflict with the anti-religious spirit. There was a general intellectual unrest. Novel theories were in the air. A new philosophy had been found as a substitute for the Aristotelian, which had served as a groundwork for the theology of the Church. Doubts were raised as to doctrines that had long been held without question. New problems were discovered, and the answers to the old were not as clear as formerly. The world was divided between the men who held an unwavering faith and the men who were trying to get a new hold upon the old truths. The result of all the unrest was, that on the one hand there were those who turned away from religion in disgust, and on the other hand there were those who were moved to seek for the faith within them a firmer foundation than any which men had to offer them. They went about groping in the dark, attempting to find something to satisfy their souls, unable either to appreciate what they were throwing away or to search correctly for the rational grounds of belief. The result was a confusion in theology that still exists among the reformed sects, in which there cannot be found one doctrine held in common that was not held by the mediaeval Church as well.

The Church could offer little help to men placed in this condition. There was a strong tendency toward a more living apprehension of the truths of religion, but there was not the gentle guiding hand to direct men. The Renaissance, with its folly and license, which had penetrated even the most sacred places, could have little feeling for these deeper principles. They were neither questions of art or classical research. They were nothing but rebellion.

Just because the Reformation did not proceed upon a dogmatic basis, and because it was to such an extent an appeal to deep religious feeling, there was the opportunity for the orator. He might never convince the people that the doctrinal statements to which he took exception were objectionable, but he could appeal to their hearts and consciences, as well as to their passions and interests. A critical discussion of the differences between the new and the old faiths would have been a useless task. People would not have been roused in any such way. Years of passionate dispute were needed to give to doctrinal differences any great influence upon the actual control of the movement; and it was only as the doctrines, formulated in haste in the midst of the strife, and thereby given a sacredness and value that did not belong to them, became subjects of controversy among theologians, that the doctrinal element assumed any great importance. In the meanwhile the popular discourse was an appeal to the deepest instincts of religion. To each section of reformed Christendom was this appeal made, differing in form and manner as it found the need different, but ever the same in being addressed to the heart rather than to the intellect, and thus ever winning sure response to its speech.

The movement in thought that is known as the Reformation, of which three causes have been mentioned, was a part of a larger movement, that was due to the causes enumerated. The feeling of nationality was not peculiar to those countries that separated from the Roman See. In France it was strong, and for nearly two centuries asserted itself, culminating in the Gallicanism of Bossuet. In Italy, on account of the divided state of the country and the fact that it was itself the land of the Papacy, the movement produced no great effect, but it was present. But everywhere the other two causes were present and effective in bringing about the reformation within the Church known as the Counter-Reformation. The same work as that of Luther and Calvin was carried on within the Church by men like St. Philip Neri and St. Francis de Sales, and the glory of canonization indicates the approval and gratitude of the Church. They attempted to bring religion down to men's hearts, and to care for the masses that were neglected. It is, therefore, by no means due solely to the reformers that the banner of religion, which seemed to be about to fall, was once more raised.

But this is not the place to investigate the causes which made the difference between the Reformation of the Northern countries and that of the Southern. The vehemence of the attack upon the ancient Church in the North has absorbed attention, and it may be that the need of reform within the Church was brought out by the men of the North; but for the student of the history of oratory the difference between the results in the two parts of Europe is of less importance than the fundamental unity of the history of thought throughout Europe in the sixteenth century.

It has been necessary to review, even at the cost of much space, these causes of the Reformation, because, as has been shown, there is an immediate connection between them and the oratory of the period. The reformers, furthermore, were in all cases preachers, and their success was due to their oratory. The results, which have been so momentous for good and evil, were so vast that the oratory of the men who were instrumental in bringing them about seems altogether inadequate when examined by itself. When the oratory of Luther, or Calvin, or St. Francis de Sales is compared with that of a later generation, it seems incredible that these utterances should have accomplished the changes in thought and life that were produced by them. Even if all due allowance be made for the effect of the powerful personalities of the speakers, the result would remain inexplicable, unless the audience to which they appealed be taken into consideration. The ordinary difficulty under which the preacher labors was not theirs. The people were excited before the appearance of the speaker. They were anxious to hear the word that was to be spoken, and felt themselves to have a personal interest in all that was said. These circumstances have rarely occurred in the history of the pulpit, but in so far as they are the creation of the preacher himself, they are the surest marks of genius and of leadership. In this art of leadership and infusing into men some of their own spirit, Luther, Calvin, and Zwingli stand among the first orators in all history. For the art of the orator is much more than the skilful construction of telling periods and finely balanced sentences. It is preeminently the art whereby men are able to impress their thought upon others and rouse them to action. And in this the leaders of the Reformation showed themselves orators of the first rank.

The greatest leader of the Reformation was Luther. It should be remembered, in connection with what has been said, that Zwingli had appeared as a reformer in Switzerland before Luther had taken up the work of a reformer at all. The work of Zwingli was based upon humanism, and not upon the deeper principles which swayed the Wittenberg teacher. The calmer, cooler, more logical and rationalistic temperament of the former was not fitted to move large numbers. He was furthermore a citizen of a small and isolated country. The affairs of Zurich were of little consequence to the rest of Europe. The Empire was not drawn into the contest. But Luther was a professor at a newly founded and important university, the subject of a powerful prince, and connected with far-reaching interests. The bold defiance of the papal authority and the patronage of the State brought Luther into a field that was vastly larger than any Swiss canton. Furthermore, his temperament was wholly different from that of Zwingli. He was a man of deep feeling. His monastic life, which was filled with tormenting doubts, had only deepened his religious emotions and rendered him more full of sympathy with the spirit of the times. Luther never rose to any great pitch of eloquence, either as debater or preacher. But there always remained the man himself, one of the strongest personalities in all history, able at once to arouse the strongest love and the most violent antipathy, painted by some as a saint and denounced by others as a monster of iniquity. A man who can be so described has in him the power of moving the world. When, however, one compares Luther with Melanchthon, the greater power of the elder as an orator becomes perfectly clear. Melanchthon was without the slightest doubt better able to construct a finished Latin oration, correct in all its parts according to the most approved models; but Melanchthon could never have created a Reformation, and was not able to control it when he was left alone by the death of Luther.

The same force of personal power comes out as distinctly in the case of Savonarola as in Luther. The man was the eloquence. He was himself a fire, and kindled into enthusiasm those who could hear him. What he might have been, if he had been placed in Wittenberg rather than in Florence, it would be idle to surmise, but limitations of the Italian political system made it impossible for Savonarola to do the work of which he seemed capable. But there was a deeper difference between the two men. Luther, in spite of his vows, married; Savonarola remained a monk to the last. Luther was able to put himself into closer touch with men, and his marriage was an evidence of his union with them in the everyday emotions of life. He was furthermore busied with the homely details of the instruction of the school-children. He wrote hymns and tunes for popular use. His home was the resort of many friends and coworkers. But the Dominican monk always remained the ascetic. His convent was his only home, his fellow-monks his only family. These differences are shown in the whole work of the two men. Savonarola sought by asceticism to win men to the faith and to purer Christianity, and his work perished with him. Luther sought to quicken interest in the affairs of life as a part of God's great plan for man. The one was a stem prophet of evil; the other was always delighting to point out the sweetness and blessedness of the Gospel. Savonarola roused an enthusiasm for righteousness sufficient to create for a time a reign of Puritanism; but the genius of Luther changed life and thought for centuries. The asceticism of the Dominican touched many a conscience and made religion a tremendous reality to the Florentines; but the healthy interest in life that is so apparent in the discourses of the Augustinian changed the religious conception of life for a nation.

Luther and Savonarola belonged to the first generation of reformers. In England, Colet and, in even greater degree, Latimer, were men of the same stamp. They were the men who laid the foundations of the new movement and won men to its side. In Scotland, the reformers were for a long time unable to make much progress, and the period of foundation extended beyond the life of the first generation.

Furthermore, there were here peculiar conditions that rendered the progress of the Reformation somewhat different from the course that it followed elsewhere.

In Switzerland the reformers of the first generation, or period, were, in addition to Zwingli, who has been mentioned, Farel and Viret. These men were able to commit Geneva to the Reformation before Calvin reached the city with which his name has been so closely associated. These men were primarily orators and belonged to that oratorical period that preceded the advent of Calvin. The cool, logical, inflexible system of Calvin would have counted for very little, apart from the fiery eloquence of Farel, his colleague and predecessor.

If the sermons and speeches of the men of the first generation be compared with those of the men of the second generation, a remarkable difference is at once apparent. There is not in many cases the same powerful appeal to the deeper feelings, and this is increasingly so with time. There is not the same fervor. There is not the same oratorical fire, although there may be greater skill in the construction of the sermons. The causes of this continually increasing change are to be found in the change in the condition in which the reformers were placed and in the needs of the reformed churches. The communities of seceders from the Catholic Church were compelled to give form to their theological position. This had been forced upon them to some extent at the time of the Augsburg Confession, but that declaration was not final. It was neither complete nor universally acceptable. Its theology needed elucidation and defence even where it expressed the general opinion. For it was an age in which men were everywhere called upon to give a systematic and scientific form to their theological convictions as opposed not merely to other schools, parties, and sects, but to unbelief, indifference, and an attempt to substitute classical culture for religion. The need of formulation was all the more pressing because the Roman Church, in dealing with the abuses that had in part caused the schism, had put forth at Trent the Roman definition of the points in controversy between itself and the new religious bodies.

But the theological discussion that was necessary for the Church as a whole could not be reserved for the scholar and the professional theologian. The people themselves were interested in the questions. Their faith depended upon these, and they had not been trained by recent events to accept their faith on authority. With the passion for nice metaphysical distinctions, as subtle as any made by the schoolmen, the laity were hardly less inspired than the clergy. The theological sermon was therefore not merely needed, it was demanded in the public worship which was the great opportunity for popular instruction.

The controversy soon passed beyond the simple form in which it was at first conducted. The presence of abuses and wrongs to be righted, the need of stimulating Christian faith and life, no longer confronted men. They were not trying to right wrongs. They lived under a regime for which they were themselves to a large extent responsible. The controversy became increasingly intellectual and the religious spirit correspondingly weaker. There were few opportunities for the exercise of oratorical arts, and few attempts were made to employ them. The history, the dogmatic treatise, and the "learned sermon" were everywhere called for, and the demand was abundantly supplied.

Calvin represents the highest type of the new style of preaching. He gave the reformed Church a systematized theology and an intellectual basis. During his constant preaching at Geneva he built up his elaborate commentaries on nearly all the books of the Bible, and thereby provided the Church with what was to a certain degree an authoritative interpretation of the Scriptures. But in comparison with the homilies of Chrysostom the expositions of Calvin, although often keen and critical, are very unimpressive productions. The influence and popularity of these discourses were due to the absorbing interest that was taken in the movement of which they were a part. The freedom and prosperity of the city depended upon the reformed faith, and the value set upon these homilies, admirable as commentaries, was in no small degree due to something else than admiration for their oratory.

In another part of Switzerland the preaching of Bullinger, Zwingli's successor at Zurich, was of great influence. But the style of his sermons as a whole can best be shown by the fact that they were used in England as a sort of theological textbook for the less well educated clergy. The instructive element predominates, and the artistic arrangement of the sermon, as apart from logical order in exposition, is but little regarded. How much the written word was supplemented in actual preaching by extemporaneous additions and appeals to the hearers cannot now be determined. The absence of all that might appeal to the fancy, imagination, passions, or emotions, renders this whole class of sermons inferior to the less learned, less logical, and less scholastic, but more hearty and effective addresses of the earlier preachers.

These characteristics of the later Swiss preaching, as opposed to the earlier, are repeated in England in the contrast between the manners of Latimer and Jewel and of the men of their respective times. The plain sermons of Latimer belong to the early period of the Reformation, which in England, on account of complications with the State, was longer than on the Continent. These sermons touched the hearts of men of every rank and won them to the faith. They were preached before the king and his court, and also before the common people. But everywhere they roused men to action, not so much by denunciation of abuses or superstitious practices as by their appeal to the simple religious feelings and moral instincts. But the sermons of Jewel, who was equally distinguished in his day, are wholly different. The controversialist here appears, with his quotations from Fathers and theologians. The so-called "Challenge Sermon," in which Jewel calls the Roman theologians to produce evidence from the early Fathers in favor of the doctrine of Transubstantiation, is replete with the most elaborate discussion of patristic references. Every possible citation is brought up and examined as to its force. Yet that sermon, which would be difficult for any but an expert theologian to follow intelligently, caused a great sensation when it was preached at St. Paul's Cross in London. Preachers became theological gladiators, and their friends and admirers cheered them as they contended in public. The keen spirit of controversy that filled all ranks of the English Church gave an interest to these long-winded popular disquisitions—that was, however, but transitory. The sermons of Luther are still readable, and might, with some allowance made for the language, be useful in the pulpit today, because they were aimed to edify the heart and soul. The lucubrations of the English divines of the later Reformation period are mines in which the antiquary and historian find a scanty reward for much labor. But this repelling trait was not due to the peculiarity of the English character or temperament. The preachers were forced into this style of preaching largely by the needs of the time and by the Protestant scholasticism that was running its course. In the next century the sermon was of a higher order and in some cases really eloquent, as in the case of Taylor, but the spirit of learned controversy inherited from the past still showed itself unmistakably. The preachers complacently emptied their commonplace books in the pulpit and their hearers were content to call it preaching. Thus in a sermon of Taylor, of very moderate length and taken quite at random, there are more than a dozen quotations in Greek and Latin from poets, philosophers, orators, and Fathers.

In the Elizabethan era, however, there was one man who deserves to be mentioned as having a style that seems to be founded upon oratorical principles. That man was Hooker, who from physical infirmity, however, was not effective in the delivery of his sermons. His contemporaries were, as a rule, content to compose sermons from an intellectual rather than an oratorical point of view. Hooker, whether consciously or not, is an exception. His magnificent periods and swelling cadences are vocal. They would have been grand and impressive in the mouth of any one capable of delivering them. Every line seems to have been composed with direct reference not only to lucidity, but also to its oratorical effect.

In the countries which did not embrace the Reformation, the art of preaching was for a long time less highly cultivated. There were of course many good and effective preachers, but preaching played no such part here as in the reformed churches. This was due to various causes. First of all there was the absence of the controversial element which required a large amount of popular instruction. There was not the same attack upon existing institutions. The reforming spirit which filled such men as St. Philip Neri and St. Francis de Sales was not contagious. They were able to win vast numbers back to the Church and to a moral and religious life. They were even able to inspire their followers with zeal. But they were not involved, as were the men in the North, in a wide-spread national movement. They were not champions of a new and popular cause. But more important were the grounds of difference due to the condition of the churches. In the reformed churches the sermon to a great extent took the place of the sacraments. To hear a sermon on Sunday was the chief appointed mode of worship. It became a sort of sacrament, a means of grace. In the Catholic Church the place of the sermon was taken by the Mass, in which every one was bound to assist. The sermon was reserved, to a great extent, for special seasons, as Advent and Lent, and was by no means common in the small country places. There was therefore very little to stimulate the cultivation of the homiletic art. There were also nothing but the mediaeval models to follow. It was not that the reformers were the only biblical preachers. The Roman preachers were for the most part equally conversant with the Bible, and the mediaeval preachers were, as a whole, far more biblical than the Protestants have been in any age. Neither was it the doctrines that made the difference; for the reformed churches differed notoriously among themselves, and yet all excelled in preaching. But the mediaeval preachers and those that imitated them were, for the most part, out of touch with the times. Their allegorical method of exegesis, while it might stimulate the fancy, did not prove conducive to real pulpit eloquence; the scholastic method, admirable in instruction, was fatal in exhortation. The reformer, unlike those who did their work within the Church, departed from traditional forms and appealed directly to the hearts of the people.

The Catholic Church, as has been said, was by no means deficient in excellent preachers in spite of the difficulties under which the art of preaching labored. In addition to those mentioned, another should be named as showing great power within the older lines, Antonio Vieyra, the Portuguese preacher. In his case, as in the case of St. Philip and St. Francis de Sales, there was an intense moral purpose that animated the preacher. The Jesuit who could give up a brilliant diplomatic career and a position as court preacher to work among the Indians of Brazil, had the spirit of St. Francis Xavier and of St. Philip of the Oratory.

The greatest development of preaching that the Roman Church, or indeed the modern world, has ever seen, took place in France under conditions most favorable to the art. There had been a certain competition and rivalry between the Catholic and the reformed preachers that stimulated both sides. The Protestants had been supported by many of the old nobility, and the Catholics by the court. With the increase in literary culture, in art and poetry, came the corresponding advance in oratory, which was so essential to the Church. The pulpit could not afford to offend the fastidious taste of the times, and the men who were appointed to high position were men of the best culture. The bishops and other prominent ecclesiastics were members of the royal court. The king himself was a patron of all that might bring renown upon his reign. He saw the importance of ecclesiastical oratory, and sought in every way to cultivate it. The court preachers were accordingly men of the greatest talents, and their rewards were the bishoprics and rich abbeys, for the path to ecclesiastical honor led through the pulpit. With the example of the court preachers before them, the inferior clergy could not remain careless of the principles of eloquence. And everywhere a constant struggle went on to attain the greatest perfection in preaching, not only as a duty lying before the parish priest, but as an art that demanded the most serious study.

The greatest of the French preachers, Bossuet, Fléchier, Bourdaloue, and Massillon, were by no means the only preachers of merit. They were those that attained a greater perfection in an art that showed many proficients and many more that achieved a respectable amount of success. Those men were more than professional orators aiming merely at pleasing; they were, perhaps, not men of the stamp of St. Bernard or St. Francis Xavier, but they were devoted priests employing every art to win men to faith and religion. No tragedian ever studied a part more carefully than the great French preachers studied their sermons. Every phrase was polished until it was brought to the highest perfection. The tone, the gesture, the very pauses, were all carefully considered and judiciously applied. The tendency toward artificiality was of course always present, and something of this may be detected in Fléchier; but these great preachers were, on the whole, free from this defect. Men of less skill and inferior taste fell into the vice of artificiality by making art their one aim and end. Intense earnestness and deep religious fervor saved the greater men. The fashion of delivering funeral orations recounting the exploits and virtues of the deceased presented another danger, but the leading preachers were surprisingly free from the vice of flattery. Bossuet recounted the glories of the life of the dead, but only to turn the minds of his auditors from the contemplation of transitory and earthly grandeur to that glory which is eternal. Massillon, in the most trying circumstances, refused to gloss over vice and astonished the courtiers by his boldness. These men were liable to all the temptations of men. They were always exposed to the most terrible temptation of a preacher,—the ease with which fame and applause might be won by being in a slight degree remiss in their duty in rebuking vice. If the example of St. John the Baptist was before them, so also was his fate. Yet no one can read the sermons of Bourdaloue and Massillon without the conviction that they never forgot the priest in the orator. They were eager to save souls, and they sought the salvation of the courtiers in the way best adapted to meet their needs and win their attention.

It was not merely within the French Church that the example of these men was powerful; it influenced the Protestant as well. Among the exiles driven from France at the revocation of the Edict of Nantes was the boy, James Saurin. In his career at the Hague he was able to transfer to the Protestant pulpit much of the French manner, adapting it to the sterner, and, possibly, more logical, method of Calvinistic theology. The success of his attempt, in bringing greater art into the pulpit and in impressing the sublime truths of religion with all the force that powerful oratory could give, showed that this method was by no means opposed to the Protestant genius or faith. His sermons were published under the most distinguished patronage and were translated into English and German at an early date, exercising a great influence on the popular style.

It might not be just to say that the sermons of Saurin caused the change in the modern style of Protestant preaching. But it is certain that he was the first to combine a sound oratory with reformed theology. In the century before Saurin, the English sermons were still fettered by the scholasticism that nearly destroyed Protestantism. Even a man of the glowing fancy of John Bunyan, when he wrote a sermon, was under the influence of this spirit that had nothing of the religious fervor of the mediaeval scholastics and had more than their tediousness. The reform dates from Saurin rather than from the English preachers. The English pulpit of the century following the Restoration was lamentably dull in spite of the great names of Barrow and Tillotson. The best preaching, though perhaps not the most learning or the best theology, was to be found among those sects which were continually attacking the Church, or among the leaders of the reforming movements within the Church. These were more eloquent because there was in their work a more powerful stimulus to oratory. The preachers of the established Church deserve the greatest credit for their defence of the fundamental principles of revealed religion against the attacks of Deism; but not until the Evangelical Revival, when the reforming spirit spread to the Church itself, was there any great revival of the art of preaching as distinguished from the composition and delivery of learned discussions on theological questions, sometimes running into a quasi-legal defence of the Apostles from the charge of forgery, and the hesitating advocacy of the fundamentals of the Christian faith. With the Evangelical Revival and the entirely different theological movement that followed it, came the great preachers. The hearts of the people were stirred, and their faith was roused to a deeper and more essentially Christian hold upon the truths of the religion they had so long professed.

JOHN WYCLIF

John Wyclif was born about the year 1320, in the village of Ipreswel, near Richmond, in the county of York. He seems to have been of respectable but not of noble lineage. He was educated at Oxford, probably at Balliol College, of which he was at one time Master. In 1365 he was appointed Master of the recently founded Canterbury Hall, and in connection with this he became involved in a dispute ending in an unsuccessful appeal to the papal court. The causes that brought about the reformatory movement with which the name of Wyclif has been chiefly associated were for the most part political and national, though other causes were not without influence. Wyclif, together with many others, resented the relation in which the Crown of England had since the days of John stood to the Papacy. Above all, he objected to the tribute that had been exacted from the realm. From this position he advanced to a doctrine of the relation of Church and State which was no less than revolutionary; for he denied, among other points, the right of the Church to hold temporal wealth. Toward the end of his life, after the schism in the Papacy, due to the return of the Pope from Avignon, Wyclif set on foot a preaching movement with the design of instructing the common people, who were, in his opinion, neglected in the parochial ministrations. But combined with this was an ever-increasing hostility to the Church as it existed. There is no doubt that this latter element contributed much to the popularity of the movement, as the Church was not in favor with the common people. Afterward he openly attacked the mendicant orders and the whole ecclesiastical institution; denied that the Church was a visible body; restricted the idea of the Church to the company of the righteous; and even denied the doctrine of Transubstantiation. In 1381 he was condemned at Oxford and in the year following at a council held at London. After his condemnation he retired to his rectory at Lutterworth and busied himself with his translation of the Bible and the composition of theological works. Wyclif died at Lutterworth on New Year's eve, 1384.

Wyclif was a great preacher, not in the sense that he was eloquent in the common meaning of that term, but that he was able to impress plain truths upon the minds of plain people. He lacked that which is essential to eloquence, imagination. His sermons were clear, simple, and forcible, built upon a theme and divided logically. But his influence upon the oratory of the Church is much greater than the production of a few masterpieces might have effected. He organized a system of popular preaching that was destined to become wide-spread. His style was adopted by Huss in Bohemia, and there became a power after its influence had almost ceased in England. From Huss the tradition was handed on to Luther.

The works of Wyclif have been nearly all published. The best edition of the Latin works is that issued by the Wyclif Society and by G. V. Lechler. The English works have been edited by T. Arnold and by F. D. Matthews. The best work on Wyclif is by G. V. Lechler, *Johann von Wyclif und die Vorgeschichte der Reformation*, Leipsic, 1873. A great deal of criticism on Wyclif is rendered useless by the prejudices of those who would either attack his position or would count him as the first champion of reformed doctrine. The accounts of Neander (*Church History*, Am. Ed., Boston, 1866, vol. 5, pp. 134-173), Milman (*Latin Christianity*, Bk. 13, chap. 6), Creighton (*History of the Papacy during the Reformation*, vol. 1.), and R. L. Poole (*Illustrations of the History of Mediaeval Thought*), are all useful and readily accessible.

SERMON ON PRAYER

by John Wyclif.

The following sermon by John Wyclif was preached from the text, John 16:33: "In that day ye shall ask me nothing. Verily, verily, I say unto you, whatsoever ye shall ask the Father in my name, he will give it you." These words are a part of the Gospel for the fifth Sunday after Easter. The sermon has been selected, not as representing Wyclif's violent attack upon the Papacy and the religious opinions of his time, for there is little of that in this sermon, but as representing another side of the preacher's work that has not been sufficiently noticed, the practical religious teaching which really lay at the bottom of the preaching movement that he set on foot. No date or place of delivery of this sermon is preserved. It probably belongs to the latter part of Wyclif s life.

CHRIST telleth in this Gospel how His disciples should be helped by virtue of their prayer, when He was ascended in to heaven. And first he saith a general word, and taking both His natures to witness that if they ask aught the Father of Heaven in His name, He shall give it them. But, as Christ saith, unto that time His disciples asked not in His name, and therefore afterward should they ask that their joy were full, and they should take. All the hardness of this matter is to know perfectly to ask in Christ's name, for he shall have that asketh thus. But since our Lord is truth and health of men that trust in Him, that man asketh in Christ's name, that asketh in truth his soul's. Christ is most lord of all, and therefore He will have despite, but unless men ask Him a great thing; for otherwise His lordship and that asking accord not to His name. And so, if thou wilt ask in Christ's name, ask the bliss that ever shall last; and since Christ is truth and reason, look thy asking be reasonable, and then may thou be sure to have the thing that thou asketh thus. And therefore Christ in this Gospel biddeth us to ask our full joy, and then shall we have it, if that we ask in reason; for no man hath but half joy, but if he be full of bliss. And this great lord will not be asked but this bliss, or means thereto; and if man ask thus in reason that he be worthy to have it, he shall have it without doubt when best time were that he had it; and he shall have on the best manner the thing that he asketh thus.

And therefore the seven askings that Christ teacheth in the Paternoster meaneth this form of asking; and by all means to ask in charity; and therefore men that live in war are unable to have their asking: but they ask their own condemnation in the fifth petition, for there they ask that God forgive them their debt that they owe to Him, right as they forgive men that are debtors unto them. And here we shall understand that each man is debtor to God, and each man oweth to each other to do him good in charity. And so failing to love God of all thine heart and all thy will, thou runnest in great debt both against God and man. And so in this fifth asking these men that war now-a-days, asking Him as they would mean,—forgive us for we are even with Thee, or else take vengeance in ire of us, as we take vengeance of our brethren. And this is no good prayer, but more asking of God vengeance; and for this cause many men are unheard in their prayer, and turned into more evil for their unskilful prayer. And such men were better to leave than to pray on such manner. For many men pray for vengeance and for world's prosperity, and in the ire of God He giveth them that they ask; but it were better to them to pray not thus, nor to have these things. And thus men of foreign lands pray God in great processions; and for unworthiness of their prayer they were better to sit at home. And, for men know not for what thing they should pray God in such causes, therefore good living profiteth, and the Holy Ghost asketh then for them. And whoever stirreth men to evil life, if they are friars that cry high, God heareth them not to good, but rather to take vengeance on them. For Christ saith, that not each man that saith unto Him Lord, Lord, shall come into the bliss of heaven, but he that endeth in right life, for he prayeth in the name of the Trinity. And thus Zebedee's sons prayed for good, but in evil manner. And so by all means right life is the best in man's prayer, for such life prayeth better to God than the voices of hypocrites.

And after saith Christ to His Apostles, that these things He saith to them in proverbs and mistily; but now is come the time when He shall not speak thus unto them in proverbs, but openly of His Father He shall tell them as best is. In that day shall Christian men ask in Christ's name unto their bliss. And now He saith unto them that He shall pray His Father for them, for they shall be like Christ and make His kingdom. Wherefore He prayeth, that the Father love these Apostles and other men that follow Him, for they loved Jesus Christ and trowed that He came from God; yea, that Christ by His manhood came of God in His Godhead. Christ came from the Father and came into the world, and now when Christ hath done His message, He forsaketh again the world, and goeth by His manhood to His Father. And Christ's disciples said to Him, Lo, now Thou speakest openly, and Thou sayest now no proverb; and therefore we know well that Thou knowest all things, and it is to Thee no need that any man ask Thee aught, for Thou knowest before the asking, what men should ask and what things leave. In this we trow that Thou come from God as His own Son.

And this belief is ground to men to have of God what that them needeth, and to know what is best for them, than if displease to the world. But, as men that are in fevers desire not that were best for them, so men here in sin covet not best thing for them. For the world said that the Apostles were fools and forsaken of God, and so it would say today of men that lived like to them, for world's joy and earthly good pleaseth to them, with means thereto, and they savor not heavenly good nor right following after Christ. And this judgment now in the world is open witness against men, that they be not whole in soul, but turned amiss to worldly things. For as a mouth of a sick man distempered from good meat, moveth him to covet things contrary to his health, so it is of man's soul that savoreth not God's law. And as wanting of appetite is a sign deadly to man, so wanting of God's wit is sign of his second death. And so judgment, that now reigneth of worldly prosperity is token of men that they are fools and savor not God's law. For the world saith commonly that if a man have worldly bliss and the world laughs at him in killing of his enemies, then God loveth him and doth miracles for his sake. But, Lord! where is our belief that we should trow in love of God, that it standeth not in this but rather hate of God! And, as Gregory saith, as a bull that shall be killed goeth in corn at his will, and is not pained nor traiveled with other beasts, so a member of the fiend is left from the grace of God, to figure his damnation, and suffered to do much harm here, to large his pain hereafter. We should leave these sensible signs and take ensample of holy men, as of Christ and of His Apostles; how they had not their bliss here. But here Christ ordained pains and hate of the world and pursuing to men that He most loved, to teach us to come after them. And thus signs of patience and pursuing in this earth should be tokens of God's love and not signs of Ante-Christ

Arnold's Select English Works of Wyclif.

GIROLAMO SAVONAROLA

Girolamo Savonarola was born at Ferrara, September 21, 1452. From his boyhood he was of a studious and meditative disposition, and without betraying any signs of his future oratorical gifts he distinguished himself early by his success in his studies. After much debate with himself as to the reality of his vocation for the religious life, he took monastic vows in 1474, in the monastery of San Domenico at Bologna. Here he gave himself up to the practice of the most extreme austerities. His duty in the monastery was the instruction of the novices, but he spent no little time in sombre reflection upon the moral state of the Church. He recorded some of his thoughts in verse, for which he had some talent. In 1482 he removed to Florence. But the moral state of the city, then in the midst of the luxury and wantonness of the reign of Lorenzo the 'Magnificent, profoundly depressed the mind of the monk. Partly as a consequence of what he saw and partly, it may be, as a result of his long brooding upon the evil of the times, a great change took place in his life. He devoted himself to apocalyptic studies, saw visions, and became convinced that he was a prophet sent from God. At San Gemignano in 1484 and in Brescia in 1486 he first distinguished himself as a preacher. In 1490 he was back in Florence with his fame as an orator already established, and in the year following he might be said to have begun what for several years proved a veritable reign in the city of Florence. He became Prior of San Marco, and after the death of Lorenzo the convent became the centre of the party opposed to the Medici. In 1492, after the election of Alexander VI. (Borgia), Savonarola's sermons became more violently denunciatory and in this year he uttered his celebrated prophecy against Florence. The power of the preacher was sufficient, for a time at least, to work what was little less than a miracle. The whole population seemed to have abandoned its frivolous pleasure-seeking and to have given itself over to pious austerities. As time went by, Savonarola became more and more unsparing in his denunciation of the personal wickedness of Alexander, and thereby he incurred his bitter enmity. The Pope soon excommunicated him, but the Prior of San Marco disregarded the bull. In the long contest with the pontiff, Savonarola appealed to a council against the Pope. One of his letters to the rulers of Europe on this subject was intercepted and forwarded to the Pope. The downfall of the preacher was now but a matter of time. The Franciscans attacked him fiercely; the town had some time since turned against the bold preacher, and his affairs were soon in a desperate condition. Finally the Seigniory, at the bidding of Rome, took up the case. He was arrested and tried. He was unable to endure the torture to which he was subjected, and recanted. He immediately withdrew his recantation; his doom, however, was already determined, and on May 22, 1498, he was burnt at Florence.

Savonarola was one of the greatest preachers that ever lived. His power in influencing vast multitudes has never been surpassed. His style, if that can be called his style which fails to give what was most essential to the man, was simple, direct, and forcible. He is not attracted by the artistic side of the subject and gives it no attention. His tremendous earnestness, his marvellous insight into human nature, his power of detecting the inmost thoughts of those he addressed, gave him a power that has, perhaps, never been equalled.

The sermons of Savonarola have been very often printed. The Florentine edition of 1845 is good. There are only a few translations of the works of Savonarola. F. C. Cowper has translated into English his *Exposition of the Miserere*. Rapp has translated into German some of his devotional works and sermons. There is a French translation of some pieces (*OEuvres Spirituelles Choisis de Jerome Savonarole*, E. C. Bayonne, Paris, 1879) in the *Bibliothlque Dominicaine*.

The most important work of recent date on Savonarola is by P. Villari, *La Storia di Girolamo Savonarola e de' suo Tempi*, 1882 (this has been translated into English). See W. R.Clark, *Savonarola: His Life and Times*, London, 1870; Milman, *Savonarola, Erasmus, and other Essays*; Rudelbach, *Savonarola und seine Zeit*, 1835; Pastor, *Geschichte der Papste*. See also George Eliot's *Romola* and Mrs. M. O. W. Oliphant's *Makers of Florence*, both of which are useful, especially the former.

SERMON ON THE ASCENSION

by Girolamo Savonarola

The following sermon was delivered by Savonarola in Florence, on the feast of the Ascension, May 12, 1496, before his power had begun to wane. It is interesting, not only as showing the constant conflict with the less strict party in the State, but as revealing the philosophical line of thought that in a trained theologian of the time underlay even his popular discourses. For Savonarola was thoroughly trained in the scholastic philosophy and, no doubt, the distinction of substance and accidents which plays so large a part in the opening of the sermon was more familiar to the Florentines of the fifteenth century than to the practical men of today. The text of the sermon was St. Mark 16:15-20, but in the long digression in which the preacher interpolates the account and application of Balaam's ass, he not only wanders far from his text, but even from any apparent connection with the subject in hand. Such a remarkable digression seems to indicate that the sermon was entirely extemporaneous, and, as such, all the more characteristic of the preacher. So far as any arrangement is to be traced, it is in the line of an exposition, and in the more ancient homiletical style which was so often followed in the exposition of the Gospels.

BELOVED in Christ Jesus, the wise men of this world divide all created things into two classes; one class they name substances, the other accidents. The substances are those things that exist through themselves without requiring anything else on which to rest, as the earth, water, air, the heavens, animals, stones, plants, and similar things. The accidents cannot exist by themselves, but only by resting on something else, as color, odor, taste, and other such things. But because our knowledge is entirely through the senses, and we are able to know anything only when its accidents fall upon our senses, we have, therefore, knowledge of the accidents rather than of the substances. The eyes are for colors, the ears for sounds, the nose for scents, the tongue for flavors, the touch for heat and cold, for hard and soft. Each sense has its own sphere of knowledge and brings what it has perceived before the imagination, and this hands it over to the reason within, which reads and illuminates the productions of the imagination, judges them, and in this way comes to a knowledge of the substances. But the reason has little light if it is separated from the body, for God has joined soul and body together; and so by means of the senses knowledge becomes definite and complete. For if the soul out of the body were richer in knowledge, it would be in vain that it should be in the body. God and Nature have done nothing in vain, and therefore the soul's union with the body ministers to its perfection.

The soul's knowledge, however, will not be complete so long as it lives in this mortal body. It does not while here come to the fundamental distinctions and causes of the substances, because it is obliged to know the inner side of things through their externals. Therefore man is able only imperfectly to know an incorporeal substance; how much less can he know the uncreated infinite being of God? But if he cannot know the being of God, he will not be able to know many other infinite things which are in Him. We ought therefore not to be surprised that there is much in God which we cannot understand, and that very many truths of the faith we cannot yet prove; since we do not yet know everything. The great God in His rich mercy saw our poor knowledge and came into our flesh and assumed it that He might work for us, die, and rise again from the dead; until after a life full of love He raised himself above the world of sense into His eternity. But so long as our Redeemer lived with His Apostles they loved too much that which they saw of Him, because they were bound down to their senses, and were therefore unable to rise to the knowledge of His Spirit. It was necessary that He should disappear in the heavens that He might lift their souls far above the world of sense up to Himself. Their natural powers could not do this; therefore He gave to His elect a light from above. Ascending on high He led captivity captive, for ascending into the heavens He took with Him the prey which the devil had made of the soul of men ever since the fall of our first parents. The Lord has given gifts unto men (Eph. 4:8), inasmuch as He has imparted to them the seven gifts of the Holy Ghost. Now they leave everything of this world, and rise above by following Christ, who gives to them for a light the light of faith. Let us speak this morning of this faith which leads to the Savior.

"Awake thou that sleepest and Christ shall give thee light." Be not held captive by flesh and sense, which hold thee fast in sleep; rise to Christ; He will give thee light. See, His flesh is above. What do ye say to that, ye wise men of this world? Everything that has weight tends downward, but His flesh is on high above all heavens. This time your laws have been set at nought. But see what hope Almighty God rouses in us: if our head has gone above, we, His members, will follow Him. In that we hope; of that we preach; on that we live. Know, O man, that if thou wilt thou canst go to Paradise, for thither has thy Savior Christ gone; but know this also, that not by thine own nature, not by means of silver and gold, not by thy virtue, wilt thou reach that place. He has given gifts unto men, and through these thou mayest reach Paradise, if thou only wilt. He has given thee the gifts of His Holy Ghost, and before all the gift of knowledge by which He enlightens thee and shows thee by that light thy goal. Thereupon He gives thee the gift of wisdom, by which thou learnest to love thy goal, and perceivest how much thou needest love. Christ then says to man: Remain in My love, leave the things of this world, follow Me to heaven. And because it is needful for thee to know that this world amounts to nothing, He gives thee experience that it may say to thee that thou must soon leave this world in which nothing lasts. Through many difficulties and doubts, man must get so far and know what to do: therefore thou hast the gift of counsel. Hold fast to this counsel, and follow Christ, who will always give thee good counsel. He will give thee not the treasures of this world, but eternal glory and undying happiness. What wilt thou do, O child of man? Leave this world, enter the service of Christ. He is waiting for thee, and will reward thy service, for He is a bountiful rewarder. Let every one then hasten to serve Him. But because each one is bound to care for the salvation of his brother, and to lead him to Christ, therefore the Lord gives thee the gift of love, by which thou shouldst warn thy brother, thy neighbor, thy friend, thy wife, every one, and with all thy strength and zeal shouldst lead them to Christ. But in this world man must go through joy and sorrow. To oppose the joys of earth, Christ gives thee fear, that thou mightest always be careful lest thou shouldst fall, and not let thy joyous days separate thee from the grace of Christ: to oppose unhappiness, He gives thee strength to resist.

What do ye want, O children of men; will ye not follow Christ who has gone up on high and has departed to prepare a place for you in glory? Thou comest not into the service of the Lord, because thou art not able to believe these words. If thou didst but believe thou wouldst stand no longer indifferent. Thou art unbelieving, thou art unthankful, and the Lord will punish thy unbelief even as on the morning of His Ascension He punished the unbelief of His Apostles. Because I have explained to you this morning this Gospel, I must punish the hardness and unthankfulness of thy heart. Thou hast refused the service of the Lord, who has ascended to prepare for thee the highest glory.

I call upon all men and women, all whose lives are ruined in sorrows and troubles. What do ye fear? He who believes that Christ is above no longer fears anything. Come then all ye into His service. Jesus reproved the unbelief and the hard-heartedness of His disciples, because they did not believe those who had seen Him after He had risen. Without faith it is impossible to please God. No doubt the Apostles said: How can we believe these women? But these women were of pure heart before God, and therefore the Savior reproved His disciples. Ye deserve still sharper reprimands. To the disciples a few women announced the news that He had risen. Ye hear all this, and in addition all the glorious revelations in which the Lord after this manifested Himself on earth. Why do ye not come to serve Christ? Ye do not truly believe, because ye are so full of sin, and despise God's commandments. Ye do not deserve the gift of faith. He who has faith should show it in his deeds, that he may have what he says he has, and may know what he has, namely, the certainty of the divine word, which cannot err, the goodness of God, and His guidance into all goodness. On account of thy sins, thou hast not the true light which would have enabled thee to see all goodness. Thou art sunk in vice, drunken with greed and luxury, and all the works of this world. Thou seekest only power and glory. And wherefore? If thou hadst faith, thou wouldst not seek such things, for thou wouldst know that faith would give thee a much higher crown. From these sins have come thy unbelief and thy hardness of heart. Therefore the words of faith do not touch thy heart: it is a heart of stone and iron. Throw off thy load of sin, and give thy will to righteousness; then will thy hardheartedness end, and God will bestow on thee the gift of faith. What wilt thou? Why standest thou so uncertain and irresolute? Why dost thou not hasten to Him, and see how He leaves thy life, how He goes into the heavens, to which He bids thee come up. Leave at length thy sensual life, and enter the pathway of Christ. Hesitate no longer, begin today, put it not off until to-morrow. If thou hast faith, thou canst not delay longer, and if thy heart is right before God, He will give thee the light of faith which will enable thee to distinguish the false from the true faith, and so when on the right road not to fall into error. Then wilt thou know for thyself that the Gospel makes good men out of those who truly believe, and thine experience will tell thee that thou hast no occasion to doubt.

A story from the Old Testament might perhaps serve as a parable and make clearer what I mean. When Balak heard of Israel's march, he was afraid, and sent to call Balaam to curse Israel for him. Balaam set out on his way with his ass, accompanied by an angel of the Lord, because Balaam was going to Balak with an evil intention. The beast sought in vain to turn into the field, and finally fell down between two walls, and suffered under blows and curses, until the prophet saw the angel and perceived his sin. Balak is the devil who would ruin the people of God; by Balaam we can understand the nobles, the prelates, the preachers, the learned, who are held captive by their arrogance. The two servants are those who follow the proud, serve them, and flatter them, especially the lazy clergy and monks, who so far as outward show goes live a virtuous life, but who live for ceremonies and take care not to speak the truth. To these belong many citizens who live apparently virtuously and hide their pride. Because they commit no sins of the flesh which can be noticed, they are full of piety in their outward ceremonies, but within full of arrogance. These are the members of the devil, for the devil neither eats, drinks, nor sleeps, he is neither a miser nor a wanton, but is within full of pride as are these. By the ass we are to understand simple people. They are led in the way of sin by the ceremonies of the lazy, since they are not thought fit for the worship of the heart, and must be led by masses, penance, and indulgences, and they throw away what might be of profit for money and for candles. The lazy give them council in their sermons: Give some vestment, build a chapel, and thou wilt be freed from any danger of going to hell.—Do not believe these mountebanks; no outward act can bring you to Paradise, not even miracles and prophecy, but only the grace of God, if you have humility and love. . . . Before the ass stood an angel with a sword. This is Christ, who speaks to the ass: Walk no longer in the path of sin, for I have ready for you a great scourge. The ass alone saw the angel; for the simple first hear the word of the Lord, but Balaam and such as are with him will hear nothing of it. The ass left the path of captivity and went out into the field, into the way of the Lord. "For the kingdom of heaven is like treasure hid in a field; which when a man found he sold all that he had and bought that field." So the simple go into the holy field of the Scriptures and say: Let me look around a little, for the flowers of this field bear fruit. Yea, our fathers, the prophets, Apostles, and martyrs bore fruit, they who died with joy for the truth. These are they who go into the field and speak the truth in the face of death. Come into the city, where the nobles and the masters taken captive by sin crowd together, cry the lazy troop of monks: O fathers, it would be well if when you spoke of these things, you touched not this string, by which you allow yourselves to fall into disgrace and disfavor.—They have said that already to me.—Our persecution begins if we begin to preach. But Jesus was willing to die for the truth of what He said; should we forsake the truth in order not to displease men? No, we will say it in every way, and with Balaam's ass go into the field.

Think not that I am such a fool as to undertake these things without good reason. I call heaven and earth to witness against me if I do not speak the truth. For against all the world is my sermon; every one contradicts it. If I go about with lies, then I have Christ against me; therefore I have heaven and earth against me, and how then could I stand? As such a trifler with holy things how should I dare rise up? Believe me, I speak the truth, I have seen it with my eyes, and touched it with my hands—believe it! If I speak not the truth, I consign myself body and soul to destruction; but I tell you I am certain of the truth, and I would that all were as I am. I say that of the truth on which I stand, not as though I wished that others had my failings as well. So come then into the service of Jesus; come to the truth, come here,

I bid you. Do ye not know how I explained the revelation of St. John? There were many who said that I spoke too much in detail, and went too deep into it. There stood the angel before the ass, and wanted it to go out into th6 field, but Balaam smote it; and ye know not how much opposition I must yet undergo. The lazy monks were the first who called me a fool and revolutionist, and on the other side stood the weak and the simple, who said in their innocent faith: Oh, if we could only do what he teaches! Then I had war with the citizens and the great judges of this time, whom my manner of preaching did not please. I was between two walls; the angel warned me, threatening eternal death from this road, and I received Balaam's blows. Ye know my persecution and my danger; but I knew that I was on the way to victory and said always: No human being can drive my cause from the world. Balaam, thou leanest thy foot against the walls, but do as thou wilt, I will crush thy foot; I leaned on the wall, on Christ, I leaned on His grace, I hoped; leave off thine anger and threatening, thou canst not get me away from the wall. I say to all of you: Come to the truth, forsake your vice and your malice, that I may not have to tell you of your grief. I say it to you, O Italy, I say it to you, O Rome, I say it to all of you; return and do penance. There stands before you the holy truth; she cannot fall; she cannot bend or give way; wait not until the blows fall.

In everything am I oppressed; even the spiritual power is against me with Peter's mighty key. Narrow is my path and full of trouble; like Balaam's ass I must throw myself on the ground and cry: See, here I am; I am ready to die for the truth. But when Balaam beat his fallen beast, it said to him: What have I done to thee? So I say to you: Come here and tell me: what have I done to you? Why do you beat me? I have spoken the truth to you; I have warned you to choose a virtuous life; I have led many souls to Christ. But you answer: Thou hast spoken evil of us, therefore thou shouldst suffer the stripes thou deservest. But I named no one, I only blamed your vices in general. If you have sinned, be angry with yourselves, not with me. I name none of you, but if the sins I have mentioned are without question yours, then they and not I make you known. As the smitten beast asked Balaam, so I ask you: Tell me, am I not your ass? and do you not know that I have been obedient to you up to this very moment, that I have ever done what my superiors have commanded, and have always behaved myself peaceably? You know this, and because I am now so entirely different, you may well believe that a great cause drives me to it. Many knew me as I was at first; if I had remained so I could have had as much honor as I wanted. I lived six years among you, and now I speak otherwise, nevertheless I announce to you the truth that is well known. You see in what sorrows and what opposition I must now live, and I can say with Jeremiah: O, my mother, that thou hast borne me a man of strife and contention to the whole earth!—But where is a father or a mother that can say I have led their son into sin; one that can say I have ruined her husband or his wife? Everybody knows my manner of life, therefore it is right for you to believe that I speak the truth which everybody knows. You think that it is impossible for a man to do what the faith I have preached tells him to do: with God it would be easy for you.

The ass alone saw the angel, the others did not; so open your eyes. Thank God, many have them open. You have seen many learned men whom you thought wise, and they have withstood our cause: now they believe; many noted masters who were hard and proud against us: now humility casts them down. You have also seen many women turn from their vanity to simplicity; vicious youths who are now improved, and conduct themselves in a new way. Many, indeed, have received this doctrine with humility. That doctrine has stood firm, no matter how attacked with the intention of showing that it was a doctrine opposed to Christ. God does that to manifest His wisdom, to show how it finally overcomes all other wisdom. And He is willing that His servants be spoken against that they may show their patience and humility, and for the sake of His love not be afraid of martyrdom.

O ye men and women, I bid you to this truth; let those who are in captivity contradict you as much as they will, God will come and oppose their pride. Ye proud, however, if you do not turn about and become better, then will the sword and the pestilence fall upon you; with famine and war will Italy be turned upside down. I foretell you this because I am sure of it: if I were not, I would not mention it. Open your eyes as Balaam opened his eyes when the angel said to him: Had it not been for thine ass, I would have slain thee. So I say to you, ye captives: Had it not been for the good and their preaching, it would have been woe unto you. Balaam said: If this way is not good, I will return. You say likewise, you would turn back to God, if your way is not good. And to the angel you say as Balaam said: What wilt thou that we should do? The angel answers thee as he answered Balaam: Thou shalt not curse this people, but shalt say what I put in thy mouth. But in thy mouth he puts the warning that thou shouldst do good, convince one another of the divine truth, and bear evil manfully. For it is the life of a Christian to do good and to bear wrong and to continue steadfast unto death, and this is the Gospel, which we, according to the text of the Gospel for today, shall preach in all the world.

What wilt thou have of us, brother? you ask. I desire that you serve Christ with zeal and not with sloth and indifference. I desire that you do not mourn, but in thankfulness raise your hands to Heaven, whenever your brother or your son enters the service of Christ The time is come when Christ will work not only in you but through you and in others; whoever hears, let him say: Come, brother. Let one draw the other. Turn about, thou who thinkest that thou art of a superior mind and therefore canst not accept the faith. If I could only explain this whole Gospel to thee word for word, I would then scourge thy forehead and prove to thee that the faith could not be false and that Christ is thy God who is enthroned in heaven, and waits for thee. Or dost thou believe? Where are thy works? Why dost thou delay about them? Hear this: There was once a monk who spoke to a distinguished man about the faith, and got him to answer why he did not believe. He answered thus: You yourself do not believe, for if you believed you would show other works. Therefore, to you also I say: If you believe, where are your works? Your faith is something every one knows, for every one knows that Christ was put to death by the Jews, and that everywhere men pray to Him. The whole world knows that His glory has not been spread by force and weapons, but by poor fishermen. O wise man, do you think the poor fishermen were not clever enough for this? Where they worked, there they made hearts better; where they could not work, there men remained bad; and therefore was the faith true and from God. The signs which the Lord had promised followed their teaching: in His name they drove out the devil; they spoke in new tongues; if they drank any deadly drink, they received therefrom no harm. Even if these wonders had not occurred, there would have been the wonder of wonders, that poor fishermen without any miracle could accomplish so great a work as the faith. It came from God, and so is Christ true and Christ is thy God, who is in heaven and awaits thee.

You say you believe the Gospel, but you do not believe me. But the purer anything is, so much the nearer it stands to its end and purpose. The Christian life purifies the heart, and places it very near to the truth. To the Christian life will I lead you, if you would have the knowledge of the truth. If I had wished to deceive you, why should I have given you as the chief of my gifts the means of discovering my fraud? I would be verily a fool to try to impose upon you with a falsehood which you would soon detect; only because I offered you the truth, did I call you. Come here, I fear you not; the closer you examine, the clearer the truth will become to you.

There are some, however, who are ashamed of the cross of Jesus Christ, and say: If we should believe that, we should be despised everywhere, especially by the wisest. But if you would know the truth, look only on the lives of those who would have to cry woe on their unbelief if they should be measured by deeds. If you are ashamed of the cross, the Lord was not ashamed to bear that cross for you, and to die on that cross for you. Be not ashamed of His service and of the defence of the truth. Look at the servants of the devil, who are not ashamed in the open places, in the palaces, and everywhere to speak evil and to revile us. Bear then a little shame only for your Lord; for whoever follows Him, will, according to our Gospel, in His name drive out the devil; that is, he will drive out his sins, and lead a virtuous life; he will drive out serpents; he will throw out the lazy who come into the houses, and say evil things under the pretence of righteousness, and so are like poisonous serpents. You will see how children can withstand them with the truth of God, and drive them away. If a believer drinks anything deadly it will not hurt him: this deadly drink is the false doctrines of the lazy, from whom, as you contend with them, a little comes also to you. But he who stands unharmed in the faith, cries to you: See that you do good; seek God's glory, not your own. He that does that is of the truth, and remains unharmed. The Lord says further of the faithful: They shall lay their hands on the sick and shall heal them. The hands are the works, and the good lay such hands on the weak that they may support them when they totter. Do I not teach you according to the Gospel? Why do you hesitate and go not into the service of the Lord? Do you ask me still what you ought to do? I will, in conclusion, tell you.

Look to Christ and you will find that all He says concerns faith. Ask the Apostle; he speaks of nothing else than of faith. If you have the ground of all, if you have faith, you will always do what is good. Without faith man always falls into sin. You must seek faith in order to be good, or else your faith will become false. Christ commanded His disciples to preach the Gospel to all the world, and your wise men call a man a little world, a microcosm. So then, preach to yourself, O man, woman, and child. Three parts the world has in you also. Preach first of all to your knowledge, and say to it: If you draw near this truth, you will have much faith; wherefore do you hesitate to use it? To your will, say: Thou seest that everything passes away; therefore love not the world, love Christ. Thereupon turn to the second part of your world, and say to it: Be thankful, O my memory, for the mercies God has shown thee, that thou thinkest not of the things of this world but of the mercy of thy creation, and thy redemption through the blood of the Son of God. Then go to the third part, to thy imagination, and proclaim to it: Set nothing before my eyes but my death, bring nothing before me but the Crucified, embrace Him, fly to Him. Then go through all the cities of thy world, and preach to them. First say to thine eyes: Look not on vanity. To thy ears say: Listen not to the words of the lazy, but only to the words of Jesus. To thy tongue say: Speak no more evil. For thy tongue is as a great rock that rolls from the summit of a mountain, and at first falls slowly, then ever faster and more furiously. It begins with gentle murmuring, then it utters small sins, and then greater, until it finally breaks forth in open blasphemy. To thy palate say: It is necessary that we do a little penance. In all thy senses be clean, and turn to the

Lord, for He it is who will give you correction and purity. To thy hands say: Do good and give alms; and let thy feet go in the good way. Our reformation has begun in the Spirit of God, if you take it to heart that each one has to preach to himself. Then will we in the name of Jesus drive out the devils of temptation. Yes, call upon Jesus as often as temptation approaches: call upon Him a hundred times and believe firmly, and the temptation will depart. Then will we speak with new tongues; we will speak with God. We shall drive away serpents; the enticements of the senses are these serpents. If we drink anything deadly it will not hurt us; if anger and lust arise in us, at the name of Jesus they will have to give way. We shall lay our hands upon the sick and heal them; with good deeds shall we strengthen the weak soul. If thou feelest thy weakness, flee to God, and He will strengthen; therefore He is thy only refuge. He is thy Savior and thy Lord, who went into the heavens to prepare a place for thee, and to await thee there. What do you intend to do? Go and follow Jesus, who is praised from everlasting to everlasting. Amen.

MARTIN LUTHER

Martin Luther was born at Eisleben, November 10, 1483. His parents were peasagottnts, his father being a miner and latterly a smith. He was brought up in poverty, but was able to attend school and later to study at the University of Erfurt. Here he took his Bachelor's degree in 150 and his Master's in 1503. He had intended to become a lawyer, but suddenly entered the monastery of the Augustinians at Erfurt. Here he was tormented with religious difficulties, with which he struggled in vain until his Superior brought him under the influence of Tauler and the German mystics. In 151 he went on a pilgrimage to Rome, where the frivolity of the papal court, which was at that time in the midst of the artistic and literary splendor of the High Renaissance, made a profound and painful impression upon him, and he returned deeply agitated to Wittenberg, where he had in 1508 been given a professorship. He resumed his lectures on the Bible, and made them even more popular. He also added to his reputation by his powerful preaching. In the midst of these labors he was disturbed by the appearance of Tetzel with indulgences which the latter disposed of in a manner that was a shameless perversion of the teaching of the Church. Luther was roused to combat He published his famous theses. At once there was great excitement, and the news of the discussion spread throughout Germany. Luther perceived, as the dispute went on, that the controversy involved the fundamental principles of religion. The tone of his writings became increasingly bitter, and he was able to enlist in his cause the political sentiments and the sentiment of German nationality. In 1520 he was excommunicated, but he publicly burned the bull of excommunication and appealed to a general council. In this appeal he merely followed the precedent set at Constance and Basle a century before. In the next year he attended the Diet at Worms, at which he was called upon to retract his heretical opinions, but this he refused to do. For this he was placed under the ban of the Empire, and to save his life his friends secreted him in the

Wartburg, where he continued his work on the translation of the Bible. In a short time Luther returned to Wittenberg and took up the hard part of his work as a reformer. He was now materially aided by the electors and other princes who sided with him. A political basis was in this way given to the Reformation, which enabled it to withstand the power of the Church of Rome in the Empire. The States which sided with him soon began to organize their respective churches, and in 1530 the Augsburg Confession gave a definite theological basis to the movement. From this time, the agitation that Luther started was beyond his control. Many were now engaged in the work, so that Luther was able to devote himself to his labors at Wittenberg. Here, in spite of his vows, he had married, and established his home. He completed his translation of the Bible, lectured, preached, and wrote incessantly, for the controversies with the Roman court were no longer affairs in which he was the sole figure. After several years of poor health Luther died at Eisleben on February 18, 1546.

Luther was essentially a popular preacher, and tried in every way to present his subject so that the simplest might understand it. He is often rude, coarse, violent, and even grotesque. But there is no mistaking his purpose. He is filled with the one thought, Justification by Faith alone, and this he aims in every conceivable way to enforce, and in his desire to be perfectly clear to every member of his congregation he draws his illustrations from every quarter. As with many others that have done a vast work as preachers, he was not eloquent in the academic sense, but he had to a marvellous degree the power of presenting a truth so that every one that heard him felt that it was the truth and that it concerned him personally.

The best life of Luther is probably that by Julius Kostlin in two volumes (1875). This has been abbreviated, and there is a good English translation. The best book on the Reformation is probably by Ranke, *Deutsche Geschichte im Zeiialter der Reformation*, of which there is an English translation made from an early edition. This work is esteemed by both Catholics and Protestants. Also to be recommended are: Seebohm, *Era of the Protestant Revolution*, 1877, and often reprinted; and G. P. Fisher, The Reformation. Schaff has written a good account of the German Reformation with very valuable bibliographical references in his *History of the Christian Church*, vol. 4.

Luther's collected works have been published many times. The best editions are: The Halle edition, by Walch, Halle, 1740-1750, in twenty-four volumes; the Erlangen-Frankfurt, by Plochmann, Irmischer, and Enders, Erlangen and Frankfurt on the Main, 1827 *sqq.*, in, so far, 101 volumes (not yet finished); the Weimar edition, by a large number of scholars, Weimar, 1883 *sqq.*

SERMON ON THE GOOD SHEPHERD

by Martin Luther.

The pastors of the early Protestant Churches were little skilled in evangelical preaching. They often read Luther's sermons instead of discourses prepared by themselves. The following sermon, one of the three on the Gospel for the second Sunday after Easter, was published, though perhaps not for the first time, in 1527, in a collection of Luther's sermons made by his friend, Stephen Rodt. The sermon is considered as typical of Luther's style, and as one of his most eloquent productions.

THIS is a Gospel full of consolation; setting forth the Lord Christ in a kind of fertile description;—teaching us what His character is, what His works are, and how He is affected towards men. And we cannot better understand it than by setting in contrast light and darkness, day and night; that is, a good and a bad shepherd; for this is what Christ does here.

You have often heard that God has ordained two kinds of preaching to the world. The one, which sets forth the Word of God:—"Thou shaft have no other gods," likewise, "Thou shaft not kill, commit adultery, or steal," and thereupon threatens that whosoever does not keep these commandments shall die. This teaching, however, does not purify any man's heart; for although a man may thereby be so restrained from these things as to show himself outwardly righteous, yet inwardly his heart is hostile to the law, and would prefer that there were no law at all. The other office of preaching is the Gospel; which shows you where that strength is to be obtained that shall enable you to do that which the law demands: this preaching does not force men, nor threaten them, but sweetly invites them. It does not say, "Do this, or do that"; but it says, "Come unto Me; I will show thee how thou art to obtain power to become righteous. Behold, here is the Lord Christ, who will give thee this." Wherefore, these two kinds of preaching are as opposed to each other as taking and giving, exacting and bestowing: and this difference is to be most carefully observed. In this way it is that God ever has governed, and still does govern the world. To carnal and rude men, who are not touched with the Gospel, the law is to be preached; and they must be driven until they be humbled and acknowledge their offences. When this is done, then the Gospel must be set before them.

These are the two offices of preaching which come from heaven. But besides these, there are others, which do not come from heaven, but are the inventions of men; which, in order to disturb consciences, have been introduced by the pope and our bishops. These are unworthy the name of shepherds, or indeed of hirelings, but are those very persons whom Christ calls thieves, robbers, and wolves. But if men are to be governed well, they must be governed by the Word of God; where they are not governed by the Word of God, there they are certainly not governed at all; moreover, Christ here assumes the other office, and describes what it is. He says that He is the principal, yea, the only shepherd: for that which He does not feed, is without pasture. Let us then look into this preaching, which is so excellent, and full of consolation.

Ye have heard, then, that our Lord Christ, after His crucifixion and death, arose from the dead, and ascended on high, and was translated into an immortal state: not that He sits idly in heaven above in self-sufficient happiness; rather He takes the kingdom in His hands, governs it, and is a King, of whom all the prophets and the whole Scriptures testify. Wherefore, let us believe, that He is continually with us, and sitting in judgment; and let us not imagine that He sits idly on high, but that He, from above, observes and governs all things, as Paul saith to the Ephesians, and especially the things of His kingdom; which is, the Christian faith; wherefore, the kingdom of Christ must go on here among us upon earth. Concerning this kingdom, we have said that it is so appointed, that we all must increase and become purer from day to day; and that it is not administered by force, but by the preaching of the mouth; that is, by the Gospel.

This preaching did not proceed from men, but was commenced by Christ Himself, and afterwards put into the hearts of His Apostles and their successors, that they might understand it, and into their mouths that they might speak of it and preach it to others. This, then, is the kingdom of Christ; it is thus that He reigns; so that all power stands and rests upon the Word of God. And those who hear and believe this Word belong to this kingdom: which Word becomes so powerful, that it effects all things that are necessary for man, and brings all good things which might be desired: for it is the power of God which can and may save all who believe on it, as Paul saith. Wherefore, if thou believe that Christ died to deliver thee from all misery, and if thou cleave to that Word, it is so sure and certain that no creature can overthrow it. And as no creature can subvert the Word, so no one can harm thee, since thou believest on it.

And thou wilt with the Word conquer sin, death, the devil and hell: and thus, thou wilt come and be drawn into that state where the Word itself is; that is, into eternal peace, joy, and life: and, to be brief, thou wilt be made partaker of all the blessings that are contained in the Word: this kingdom, therefore, is wonderful. The Word itself is present, and is preached by a living voice before all the world: but its power is quite hidden: nor can any one perceive that it is so active, nor know that it is so powerful, but he who believes it; it must be felt and tasted in the heart itself.

We ministers can do nothing else than become the mouths and instruments of our Lord Christ, through which He sensibly preaches His Word. He permits the Word to be proclaimed openly, that all may hear it. But for the heart itself to digest it and feel it within, that is the operation of faith, and is the mystical work of Christ; which He works, according to His divine knowledge and good pleasure. And this is what He saith: "I am the good Shepherd." For who is a good shepherd? "A good shepherd," says Christ, "layeth down his life for his sheep; and I also lay down My life for My sheep." In this virtue He comprehends all things at once, and sets before us a sweet parable of the sheep. You see that this animal is altogether foolish and is the simplest of all beasts, so that if one would speak of some simple person, he says, "He is a sheep!" Nevertheless the sheep has this characteristic more than any other animal, that it quickly hears the voice of its shepherd; nor will it follow any other than its own shepherd. And it is so devoted, that it will cleave closely to only its own shepherd, and seeks help from him. It cannot help itself, nor procure its food, nor defend itself from wolves, but depends absolutely upon the care of another.

The nature of this animal Christ uses as a parable, and makes Himself the shepherd; wherein He beautifully sets forth of what nature His kingdom is, and in what it consists. As though He had said, My kingdom is nothing else than that I rule My sheep; that is, poor, miserable, and troubled men in this world, who will know and find, that apart from Me, there is no succor nor counsel to help them.

Moreover, to set this forth more clearly, and that it might be the better understood, let us adduce a saying from the prophet Ezekiel, who speaks against evil shepherds who are opposed to Christ: saying, "Should not the sheep be fed by the shepherds? why have ye not fed them? Ye have partaken of the milk of the sheep and ye have clothed you with the wool: ye kill them that are fat, but ye feed not my flock. The weak have ye not strengthened; neither have ye healed that which was sick; neither have ye bound up that which was broken; neither have ye brought again ' that which was driven away; neither have ye sought again that which was lost; but with force and with cruelty have ye ruled them. And they were scattered because there was no shepherd; and all the beasts of the field have devoured them. My sheep are scattered over all the mountains, and over the whole earth." God here rebukes the shepherds who do not properly feed the sheep. See, now, how He writes. His most serious concern is that the weak, the sick, the broken, the driven away, the lost, should be strengthened, healed, sought out, and not scattered about. This, says He to the shepherds, is what ye ought to have done, but ye did it not. Wherefore, I will Myself do it,—as He saith a little after, "I will seek that which was lost, and bring again that which was driven away; and will heal that which was sick, and will make it again sound."

Here you see that the kingdom of Christ is such, that He is occupied in the care of the weak, the sick, and the broken; and that He takes them to Himself, that He may help them. This preaching is indeed full of great consolation. But there is one deficiency in it, for we have not a sufficient sense of our calamitous state; for if we felt that, we should flee to Him. But what did those shepherds? They ruled with rigor: they enforced the law of God with great tyranny: to which they added moreover their own inventions, as they still do: and if you do not keep them, they immediately cry out and condemn you, so that their administration is nothing else than a continued driving and commanding. Such is not rightly feeding and ruling souls, says Christ; and He is no such shepherd. For in this way, no one is helped, but rather is entirely ruined, as we shall hear. Let us, therefore, now go over the description of the prophet in all its particulars. '

First, he says that the weak sheep are to be strengthened. That is, consciences which are weak in the faith, and are of a sorrowful spirit, and are disheartened, are not to be driven and told, "Thou must do this. Thou must be strong: for if thou be weak, thou wilt be lost." This is not to strengthen the weak. As St. Paul says to the Romans, "Them that are weak in the faith receive, and disturb not their consciences." And immediately after he says, "We that are strong ought to bear the infirmities of the weak." Wherefore, they are not to be driven with strictness, but are rather to be consoled, that though they are weak, they should not on that account despair; in time, they will become stronger.

For the prophet Isaiah speaks thus sweetly concerning Christ: "A bruised reed shall he not break, and smoking flax shall he not quench." The "bruised reed," signifies weak and bruised consciences; which are easily shaken and driven to desperation. These He does not trample under His feet; this is not His manner; but He gently and carefully deals with them that He may not break them. "Smoking flax," which as yet hardly burns, and is more smoke than fire, signifies those same weak ones; whose spirit shall not utterly despair, for He will not entirely extinguish them; nay, He will by degrees fan them to a flame, and will strengthen them more and more. That is a great consolation to him who understands it. He, therefore, who does not gently lead the weak consciences, is certainly no good shepherd.

Secondly, saith the prophet, "That which was sick ye ought to have helped." Who then are the "sick"? Those who suffer infirmities that are apparent in various bad works. The first concerned the conscience when it is weak. The second concerns the eternal walk in life: that is, when any one, in fits of self-will and wrath, is driven headlong this way or that in a passion; or commits at times other foolish sins of the same kind; even as the Apostles at times offended in gross instances. Those, therefore, who show their infirmity in external things before men, so that they are offended and say, that they are men of bad and morose spirits, these God does not reject; for His kingdom is not ordained that none but those that are sound and of perfect health are therein, because these pertain to the life to come. But Christ is seated on high to receive these helpless ones, and help them.

Wherefore, although we are weak and sick, we should not despair nor say that we are not in the kingdom of Christ. Nay rather, on the contrary, the more we feel our weakness, the more ought we to draw near the kingdom. For it is for this very end that He is there, that He might help us and make us well. If therefore thou be sick, and a sinner, and feelest thy need, thou hast the greater cause to say to Him, "O Lord, I come unto Thee just because I am a sinner; that Thou mightest help me and make me righteous." Thus thy very necessity drives thee to Him. For the greater thy disease is, the more necessary is it for thee to get thyself healed. This will Christ have, and He, therefore, invites us to come joyfully to Him. But those who are not such shepherds, think that they can make men righteous by loud bawling and driving: whereas, by such means, they only make them worse. Hence it is, that we see in this day that this preposterous way of instructing men only tends most miserably to confound all things; as the prophet here complains.

Thirdly, "That which was broken have ye not bound up." To be "broken," is when a man's leg is broken in two, or he has received any other hurt; that is, when the Christian is not only weak, and has an infirmity, so that at times he offends, but falls into grievous temptations so as to break a leg, as if it should happen that he should fall and deny the Gospel, as Peter did when he denied Christ. Now if any one so sins, so as even to be driven quite back, or to fall prostrate on the ground, yet he is not to be rejected, as if he belongs not at all to Christ's kingdom. Christ must and will be ever like Himself: and in His kingdom must remain mere grace and mercy: so that He will ever continue to help those, who feel their misery and wretchedness, and who desire to be rescued from their sufferings: and thus it will always be a kingdom of help and comfort. And He will be a comforting, gentle shepherd, who invites and allures every one to come to Him.

Moreover, all these things are administered by the Gospel only. By this the weak are made strong, the sick healed. For the Word is of that nature, that it serves for all things which the conscience lacks, and gives to all so much comfort, that however great a sinner one may be, one need not despair. Christ alone therefore is the true and real shepherd, who heals every wound, and lifts up every one that is fallen. He who does that not is no shepherd.

Fourthly, the prophet saith, "That which was driven away, ye brought not back." What is that which is "driven away"? Truly, the soul that is despised and brought to shame; which is thought to be utterly lost. But Christ is not willing that persons of this kind shall be dealt with harshly. For He does not so contract His kingdom as to admit none but the strong, the whole, and the altogether perfect, to dwell therein; that perfection pertains, as had been said, to the future kingdom after this life. But now, because He rules, His present kingdom shall be nothing but grace and sweetness, even as God declared to the future race of Israel that the promised land should flow with milk and honey; which also St. Paul confirms when he says, "On the less honorable members of the body we bestow more honor."

Fifthly, the prophet saith in conclusion, "That which was lost ye have not sought out." "That which is lost," signifies that which is condemned, so that one thinks that it will never return. Such are the publicans and harlots in the Gospel; and such among us are the profligate and the lawless. These are in no wise to be disregarded, but to be called back by all possible means. Even as we read that Paul did, when he delivered over two unto Satan, as he says to Timothy, "I have delivered them unto Satan, that they might be chastened, and might no more blaspheme." And also to the Corinthians he says, "I have resolved to deliver such an one unto Satan for the destruction of the flesh, that the spirit may be saved in the day of the Lord Jesus." These he cast out as condemned, but afterwards he restored them.

Wherefore Christ must be preached, that He rejects no one, however weak he may be, but is never ready to receive all unto Himself, to comfort and strengthen them; so that we may always think of Him as the pattern of a good shepherd. For hearts will of their own accord go to Him, so that men are no more to be urged, and driven, and compelled. For the Gospel attracts and invites so that they find a pleasure in it and go to it in all confidence. From this there springs up in them a love and affection for Christ; so that now, they do gladly what they should, which formerly they had to be driven and compelled to do. If we are driven to do anything, we do it with displeasure and against our will; and such an obedience as this God cannot endure, therefore is it lost.

But when I see that the Lord is so favorably inclined towards me, He takes from me my heart, so that I must run to Him; and, from this time, my heart is filled with all pleasure and joy.

Here then observe what an accursed thing it is for one man to judge another. The kingdom of Christ, as we have heard, is for that end established, that it might have respect unto sick souls, and might render them righteous. Wherefore, all those must be in error, who regard only the strong and the holy. And hence, the chief of all knowledge is to know Christ aright. For it is engendered in us by nature to be ourselves filled with sins within, and yet to wish all men to be holy; and we gape and look upon strong Christians only, and will not look at the sick and weak; persuading ourselves, that if they are not strong, they are not Christians; and those who are not entirely holy, we hold for wicked, when we are all the while far worse than they. This arises from our evil nature, and from our blind reason, which is ever measuring the kingdom of God according to its own apprehension, and imagining that those things which appear vile in its own eyes are vile in the eyes of God.

Wherefore, all these things must be far removed from sight. For if thou lookest upon them much thou wilt at length arrive at that state of mind that thou wilt think: "Alas, where shall I remain? If only such can be Christians, who are strong, perfect, and righteous, when shall I ever attain unto that state?" And thou wilt make it so that thou wilt never attain it. Wherefore, thou must come at last to this point, to say: "O Lord, I feel that I am thus infirm, thus sick and broken in mind: nevertheless I will not let myself wander; I will come to Thee that Thou mayest help me, for Thou art that good and gentle Shepherd; I believe Thou art that, therefore will I put no trust in my own works."

Therefore we should be wise, that we may learn to know Christ rightly and to know that His kingdom is nothing else than a hospital where lie the sick and languishing, who need to be nursed. But this knowledge very few receive; this wisdom is very deeply hidden; so that, oftentimes, those who are partakers of the Gospel and of the Spirit are very deficient in it. For this is the highest wisdom that can be had. Wherefore, although men look into the Scriptures and see that those Scriptures extol the kingdom of Christ, and say what a splendid thing it is, yet they do not clearly see what the words really mean, nor do they observe that in this lies the true wisdom, which far surpasses all human wisdom. For our wisdom is not ours in order to deal with the wise, the prudent and clever people, and talk about it and preach it, but to deal with fools and imprudent men, and win them to it; not, however, that we may gratify ourselves thereby, but rather that we may help men out of their sin and folly, so that they attain unto righteousness and a sound understanding.

Hence it is evident that Christian wisdom consists in this: that we raise not up our eyes on high, and look at what is exalted and wise, and see in that an image of ourselves; but rather, that we turn our eyes downward and see what is lowly and foolish. He who knows that, should thank God. For by this knowledge he is become such an one that he can rightly accommodate himself unto everything that happens in the world. Wherefore, you will find many, even those who are preachers of the Gospel, that have not yet attained unto this wisdom. For hitherto we have been instructed, and we have been accustomed to believe, that no one dare come unto Christ unless he be first perfectly pure. Wherefore, thou must unlearn this persuasion, and lay hold upon a true understanding that thou mayest know Christ rightly: that He is the true Shepherd, of whom we have already heard.

And now, He compares the good shepherd with a bad shepherd, or an hireling, and says: "A good shepherd giveth his life for the sheep, but an hireling, who is not the shepherd, whose own the sheep are not, seeth the wolf coming, and leaveth the sheep and fleeth, and the wolf catcheth them and scattereth the sheep. The hireling fleeth because he is an hireling, and careth not for the sheep." And even as He alone is Christ, and yet He gives us the same name, so that we are called Christians; so, although He be the only shepherd, yet He gives the name to those who are to exercise in the Christian Church the office of preacher. So also, He forbids us to call any one upon earth by the name of Father, because One is our Father, who is in heaven. And yet, nevertheless, Paul calls himself the father of the Corinthians, when he says, "In Christ Jesus I have begotten you through the Gospel." Thus also God declares that He alone is Father, and yet He permits men to be called by that name, and that they also should be fathers; which, however, they have not from themselves, but from Christ. So also we are called Christians; but on this account only, because we have nothing of ourselves, but receive all as given through Christ. "But the hireling," saith He, "who is not the shepherd, and whose own the sheep are not, when he seeth the wolf coming, leaveth the sheep and fleeth." This is, indeed, a hard saying, that some who preach and handle the Gospel purely, and who comfort and heal the sheep, yet, at last, suffer them to be tom away, and themselves flee when the sheep most need their help. As long as no wolves appear, they are diligent and feed well the flock; but as soon as they see the wolf rushing in upon the sheep, they desert the sheep. They have well fed the sheep, so that the sheep are strong, sound, and fat; they are, therefore, all the more acceptable to the wolf, for whom these men have fattened them. But what is the meaning of all this? The meaning of Christ is this: In His kingdom, which consists in nothing else but in strengthening the weak, in healing the sick, and in giving courage to the fearful, and so forth, the Holy Cross shall by no means be wanting. For when it shall be preached that Christ alone must take to Himself us who are poor miserable sheep; that He only must strengthen, heal, and help us, and that of our own powers and our own works we can in no respect help ourselves; so that thereupon must disappear all our own works, and all that by which the world pretends that it does much for God's worship; such preaching as this, the world cannot bear. For it is the nature of the Gospel that it brings with it the Holy Cross. Whosoever shall confess this before the whole world, must do it at the peril of his life. .

If therefore these things are so, we have here a separation of the good shepherd from the bad, in the most open manner. He that is an hireling only preaches the Gospel as long as he hears himself called a learned, good, and holy man. But afterwards, if he is attacked and is called a heretic and a rogue, or is made the subject of public ridicule, he either recants or runs away and leaves the poor sheep alone in their misery; and now they are in a worse state than they were before. And what avails it that the sheep were formerly well fed? Whereas, had they been true shepherds, they would rather have lost their lives beside the sheep, being ready at any time to lay down their lives for the Gospel's sake. And hence those are in no respect true shepherds who preach so that they may derive from it honor, wealth, and profit. These are certainly hirelings. They seek their own gain by the means of true doctrine and the Word of God; but they hold to these no longer than they have honor and reward. But when the wolf comes, they draw back and deny the Word, or betake themselves to flight, and leave the flock of sheep with mouths wide open and longing for pasture and the shepherd, who should defend them from the wolves, but no one is there, and they are deserted, when there is most need of some one to strengthen them.

This continually happens in our day. When it happens that we are attacked and persecuted, then preachers shut their mouths and betake themselves to flight; while the sheep are scattered in a miserable manner, and are carried and driven away in every direction. May God grant that some shepherds at least may remain and be ready to shed their blood in defence of the sheep.—Thus hath Christ portrayed hirelings.

He saith moreover:

"I am the good Shepherd, and I know My sheep, and am known of Mine."

These are deep words; and it would take up a great deal of time to discuss them thoroughly. He is here speaking of that peculiar office which belongs to Him. I know My sheep, he saith, and they in turn know Me. How comes this to pass? He shows how it is immediately afterwards:

"As the Father knoweth Me, even so know I the Father."

And how knoweth He the Father? Not by human, but by divine knowledge. Upon former occasions, I have sometimes spoken upon this more largely. The sum of the matter is this: Christ knows us as His sheep, and we, on the other hand, know Him as our shepherd. We have already heard what a good shepherd is, and, on the other hand, what the poor weak sheep are. He looks upon us as sheep that are weak, sick, and have broken limbs: that is, He cares not that His sheep are thus weak and sick, despised and rejected; but takes them to Him and heals them. For although they be so diseased and unsound that the whole world thinks they are no sheep of His, yet this is only the knowledge of the world. Christ does not thus know His sheep. He does not look to see how they are, but only whether they are sheep, that they have the name of sheep, that they are called sheep. His eyes are on the sheep, not on the wool.

In a word, those are real shepherds, and they follow Christ, and know sheep as He knows them, who keep their eye upon the person, and not upon the diseases, and who thus make a difference between the sheep and the disease.

"My Father," saith Christ, "knoweth Me, but the world knoweth Me not. When that time shall come, that I shall die by an ignominious death upon the cross, then will they all say; 'What I is this the son of God? No! He must be some condemned wretch, whose soul and body belong to the devil!' So will the world look upon Me and regard Me. But My Father shall say, 'This is My beloved Son.' He is My King, and My Savior. He will not look at My affliction, My wounds, My cross, and My death, but on the person that I am. Wherefore, although I may be in the very belly of hell, and in the very jaws of the devil, yet I must of necessity be delivered therefrom, for My Father will not forsake Me. And thus it is that I know My sheep, and they know Me. They know that I am the good Shepherd, and they recognize Me as such, therefore they come to Me and cling to Me; they are not troubled that they are weak and sick; they know well that I would have them such sheep."

And now He concludes and says: "Other sheep I have which are not of this fold. These also will I bring, and they will hear My voice, and there shall be one flock and one shepherd." Some have so interpreted this Scripture, as if it is to be fulfilled in the last days, when Antichrist shall come with Elias and Enoch. But this is not true, and it is the devil who has made it so that they might believe, that all the world should become Christian! The devil has been at work to obscure the true doctrine, that no one might be able to understand it. Wherefore, beware of this imposture. For this Scripture was verified and fulfilled soon after the ascension of Christ, and is still being fulfilled. When the Gospel was first promulgated, it was preached to the Jews, and that people was the fold. And where He says, "Other sheep I have which are not of this fold, them also I must bring," He here shows that the Gospel must be preached to the Gentiles also, that they also might believe on Christ, that of the Jews and Gentiles there might be one Church. Which thing Christ afterwards wrought by the Apostles, who preached to the Gentiles, and converted them to the faith. So that now there is one Church, one faith, one hope, one love, one baptism, and so forth. And the same work is still going on, even till the last day. Wherefore, ye must not think that all the world and all men will believe on Christ. For we must always have the Holy Cross; those who persecute the Christians must be the greater part of the world. But the Gospel must still continue to be preached, that some may be continually won over to Christianity. For Christ's kingdom is not yet finished, and is not complete.—This is a compendious explanation of this Gospel.

HULDREICH ZWINGLI

Huldreich Zwingli was born in Wildhaus, Switzerland, January 1st, 1484. He was a pupil of the learned humanist of Basle, Thomas Wyttenbach. The bent that he received from this master he retained through life, and the influence of the classical spirit is to be clearly traced throughout his works. After a pastorate of ten years in Glarus, he removed to Einsiedeln in 1516. Here he began his work as a reformer. The town was the goal of many pilgrims on account of the presence of the miraculous image of the Virgin, and the practices associated with the pilgrimages roused the indignation of Zwingli, who attacked the whole system. This was before Luther's breach with the Roman court. But after the appearance of Luther in the role of a reformer, and especially after the extension of the indulgence traffic to Switzerland, Zwingli boldly came forward in opposition to the ancient faith. By the year 1525 the Reformation, according to the ideas of Zwingli, was practically victorious at Zurich, and the movement spread rapidly to Basle and the other cantons. A prominent feature of the Reformation in. Switzerland was the great number of public disputations that were held, and in these, for various reasons, the reforming party was generally the victor. In 1529 the Reformation was complete in Basle, St. Gall, and Schaffhausen. In consequence of the stand taken by Zwingli and the reformed cantons, and also on account of jealousies of long standing, the Catholic cantons entered into a league with Austria against the reformed cantons. This was, however, of short duration. War, nevertheless, broke out between the two parties, and in a battle at Cappel, October 11, 1531, Zwingli, who was acting as chaplain in the army, was among the slain. As a result of this battle, the Catholic party was able to win back much of the territory that had been lost. The theological system of Calvin subsequently took the place of Zwingli's in those places where the reformed faith survived.

As an orator, Zwingli was thoroughly versed in the classical masters, whom he studied diligently in order to fit himself to be a preacher. In this he was perhaps alone among the reformers that separated from the Roman Church. He always remained a scholar, and retained the habit of quoting Greek and Hebrew in his sermons. He was a man of tender sentiment, but at the same time was full of fire and energy. He used the Swiss dialect in his preaching.

The works of Zwingli have appeared in several editions, of which the best is that of Melchior Schuler and Joh. Schultheissen in 8 vols., Zurich, 1828, etc. The life of Zwingli has been written by J. J. Hottinger, Zurich, 1843 (translated by T. C. Porter, Harrisburg, 1857); by W. Roder, St Gall, 1854; by R. Christoffel, Elberfeld, 1857; by J. C. Morikefer, Leipsic, 1867-1869, 2 vols., and by R. Staehelin, Basle, 1895-1897, 2 vols.

SERMON ON MARY, THE PURE MOTHER OF GOD

by Huldreich Zwingli

The occasion of the following sermon, from which the portion referring to the Annunciation has been taken, is given by Zwingli in the preface to the sermon. According to this, he tried, wherever he thought he saw superstition, to restore the faith to its original purity. He had done this regarding the "superstitious" reverence to the Blessed Virgin. Thereupon his enemies took occasion to charge him with having deprived her of the honor that was justly due her, and even of having despised and reviled her. In the sermon from which the following selection is taken Zwingli endeavored to show the honor that was due to the Blessed Virgin and the manner in which men should honor her. The sermon was preached at Zurich in the autumn of 1522.

WHEN the fulness of time was come according to the divine determination, God sent His messenger Gabriel to the maiden named Mary, who was espoused to a pious man called Joseph. But in this the wisdom of God was manifested in that God did not intend that the marriage with Joseph, to whom she was espoused, should take place that children might be born, but that the Virgin Mary, after she was found to be with child, might not be stoned according to the law of the Jews, for that commanded that she who bore a child and had no husband should be stoned. Joseph was so honored that he might be able to shield her from the severity of the law. Furthermore, she was married to Joseph that she and the child might always have a guardian and protector. For by herself a woman is a poor helpless thing.

Joseph, however, was given to her and married to her that she might always have some one to help her; for when she was commanded to flee or move from one place to another, Joseph was there to prepare all things needful. Thus she was obliged to flee into Egypt, and again from Egypt she removed to the land of the Jews, and from Judea into Nazareth, a city of Galilee. For all this Joseph was needed. So much in brief of the marriage of Joseph.

In this we see the great grace that God showed to Mary, in that He chose her, before all other women and virgins of the whole world, to be the mother of His Son. And He did this without any reference as to whether she was of lowly birth or a high-born virgin. Although she was of the family of David, she was still poor and not at all high born according to human estimate, as she herself sings: "God hath regarded the lowliness of His handmaiden." However high the house of David might be regarded by God and men, at that time it did not stand in high position or honor, according to worldly honor, for no one of the house of David was at that time reigning. Just as today we have no regard for those of noble lineage, be they ever so high born, if they have no possessions or power. She was also noble in that the prophets, filled with the spirit of God, had spoken of her of old time. Isaiah said: "Behold a virgin shall conceive, and bear a son, and his name shall be called Immanuel, God with us." Yea verily, God with us, in that He has taken upon Him of a pure virgin our human nature, and has become for us our brother and a propitiatory sacrifice. The same prophet also said: "There shall come forth a branch out of the stem of Jesse, and a flower shall grow out of his roots." This branch is the holy Mary, this flower is Christ.

When the angel came in unto Mary, he greeted her with these words: "Hail, thou art full of grace! The Lord is with thee, blessed art thou among women." Here it is to be noticed that this word "full of grace" is translated from the Greek word "kecharitomene," which means beloved, or filled with grace, highly favored, whereby we understand that the word "full of grace" should not be taken to mean that she was from herself full of grace, but that all the grace with which she was so rich and full was from God. For to be full of grace is nothing else than to be highly favored of God and to be chosen before all other women. For grace is only the favor of God. So if I should say that God has given much grace to men, I should say nothing else than

God has been very favorable to men and done loving things for them. Therefore is the pure Mary full of grace from God, as she herself sings: "He hath done to me great things." She says not: "I am great from mine own grace," but "the Almighty hath done to me great things." For immediately afterward she adds: "He hath regarded the lowliness of His handmaiden, for behold from henceforth all generations shall call me blessed."

We have also said: "blessed art thou among women" that there may be no doubt what the word "blessed" might mean. I have said: "highly praised art thou above all women"; for the Greek word "eulogumene" means highly praised or blessed. I will not, however, discard the word "blessed," yet we should understand that the phrase: "blessed art thou," means, highly praised art thou. Here the Angelic Salutation ends, that is, the angel said no more in his salutation than these words: "Hail, thou art full of grace! the Lord is with thee, blessed art thou among women." What follows has been added partly by the pious Elizabeth, and partly by devout Christians. Elizabeth added: "Blessed" (understand thereby, highly praised) "is the fruit of thy womb." Devout men have added: "Jesus Christ, Amen." But that phrase: "blessed is the fruit of thy womb," is of no less value because the angel himself did not speak it. The words are also spoken of the Holy Ghost, as Luke plainly states, saying: "And Elizabeth was filled with the Holy Ghost and she spake out with a loud voice, and said: 'Blessed art thou among women, and blessed is the fruit of thy womb.'" "Jesus Christ" is also added by the Holy Ghost, for no one can call Jesus Lord but by the Holy Ghost. Yet herein is nothing strange, for the Greeks add still more after the words: "blessed is the fruit of thy womb," namely: "for thou hast borne the Saviour of souls."

And here there will be some who are displeased and will take occasion to complain: See, thou art giving us the Ave Maria. I answer: I do not give it to you, but the Evangelist Luke, he it is that gives it to you. Read the first chapter of Luke, from which it is taken. But some will still say, the angel did not say it all to Mary. But on that account it is none the less good. It should none the less be said one part with the other. And it is by no means wrong that we call it the Angelic Salutation, for the beginning and the greater part is the angel's.

When the chaste and modest Mary saw the angel, she was troubled at his saying and cast in her mind what manner of salutation this should be. The angels of God have always appeared in the likeness of beautiful men, and in this way the angel appeared to Mary. Therefore she was afraid, for she had had nothing to do with any young man, that he should come to her secretly. Therefore she was afraid when she saw the beautiful figure of Gabriel and heard his friendly salutation; for she was innocent of any knowledge of gallantry or wantonness, and there appeared to her, nevertheless, this beautiful youth. Therefore she wondered what manner of salutation this might be. She knew not the society of any man nor of any man's affection for her; yet she heard from a man, as she first thought him, a friendly salutation. Herein we have a manifestation of the pure and unspotted soul of Mary, who knew nothing of sin, yea, was so far from all wantonness that, as Ambrose says, she was afraid at even the salutation of an angel. But the Heavenly Father did not allow her to remain in error, but at once instructed her further by the angel: "Fear not, Mary, God has revealed His grace to thee. Behold, thou shalt conceive in thy womb, and bring forth a son, and shalt call His name Jesus. He shall be great and shall be called the Son of the Highest, and the Lord God shall give unto Him the throne of His father David; and He shall reign over the house of Jacob forever; and of His kingdom there shall be no end."

See what a great work the almighty God begins with the humble Mary. Think not that if the Spirit of God had not enlightened her understanding and faith, she would have been able of her own soul's strength to have believed the angel. She would have regarded the speech of the angel rather as a deception or as a slander. For she, by no means, thought so of herself that she should be the mother of so great and excellent a son, for the great promise was certainly far above her lowliness. From this we learn, however, that the understanding of the Word of God and faith in it, is not of any human reason or power, but cometh of the grace of God, which illuminates our minds and trains us. Therefore Mary spoke with reason: "He that is mighty hath done to me great things, yea verily great things, for He hath so graciously spoken to me His lowly handmaiden, who never thought or imagined such a thing before He thus dealt with me. He has also drawn my heart to Himself so that I have believed in Him; and He has therefore done that which is above the course of nature; He has made a virgin the mother of His Son, the Lord of all things, the Redeemer of men. He has not been pleased, in thus dealing mercifully with the human race, to accomplish his purpose by the daughter of an emperor, or King Herod, or the High Priest, but by me, a simple lowly maiden. She it is who was not esteemed by the world that He hath raised on high, that on account of the honor and good things that He has given me, all men may be astonished and shall call me blessed, that I, a bride of God, the Heavenly Father, and a dwelling-place of the Holy Ghost, have in this world borne without a human father, and for the salvation of all men, Him who from all eternity in Heaven was born, according to his Godhead, of the Heavenly Father without any mother. Oh, the indescribable wisdom and grace of God, who has so wisely and mercifully thought on us wretched men, that we may be united to Him through His Son, and as the beginning of His gracious work, I have been made the spouse of God, that the heavenly conception and birth of the Saviour might make men partakers of divine grace, which He has given unto me, not according to my deserts, but according to His grace!" Therein let all the world see what love the gracious God hath to us; that He of His own motion, when we were still in disfavor with Him, began to make friendship with us.

But that to Jesus the throne or power of David should be given, is not to be understood of a worldly kingdom, but of a kingdom of faith; by which the whole world has been made subject unto Him. That is, that through faith all men have received mercy of God as great, as certain, and as true as that shown to David. For David committed a great murder in the case of the brave Uriah, but God forgave him that and promised that He would make a covenant with the human race according to the mercy shown to David: "I will make with you an eternal covenant, even the sure mercies of David"; that is, I will make with you a true covenant; I will be merciful to your sins as I was with David. And as David received the promise from God that one of his seed should always possess his throne or kingdom, so is this truly accomplished in Christ Jesus, not after an earthly, but after a heavenly manner. For through the Lord Jesus have all races of men been blessed, as was also promised to Abraham. He is therefore an eternal king and father of all those that take refuge in Him that their sins may be forgiven, even as David was forgiven his sins.

By this we should learn from Mary the unshaken faith by which she did not doubt the word of the angel, although she never saw her Son attain an earthly kingdom. On the contrary, she saw Him shamefully abused and put to death. Nevertheless she in no respect doubted the word of God. Let him therefore who would honor her highly, imitate her faith, and not fall from the Lord Christ Jesus.

When the holy Mary believed the word of God announced by the angel, she would further know how the birth might be brought about, since she knew no man, that is, she had no intercourse with any one of such a sort. The angel answered her: "The Holy Ghost shall come upon thee from above and the power of the Highest shall overshadow thee, therefore that holy thing which will be born of thee shall be called the Son of God." This is the meaning of the angel: Mary, I announce to thee a new sort of birth, which has nothing in common with the sinful birth of men. What is by thee conceived will come of the Holy Ghost, who will make thee fruitful; the power of God also will come over thee and work upon thee so that that holy thing that shall be born of thee shall be called the Son of God. Therefore was it made known not merely to men, believing and unbelieving, but also the devils, that He is a Son of God. He informed her further of another birth, impossible according to the course of nature before and since, that Elizabeth, who had never borne, and therefore was called barren, had now in her old age conceived a son and was already six months with child. Thereby Mary should understand that it was not impossible for God to do this; for all things must obey the promise of His word, although it might be against nature. For the course of nature cannot compel God, the creator and ruler of all things, that He must work according to it, but nature, which has her course from God, must let her Lord God compel and lead her; nature suffered no more wrong if her course was hindered or changed than if a certain laborer in a household takes up another kind of work and a more skilful is called by the master of the house. That is called by us a miracle, or wonder, but in itself that is according to the working of God and is no wonder. For to God there is nothing impossible; in His hands are all things and with them He may do as He please and command them as well, so that they may not say: "Why hast thou made me so?" as Paul shows.

On this assurance of the angel the spotless virgin relied, firmly believing that God promises nothing that does not come to pass, and she said to the angel: "*Ecce ancilla domini*," that is: "Behold, I am the handmaid of the Lord. Be it unto me according to thy word!" Mary called herself a handmaid of the Lord from that hour in which she believed the words of the angel; for so mighty are those words that when once they are made known to man he believes them firmly, and they make him obedient without any ambition or temporal promises, therefore man freely rests on the simple words and grace of God. This Mary showed quite joyfully, in that, unlike women that marry, or maidens, she did not ask of God this or that gift, or how she was to be regarded afterwards, but gave herself to Him with humble words and mind, and called herself nothing else than the handmaid of the Lord, and asked God to do to her according to the word of the angel. From this we ought to learn that we should have a mind and soul wholly trusting in God, that we should give ourselves so to Him that we should not ask what reward there is to be for us for this or that work; but with the trustful Mary say: "Lord, I give myself to Thee to be Thy servant; do with me hereafter according to Thy will! Thy will be done, not mine. If we live or die, Lord, we are Thine. If I desired great things of Thee perhaps that were foolishness; for we ask of Thee as the sons of Zebedee asked. But Thy Spirit, which speaks for us and represents us, will so better things that we shall do less out of ignorance. Therefore grant me such faith, that I may let myself rest on Thee alone, freely and without reserve, and let Thee determine my reward according to Thy good pleasure."

But there are many, alas, yea, the larger part of those that are called spiritual, that do nothing except for the mere reward. They also think that when they give alms they will know beforehand how much it will be worth, how much it will cut down their debt of sin, and if there is not much reward they are not diligent in doing anything. So also in other things: they say for instance a Paternoster, but they want to know at once how much it will count for them. And the simple people have learned such rubbish from us. Yes, we have taught them such error, in that we in the indulgences (with a right deceitful pretence) have offered and shown them how very cheap all good works were, how much each was to be worth. And always the basin, or tin box, or money chest stood beside us. For this reason no one has asked what is the will of God, but how they may be able to pay for and be absolved from the sins that they have committed, until it has come to pass that every madman has been hawking about fancies about sin, hell, and the kingdom of heaven as if they were selling a horse, or a pig, or an ox. None thought, however, that he should turn to the mercy of God, and direct himself according to the will of God, from which spring the fear of God and contempt of one's self; but all have made their sins a matter of trading: Ho! do these sins I steal, rob, murder, kill; you will be all right with this prayer, this pardon-money, or this pilgrimage. Oh, the dreadful murder of souls! Why have we not taught that one should certainly trust in the grace of God, and count our works as of no value: or that they are not ours, be they ever so good, but God's? For if the works were good according to the judgment of men, we would value our works so high that no one would be able to reward us. Therefore should we learn our humility from Mary: to submit ourselves wholly to God, so that if God speaks a word, we submit ourselves to it and believe it; although according to our understanding it appears impossible, we can say with her: "Lord, my mind is weak; but what Thou sayest, must take place. I am Thy servant; be it unto me according to Thy word!" Now will every foolish question cease, for every one would know before he does anything good (that is, what we call good) how much it will help him, but we will rest ourselves with trustful hearts wholly and unconditionally on the grace of God, who knows what we need before we ask Him, and knows what is proper to give us.

HEINRICH BULLINGER

Heinrich Bullinger was born July 18, 1504, at Bremgarten, a small town about ten miles west of Zurich. He was educated at Emmerich and later at the University of Cologne, where he became acquainted with the principal patristic writers. He also read the works of Luther, and was much influenced by them. He did not, however, break with his faith, but, having taken his degrees, returned to his home, where he was soon employed as a teacher in the monastery at Cappel. In 1523 he came under the influence of Zwingli and began to preach the reformed doctrines. After the victory of the Catholic cantons at Cappel he was forced to fly to Zurich, where he was made preacher in the Cathedral, filling the post his master had held until his death. He was tireless as a preacher and took part in many of the disputations that were held throughout the country. In these he was a zealous upholder of the Zwinglian doctrine of the Lord's Supper, in opposition to the Lutheran and Calvinistic views. From 1554 to 1564 he was busily engaged in controversies, but he was able to extend sympathy and assistance to the English fugitives then at Zurich, among whom was Jewel. The Italian re-formers who resorted to Zurich also found with Bullinger a warm welcome. Heinrich Bullinger died after a painful illness, September 17, 1574.

Bullinger has always been esteemed one of the greatest preachers of the Reformation period. His influence was no less in England than in his native country, this being due, no doubt, to his relations with the English fugitives. His sermons, arranged in five decades, acquired a remarkable prominence in England. Their value in the eyes of the Church may best be shown by the following order of the Convocation of 1586: "Every minister having cure, and being under the degrees of Master of Arts, and Bachelor of Laws, and not licensed to be a public preacher, shall before the second day of February next, provide a Bible, and Bullinger's Decads in Latin or English, and a paper book, and shall every day read one chapter of the holy scriptures, and note the principal contentes thereof briefly in his paper book, and shall every week read over one sermon in the said Decads and note likewise the chief matters therein contained in the said paper; and shall once in every quarter (viz. within a fortnight before or after the end of the quarter) shewe his said note to some preacher nere adjoyninge to be assigned for that purpose."

Many of Bullinger's works have been translated into English. The Decades have been reprinted in four volumes by the Parker Society, Oxford, 1849, etc. A biography is prefixed to the fourth volume of that edition.

SERMON ON FAITH

by Heinrich Bullinger

The following sermon appears in the first Decade of Bullinger as published by the Parker Society. No details have been preserved as to the time or place of its original delivery.

BEING cut off with the shortness of time, and detained by the excellency of the matter, I could not in my last sermon make an end of all that I had determined to speak touching faith: now therefore, by the grace of the Holy Spirit, I will add the rest of the argument which seemeth yet to be behind. Pray to the Lord that that which by man's voice is brought to your ears, may by the finger of God be written in your hearts.

True faith is ignorant of all division; for "there is," saith the Apostle, "one Lord, one faith, one baptism, one God and Father of all." For there remaineth, from the beginning of the world even unto the end thereof, one and the same faith in all the elect of God. God is one and the same forever, the only Well of all goodness, that can never be drawn dry. The truth of God, from the beginning of the world, is one and the same, set forth to men in the word of God. Therefore the object and foundation of faith, that is, God and the word of God, remain forever one and the self-same. In one and the self-same faith with us have all the elect ever since the creation of the world believed, that unto us through Christ all good things are freely given, and that all truth necessary to be believed is declared in the word of the Lord: wherefore the faithful of the old world have always settled their faith on God and His word; so that now, without all doubt, there cannot be any more than one true faith.

I know very well, that in the world there are sowed many and sundry faiths, that is to say, religions. For there is the Indian faith, the Jewish faith, the faith of the Mahometists, and the faith of the Georgians; and yet notwithstanding there is but one true Christian faith, the abridgment whereof is contained in the articles of our belief, and is taught at the full in the sacred scriptures of both the Testaments. I know also that there are sundry beliefs of men, resting upon sundry things, and believing that which is contrary to true faith; but yet, nevertheless, there remaineth but one true belief in God and His word—an undoubted persuasion and confidence of things most true and assuredly certain.

This confidence doth grow with increase in the minds of the faithful, and, contrarily, decreaseth again and utterly faileth. And for that cause the Apostles besought the Lord, saying: "Lord, increase our faith." And Paul the Apostle doth in his writings everywhere wish to the faithful the increase of the spirit and faith. David also before him prayed, saying: "O God, create a clean heart within me, and take not Thy Holy Spirit from me." For he had seen how that from Saul, whom he succeeded in the kingdom, the good Spirit of God was departed, and that instead thereof the wicked spirit had entered into his mind, which tormented him very pitifully. Hereunto belongeth that saying in the Gospel: "To every one that hath shall be given, and from him that hath not shall be taken away that which he hath not"—or that he maketh no account of—"and shall be given to him that hath." Neither was it in vain that the Lord said to Peter: "I have prayed for thee, Peter, that thy faith fail not." For Paul speaketh of some in his time that "made shipwreck of their own faith, and overthrew the faith of others." And to what end, I pray you, do we daily hear the word of God, and make our humble petitions to the Lord, but because we look for increase of godliness, and His aid to keep us that we fall not from true faith? Verily Paul to the Thessalonians saith: "We pray earnestly day and night to see you personally, and to supply that which is wanting in your faith." And a little before he said: "For this cause I sent Timotheus, that I might be certified of your faith, lest by any means the tempter had tempted you and so our labor had been of none effect." The same Apostle also, in his Epistle to the Ephesians, saith: "Christ gave some apostles, some prophets, some pastors and teachers, to the restoring of the saints, unto the building of the body of Christ, until we all meet together in the unity of faith and the acknowledging of the Son of God, unto a perfect man, unto the measure of age of the fulness of Christ, so that now we be no longer children." Therefore, so long as we live, we learn, that our faith may be perfect; and if so be that at any time it shall be weakened by temptations, that then it may be repaired, and again confirmed. And in this diversity, in this increase and weakness of faith, there is no partition or division; for the self root and substance of faith doth always remain, although it be at some time more, and at some time less. In like manner, faith is not therefore changed or cut in sunder, because one is called general faith, and another particular faith. For general faith is no other than that which believeth that all the words of God are true, and that God hath a good-will to mankind; particular faith believeth nothing contrary to this; only that which is common to all the faithful applieth particularly to himself, believing that God is not well-minded toward others alone, but even unto him also. So then it bringeth the whole into parts, and that which is general into particularities. For whereas by general faith he believeth that all the words of God are true, in the same sort by particular faith he doth believe that the soul is immortal, that our bodies rise again, that the faithful shall be saved, the unbelievers destroyed, and whatsoever else is of this sort taught to be believed in the word of God.

Moreover, the disputation touching faith poured into us, and faith that we ourselves get, touching formal faith and faith without fashion, I leave to be beaten out of them which of themselves do bring these new disputations into the Church. True faith is obtained by no strength or merit of man, but is poured into him of God, as I declared in my last sermon; and though man obtain it by hearkening unto the word of God, yet nevertheless it is wholly imputed to the grace of God; for unless this grace do work inwardly in the heart of the hearer, the preacher that laboreth outwardly doth bring no profit at all. We read in the third chapter of. St. Augustine's book, *De Prcedestinatione Sanctorum*, that once he was in error, because he thought that faith, wherewith we believe in God, is not the gift of God, but that it was in us as of ourselves, and that by it we do obtain the gift of God, whereby we may in this world live rightly and holily. But this he confuteth in that book at large, and that substantially. So then true faith, which bendeth on God alone, and is directed by the word of God, is formal enough, or sufficiently in fashion. Verily, the form of faith is engraven in the heart of the faithful by the Holy Ghost. And although it be small, and doth not grow up to the highest degree, yet notwithstanding it is true faith, having force in it as it were a grain of mustard-seed. The thief that was crucified with our Lord believed in the Lord Jesus and was saved, al-though the force of faith was strong in him but a very small season and brought not forth any great store of fruit of good works; finally, that faith of the thief was not any whit diverse or contrary from the faith of St. Peter and St. Paul, but was altogether the very same with theirs, although their faith brought forth somewhat more abundantly the fruit of good works. Peter and Paul were frankly and freely justified, although they had many good works; freely was the thief justified, although his good works were very few or none at all. Let us hold therefore that true faith is one alone, which notwithstanding doth increase and is augmented, and, again, may decrease and be extinguished.

There remaineth now for me to declare the virtue and effect of true faith. This hath the holy Apostle Paul done very excellently well, yea, and that most absolutely, too. But although, in the eleventh chapter to the Hebrews, he hath said very much, he is compelled notwithstanding to confess that he cannot reckon up all; therefore at this time I mean to rehearse a few virtues of faith, leaving the rest, dearly beloved, to be sought out and considered of yourselves.

True faith before all things bringeth with it true knowledge, and maketh us wise indeed. For by faith we know God, and judge aright of the judgments and works of God, of virtues and vices. The wisdom that it bringeth with it is without doubt the true wisdom. Many men hope that they can attain to true wisdom by the study of philosophy; but they are deceived as far as heaven is broad. For philosophy doth falsely judge and faultily teach many things touching God, the works of God, the chief goodness, the end of good and evil, and touching things to be desired and eschewed. But the very same things are rightly and truly taught in the word of God, and understood and perceived by faith. Faith therefore is the true wisdom, and maketh us wise indeed. For Jeremy also saith: "Behold, they have cast away the word of the Lord; what wisdom therefore can be left in them?" The wisdom of Solomon is worshipfully thought of throughout the whole compass of the world; and yet we read that the Lord, in the Gospel after St. Matthew, uttered this sentence against the Jews: "The queen of the South shall rise in judgment with this generation and shall condemn it; because she came from the ends of the world to hear the wisdom of

Solomon; and behold, there is one in this place greater than Solomon." Christ is preferred before Solomon, and the wisdom of Christ before the wisdom of Solomon. But it is well known that the wisdom of Christ, the Son of God, cannot be attained to without faith. Faith therefore bringeth with it the most excellent wisdom. But herein this wisdom of ours deserveth a singular praise, because they that desire it are not sent to foreign nations, with great cost and labor, to learn it; as to the priests of Egypt, the gymnosophists of India, the philosophers of Greece, or to the rabbins of the Jews. God hath dispersed the word of God throughout the whole world, so that now the word of faith is in the hearts of all the faithful. For Paul the Apostle saith: "Thus saith the justice that is of faith, Say not in thy heart, Who shall ascend into heaven? that is, to fetch Christ down from above. Or, Who shall descend into the deep? that is, to bring Christ from the dead again. But what saith he? The word is nigh unto thee, even in thy heart: this same is the word of faith, which we preach; for if thou confess with thy mouth the Lord Jesus, and dost believe with thy heart that God hath raised Him from the dead, thou shalt be saved."

Faith therefore doth not only make us wise, but happy also; the Lord himself bearing witness thereunto, and saying to His disciples: "Happy are the eyes that see the things that ye see. For I say unto you, that many prophets and kings have desired to see the things that ye see, and to hear the things that ye hear, and heard them not." We shall therefore find in faith a most certain determination of the most notable question stirred in, since the beginning of the world, of learned and most excellent wits; which is, by what means a man may live, be happy, attain to the chief goodness, be joined to the chief good-ness, and so be justified. There have been, yea, and yet are, divers opinions touching this matter, contrary the one to the other. But we do briefly and truly affirm, that by true faith a man doth live, is happy, attaineth to the chief goodness, is conjoined to the chief goodness, and also justified; so that God dwelleth in us and we in Him; and that by faith we are both happy and blessed. What, I pray you, could have been spoken more excellently, worthily, or divinely, touching true faith? For see: faith quickeneth us, maketh us happy, joineth us to the chief goodness, so that He in us and we in Him may live; and faith doth also fully justify us.

But now it is best to hear the testimonies out of the Scriptures. Faith maketh us happy. For to St. Peter, confessing the Lord Jesus by true faith, it is said: "Happy art thou, Simon, the son of Jonas. Flesh and blood hath not revealed this to thee, but my Father which is in heaven." St. Paul, for the proof of faith, bringeth in that sentence of David: "Happy are they whose iniquities are forgiven, and whose sins are covered. Blessed is the man to whom the Lord shall impute no sin." Faith quickeneth or maketh alive. For "the just liveth by faith." This doth Paul very often in his writings allege out of the prophets. The same Paul also saith: "The life which now I live in flesh, I live by faith in the Son of God, who loved me and gave Himself for me." Faith joineth us to the eternal and chief goodness, and so maketh us to enjoy the chief goodness, that God may dwell in us and we in God. For the Lord Jesus Himself in the Gospel saith: "He which eateth my flesh and drinketh my blood dwelleth in me, and I in him. As the living Father sent me, so also I live by the Father, and he that eateth me shall live by me." But to eat and drink the Lord is to believe in the Lord, that He hath given Himself to death for us. Whereupon John the apostle saith: "We have seen and do witness, that the Father hath sent the Son, the Savior of the world. Whosoever shall confess that Jesus is the Son of God, God dwelleth in him, and he in God." Wherefore also Paul saith: "I live now; not I, but Christ liveth in me." Moreover faith doth justify. But because the treatise thereof cannot be fitly and fully made an end of this hour, I mean to defer it till the next sermon that shall be.

At this present, dearly beloved, ye must remember that there is but one true faith, that is, the Christian faith. For although there be said to be many faiths, that is, religions, yet notwithstanding there is only one true and undoubted faith. And that doth increase, and again decrease, in some men. As for those in whom it is rightly and godly observed, in them it showeth forth sundry virtues. For it bringeth with it true wisdom; finally, it quickeneth, and maketh us blessed and happy indeed. To God, the Father, the author of all goodness and of our felicity, be all praise and glory, through Jesus Christ our Lord, for ever and ever. Amen.

JOHN CALVIN

John Calvin was born at Noyon in Picardy, July 10, 1509. His father, Gerard Chauvin,—Latinized by his son to Calvinus,—was first a cooper, and afterward an official of the bishop's court. In his youth Calvin was designed for the priesthood and was educated accordingly, but later his father set him to study law. But the original bent of his genius was not to be defeated. In 1532 he was in Paris, busy with theology, having already embraced the reformed doctrines. In consequence of his teachings he was obliged to leave Paris. In 1535 he issued the first edition of his Institutes, in which his theological system is substantially set forth, and in the next year he went to Geneva, which was from that time the principal scene of his activity. Farel had already introduced the reformed faith, and needed the cooperation of a man of Calvin's temperament and powers. The two preachers were expelled, however, two years later, but returned in 1541. From this time Calvin's rule in Geneva was undisputed. The city became a theocracy more strict than any ever known. The will of the clergy was absolute. The citizens were punished with fine, imprisonment, or exile for criticism of doctrine put forth by the authorities. But the city at the same time became exceedingly prosperous under the wise and energetic though tyrannical rule of the clergy. Schools were founded, abuses corrected, even the sanitary condition of the city was improved,—something very remarkable in those days. Calvin's life was one of incessant activity. His health was always poor, and his last years were spent in great suffering. He died in 1564.

Calvin was a powerful and Indefatigable preacher. He frequently preached every day for many weeks in succession. His style as a preacher is that of his theological writings, clear, calm, and logical. He has no imagination, nothing of what might be regarded as the first element of eloquence, and in this he was a remarkable contrast to Luther. But the two reformers had this in common, that they were both men of iron will. Calvin never faltered. His strict consistent logic carried weight.

Added to this was the personality of the man, that element which the ancients prized so highly in orators. His genuine piety and intense earnestness rendered his every utterance telling. Of his preaching, Beza, his friend and biographer, says, "Every word weighed a pound."

Editions of Calvin's collected works appeared at Geneva, 1617, and Amsterdam, 1671. The best edition, however, is that contained in the *Corpus Reformatorum*, Brunswick, 1863-1896, of which fifty-six volumes have appeared. The works include, in addition to his *Institutes* and other theological and dogmatic treatises and controversial pamphlets, commentaries of remarkable merit on nearly the entire Bible. The *Institutes* have been translated into almost all modern languages. The commentaries and a large number of sermons have been translated into English. The earliest life of Calvin was written by his friend Theodore Beza. Among the modern works of value are Staehlin, *Johannes Calvin, Leben und Ausgewdhlte Schriften*, 1863; Dyer, *The Life of John Calvin, Compiled from Authentic Sources*; M'Crie, *The Early Years of John Calvin*, 1880; P. Henry, *Das Leben Calvins*, 1835-1844 (translated by Stebbins, New York, 1854). See also Tulloch, *Leaders of the Reformation*, and the remarkable article in the third edition of Herzog's *Realencyclopädie*.

THE PRIVILEGE OF BEING IN THE CHURCH OF GOD

by John Calvin

The following sermon was published by Calvin, September, 1552. It is one of four which he addressed "To all Christians who desire the advancement of the kingdom of our Lord Jesus Christ." The animus of the sermon and the thought underlying it may best be expressed in the words of Calvin himself, contained in the "Author's Epistle."

The object of the third sermon is to show how valuable a privilege it is not only to be permitted to serve God purely, and make public profession of this faith, but also to belong to a regular and well-managed church, where the word of God is preached and the sacraments are duly administered; seeing that these are the means by which the children of God may be confirmed in the faith, and are incited to live and die in the obedience to His law. It seems to me that the discussion of this subject was very necessary at present, because there are many imaginary Christians who make a mock of those who take the trouble of coming into a strange and distant land, in order to enjoy this privilege.

"I have asked one thing of God, and it will I seek after—to dwell in the house of the Lord all the days of my life , to see the beauty of the Lord, and behold His temple ."—Psalm 27:4.

WE find a strange diversity in the wishes of men; and yet there is one point in which they all agree and are alike. It is in finding their amusement here below in the world. Every one has, indeed, his own end, his own particular method; but in all quarters this vanity prevails, the vanity of seeking well-being and felicity only in this corruptible life. This shows that men are in a very degraded state: for we were created for a quite contrary end, namely, while living in the world, to aspire to the kingdom of God; and this is the reason why the present life is termed a passage or path. Wherefore, in the case of every one who would not of his own accord defraud himself of the eternal heritage of God, the point at which he must begin is by cutting off all foolish and fickle desires which might tend to engross him and bind him to this world, that his principal desire may be to go to God, and there may be nothing to hinder him at least from tending thither. I say at least, inasmuch as it were very requisite that all earthly affections, which do nothing but distract us from God, were completely plucked out of our hearts, so that we might be able to speed quickly in the journey which we have to make.

But because we are far from possessing such purity, it remains, in the second place, to surmount all the hinderances which retard us, and pursue our course at all events so that in the midst of our weaknesses we may nevertheless prefer the heavenly life to all that the world can bestow. The next thing is, to consider what the means are which may enable us to succeed.

Now, it does not belong to us to devise means. We must take the means which God has appointed, and of these the principal are here mentioned by David, namely, The order and government which God has established in His Church; or, to express it otherwise, that we be taught by His word—that we worship Him with one accord, and call upon His name—and that we have the use of the sacraments to assist us herein. Such is the way in which we must exercise ourselves in order to be more and more confirmed in the faith, in the fear of God, in holiness, in contempt of the world, and in love of the heavenly life.

Accordingly, it is with a view to this David declares that he desires above all things to dwell in the temple of God. For under the term temple he comprehends the liberty of worshipping God purely with the faithful, of making a confession of faith, praying, and partaking of the sacraments. At this time God had chosen a certain place where men should offer sacrifice and pay homage to Him, accompanied with the declaration, that they held Him to be the only God; where they might be instructed in His law, and behold the symbols of His presence. And, in fact, he sufficiently explains what he has in view in desiring to dwell in the temple, when he adds, that it is to see the beauty of God. Herein he shows that the temple was nothing in itself, and that his attention was fixed on the use to which it was devoted. Did we imagine that he was amused with a material building, we should do him much wrong and injury, for then his wishes might be imputed to superstition and not ascribed to virtue. We must hold it certain then, that he is declaring the high value which he sets on the external order by which the faithful are brought into the Church. In one word, he intimates, that it is an inestimable blessing and privilege to be in the Church of God, so as to share in the means by which this kind Father has enabled His children to approach Him.

Let us observe well who it is that speaks. It is not a poor, ignorant, coarse, and illiterate individual, but a prophet as excellent and as much illumined by the Holy Spirit as any one that has ever existed. He speaks not of what is useful and good for the common herd of men, but he declares in regard to himself, that there is nothing he more desires than to be able to attend the assembly of the people of God, to the end that he may be always more and more edified by the doctrine of salvation which is there preached, and by the sacraments. Nor does he make this protestation here only, but in many other passages, as in the preceding Psalm, when he says, "O Lord, I have loved the habitation of Thy house, and the place where Thy glory has its abode." Again, "As the hart longs to refresh itself in the water, so my soul longs after Thee, O God; my soul burns with thirst in seeking God. When will it be that I shall come to appear before the face of the living God?"

It was surely enough to have said thus much, but his desire transports him still higher, for he adds, that he had fed upon tears while he was deprived of the privilege of coming to the temple. He adds, moreover, that his heart melted away when he thought of the time when he went to the temple, praising God among the body of the faithful. After groaning deeply, stating his plaint, and giving utterance to his regret, he finds no better consolation than the hope which he entertains that God will restore to him the privilege which he has lost. He exclaims, "My soul, why art thou troubled, and why art thou so tumultuous within me? I shall yet see the face of the Lord." He repeats the same thing in Psalm 43; but the strength of his feeling on the subject is most forcibly declared in Psalm 84. For, after exclaiming that his heart and body thrill with the eager desire he had to enter the courts of the Lord, he adds the reason, that "those who dwell in the house of God are happy, because they praise Him that is, because with one accord they acknowledge His mercies and glory in Him, while they make confession of their faith.

Seeing that David, who was so far advanced in all holiness, and was even as an angel of heaven dwelling in the world, felt he had so great need of being aided and stimulated by the means of grace which God has given to His people, I would ask, In what case must we be—we who are so rude and so earthly, whose faith is so small, and whose devotion is so meagre and cold? We might easily conclude, that even though David, from the perfection to which he had attained, should have been able to dispense with such inferior aids, yet to us, considering our infirmity, they are more than necessary. But then, those who are the most perfect are much better acquainted with their deficiency than those who have made no progress at all. Is David richly endowed with evangelical virtues? That only makes him feel with greater force how requisite is it for him to be more inflamed by the preaching of the law, by the sacraments, and by other similar exercises. On the other hand, those worthless boasters, who in the present day hold all those things in no account, show plainly that they are not imbued with one particle of Christianity.

The persons I refer to are the closet philosophers who live under the Papacy. It is rather odd, they say, if one cannot be a Christian without trotting to Geneva to have one's ears stuffed with sermons, and to use the ceremonies which are practised there! Cannot we read and pray to God apart by ourselves? is there any necessity for going into a church to be taught, while each has the Scriptures in his own house? To this my answer is, that we do not lay down a law for any one to stir from the place where he is. May, when a man will live purely, and serve God as he ought in the midst of the Papal tyranny, I prize him a hundred times more, other things being equal, than ourselves, who are at liberty and in repose.

But here two questions are to be considered: first, Whether they who, feeling their infirmity, come and seek in a Christian church such confirmation as David in his time attributed to the temple at Jerusalem, do not do well? and, secondly, Whether all in general, even those who are forcibly detained, may not well sigh on seeing themselves destitute of the ordinary means which were to conduct them to God? Beasts which have no reason will bray for their pasture; and will those, who call themselves "children of God," feel no anxiety for that which is to nourish and maintain their faith? May, not contented with disdainfully trampling these precious gifts of God under their feet, they jeer at those who run into a foreign land to seek and enjoy them. In regard to their pride, which makes them imagine that sermons, public prayer, and the sacraments, are to them a kind of superfluous thing, no other evidence is necessary to condemn them and banish them from the Church of God.

Accordingly, Paul does not say that the order which our Lord has put into His Church is merely for the rude and simple, but he makes it common to all, without excepting a single individual. He says, "He had ordained apostles, pastors, and teachers, for the establishment of the saints, for the edification of the body of Christ, till we all come in the unity of faith, to a perfect man, to the measure of the full age of Christ." Observe well, it is not said that God has left the Scriptures for every one to read, but has appointed a government that there may be persons to teach; under this comprehending all the rest, which in a manner depend upon it. Though an individual reads in private, that does not hinder him from listening in public. And whom does he address? Great and small indifferently. Does he say that it is for one day? On the contrary, he commands the same course to be followed until death; for now is the time of our complete preparation. Those then who deign not to rank themselves with those who are to profit in all faith and virtue by the common order of the Church, could not take a more effectual means of cutting themselves off from the company of the children of God! It is vain to cavil. The declaration of St. Paul is too manifest, that no man belongs to the body of Christ, or should be kept in it, who does not submit to the general rule. Wherefore, brethren, let us humble ourselves, and not tempt God by thinking we are able to fly without wings.

But some one will say, Possibly David was speaking with reference to the time of figures; because God then governed His people after the fashion of little children, as St. Paul says, and therefore his longings after the temple are not applicable to us in the present day, seeing we are compared to those who have ceased to be children, and have become full-grown men. To this I answer, in the first place, that the necessity of being instructed by sermons, confirmed by the sacraments, and exercised by public prayer and confession of faith, is common to us with the Fathers of old. And to this effect are the numerous promises which occur principally in the prophet Isaiah, where God says, that His Church will have an infinite number of children, and that after she has conceived and borne she will nourish them. It cannot be denied that this is applicable to the kingdom of Jesus Christ and to our time.

God expressly sends His children into the bosom of the Church. Why so? Just because this is the order He has established whereby to gather together His children as it were by flocks. This is very well expressed by a fine similitude which the same prophet employs, saying, that Christians will be like pigeons returning in flights to their dove-cot. And what, pray, is this dove-cot, but just every place where the word of God is preached, where the sacraments are administered, and the name of God is proclaimed? In fact, those who imagine themselves so robust as to have no need of this external guidance, take a very wrong view of their condition. For why has God given us the sacraments, but just because, clothed with our bodies, we are too dull and heavy to apprehend spiritual things, without being aided by visible signs? Angels, it is true, have the reality which the sacraments figure, and that suffices them; but God must come lower down to us, because of our rudeness. Let imaginative Christians divest themselves of their bodies, and make themselves angels of heaven, and then they will be able to dispense with those little helps of which they make such small account.

It is true that the grace of God is not bound, nor is the virtue of His Spirit so enclosed either in the sacraments or in things external as that He cannot when He pleases act without any medium, but here we treat of the perpetual order which He has established in His Church, and not with what He does extraordinarily by miracle. Those, therefore, who are deprived of the use of the sacraments, and of the liberty of being able to call upon His name, and feel not their misfortune and misery so as to groan over them, are more stupid than the brutes I

I say, moreover, that if David in his time had just cause to say, "O Lord, how desirable Thy temple is! Happy those who dwell in Thy house! My soul is on flame with the desire which it has to enter the courts of the Lord," we in the present day ought to be doubly moved and inflamed. For what were the blessings of the temple which David regretted so much, as to be weary of his life when he saw himself deprived of them? No doubt, in substance they were those which we have in the present day; but we know that they were obscure shadows, in which God did not display His grace with anything like the fulness in which we have it at present.

God manifests Himself to us so familiarly in the order of His Church, that the heavens, so to speak, are opened to us. The sacraments do not show us Jesus Christ from a distance, so under the law, but set Him before our eyes. We must, therefore, be very ungrateful if we do not prefer these blessings to all that David could find of old in the temple of Zion. We are no longer in the court, as David terms it. There is no veil hung up to keep us at a distance from the sanctuary. In one word, we show very little respect to the infinite magnitude of the blessings which God bestows upon us, when at the very least our longing is not equal to that of David. This I say merely by way of doctrine. The application will come afterwards in its own place.

It remains to see more distinctly what this longing was, that we may conform to it as our rule. "One thing," he says, "have I asked of the Lord." In speaking of one thing only, he intimates that he was so strongly attached to it, that he has left all other things behind, as if he had placed them in oblivion. Was it that he was otherwise in possession of all his wishes, and that this was the only point in which he was deficient? On the contrary, he was a fugitive from the land of his birth, banished even from his father's house, and the society of his relations and friends; he was stripped of all his goods, deprived of all his offices and honors, which had been great; he had been robbed of his wife. In short, here is a man who is desolate in everything and in every respect, and yet it is the want of one thing only that he regrets—that of access to the temple. On the other hand, when he thanks God for all the blessings which He has bestowed upon him, after speaking of eating and drinking, of rest and bodily convenience, he sums up the whole with saying that he will "dwell in the temple of God," thereby declaring that though at his ease and in possession of all luxuries, he has nothing more precious than the privilege of going with the body of the faithful, and thereby being conducted to the sovereign good.

Observe well, then, that David, alike in his afflictions and in his prosperity, always displayed the same courage in endeavoring to enjoy the privilege which God had given to the children of Israel; and this is no small virtue. We see some persons who, when pressed with misfortune and in anguish, will remember God; but the moment they are delivered and find themselves at their ease, His name is no more mentioned. What is worse, they kick against Him like horses too well fed. Others are so annoyed and feel so despitefully towards God in their adversity, that they cannot bear to hear Him spoken of. Is David cast down into such depths of poverty that he is to all appearance the most miserable creature in the world?—So far is he from being so overpowered by distress as to be annoyed and disdainful when others speak to him of God, that it is the only subject in which he finds consolation! Even though he cannot think of God without lamenting his being banished from His temple, and shut out from the use of the sacraments, and the other exercises of the faith, he has no greater pleasure than in expressing regret for the loss. Has he surmounted all his difficulties; has he vanquished all his enemies, so as to be in peaceful possession of his kingdom, and dreaded by all? Has he the means of plunging into all kinds of pleasures? He still remains steady to his purpose—his true happiness is in having access to the temple, to participate in the service of the Church.

We see, therefore, that it was not without reason David declared that he had asked "one thing"; for so dear was it to him that he would at any time have given all the rest in exchange for it. Let us now consider who among us has such discretion as David. Will those who are satisfied with the good which is in their hands, prize the liberty of being able to call purely upon the name of God, of hearing His word preached, and of using the sacraments, more than their domestic repose? There are very few who do so; nay, rather, their fat makes them sleepy, or they only think of making good cheer. In short, the fashion nowadays is to prize a well-stocked larder more than the temple of God!

If we speak of troublous times coming, every one will fear to be pillaged by war, to suffer damage, molestation, and annoyance; but as to losing the preaching of the doctrine of salvation, the use of the sacraments, and such helps as are given us to draw near to God, they make no mention of it; and, accordingly, we perceive not that those who are deprived of such privileges give themselves much concern. If their income does not last them out the whole year, and keep up such a style as their ambition longs for, if their gains and traffic are diminished, if their credit decays, they torment themselves out of all measure; and yet the ordinary nourishment of the children of God (the want of which ought to make them feel famished) is a mere nothing to them! God, however, plainly shows by the threatening which He denounces, that no worse evil can befall us: He says, "1 will send them a famine, not of bread or of water (as if He had said, that were a small matter), but of hearing My word!" Wherefore, brethren, let us beware of allowing ourselves to be stupefied by Satan and the world, and let us always hold this privilege in estimation above all others—the privilege of being entertained among God's flock, under the external order and guidance which He has appointed among His people.

This is still more strongly expressed by what David adds: he will "seek after" the things which he has asked. Hereby he intimates that he has not had a sudden fit of devotion, which will by and bye cool away, but that he has been, and will be, constant in the pursuit of this blessing. We see some persons whose affections for a short time are so lively, that to all appearance they are ready to quit all things to-morrow; but the constancy of which David speaks is a rare quality. Nay, the great majority, instead of stirring the fire to kindle up the good zeal with which God has inspired them, extinguish it of their own accord.

We have a similar testimony to David's zeal in another Psalm, which I have already quoted. Because it might have been alleged that though he was chased from the land of Judea, there were many other places to which he might retire, he exclaims, "Thy altars, O Lord of hosts, my God and my King!" As if he had said, he could find no place delightful, although he possessed all the palaces of the world, while he had no admission to the temple of God. He complains that the sparrows and swallows there find a place to make their nests, and that he is worse off than they. How so? Is it because he has neither room nor kitchen? He does not allege that, but he finds no good or proper dwelling, seeing he is kept back from the altars of God.

It is very certain that if this doctrine had gained an entrance into our heart, we would not be as we are—some irregular, and others totally abandoned in regard to the means which God has placed in our hands to forward us in the path of everlasting life. What! some from ambition cling to high estates and dignities, or are stimulated to acquire them; others are inflamed and hurried along by avarice; many have nothing at heart but their pleasures and giddy delights. All have their desires and longings, but yet none exclaim, "Thy altars, O Lord!

where are Thy altars, my God, my King?" And, in fact, worldly vanities rule too strongly over them to allow God to be obeyed.

There is weight in the expression, when David says, that he has "asked God" for the thing of which he speaks. It is easy to make such a fair show before men as to make it be imagined that we are all on flame. But here David shows a way by which a man will be able to say that he sincerely desires to belong to the flock, I mean, by continuing to have the longing when he has God only for witness. When we come before such a Judge all hypocrisy must cease, and there must be nothing but truth and plain dealing. Would we then follow the example of David? Let each retire into his own conscience, and laying his case before God, say, "Lord, Thou knowest how I prize the privilege of being in Thy house above all worldly blessings!"

Moreover, we are here admonished not to keep champing the bit by confining ourselves to groans and lamentations. We must send up our sighs directly to Him who can relieve our distress. In fact, we ought to understand that the fearful confusion prevailing at present throughout the world, in that the whole service of God is corrupted, the Word of God falsified, the sacraments bastardized, is a just punishment for our sins! To whom then shall we have recourse to enjoy pure doctrines and sacraments, and the liberty to call upon the name of God, and make confession of our faith, but to Him who chastises us by depriving us of our blessings?

But let not the rigor of God's chastisements have the effect of dissuading us from going to Him: far less let it have the effect of making us kick against the pricks, and disdain to seek the cure at the hands of Him who makes the sore. David assuredly knew very well that he was not banished from the land of Judea without the providence of God, and yet he fails not to go to Him and lay his complaints before Him; not that he did not feel it to be a hard and heavy trial to see himself banished apparently by God. But the faith which he has in the promise which had been made to him, raises his thoughts upward to supplicate God that He would restore forever what He has taken from him for a time.

Methinks I have already sufficiently applied the doctrine of the text to ourselves, and the circumstances of the present time, were it not that some minds are so rude and dull, that it is impossible to make them take in anything until it has been minced and minced again into minute fragments! Though, to say the truth, it is neither rudeness nor obscurity of doctrine that hinders them, but they twist themselves about in search of all possible and imaginary subterfuges to darken that which in itself is perfectly clear. This opposition to the doctrine obliges us to spread it out, and shew more fully how it applies to the present time.

I admit that there is no longer any material temple to which we must make a pilgrimage to sacrifice to God; but that now we are His spiritual temples, and that we ought in every place to lift up pure hands to heaven. Still the injunction to invoke His name in the company of the faithful remains in force forever: for this forms no part of the figures of the Old Testament, but is the rule which our Lord Jesus has given us until the end of the world. Wherefore, although we differ from David in regard to the temple of Zion and the sacrifices, we are like him in that we have to pray to God in common, and assemble together to make confession of our faith.

It is very true that we are no longer like little children kept under the tutelage of the law of Moses, but are men, and will continue so till God shall take us away out of the world. Hence, although the shadows and figures which existed in the time of David are no longer applicable to us, it is still necessary for us to be urged and led by the preaching of the Gospel and by the sacraments. If any one maintains the contrary, experience alone is required to confute him; for the ablest make it abundantly manifest how necessary it is that God aid their weakness.

The point we are now discussing is not, whether God can conduct His people without any inferior means, but how He is pleased to conduct them. Now, it is certain that, seeing our weakness, He has given us a kind of props or staves for support. What folly is it then, I ask, when we feel our limbs failing, to refuse to lay hold of props, as if they could not be of any use to us! Let us understand, then, that whatever difference there may be between us and the Jews, the doctrine which David here lays down is common to all. All we have to do is to change the word *temple*, because we are no longer tied to a particular spot. The view which David took of the matter touches us no less than it did him. It is true that the haughty and arrogant care little about assembling to hear sermon, to engage in public prayer, and receive sacraments; but this is the fault of not examining their consciences. On our part, independent of the ordinance which God has made on the subject, let it be enough for us that He is pleased to maintain our faith by such humble means; and, moreover, as we have said, that we are sensible of the benefit which we derive from them.

Be this as it may, since St. Paul declares that the way to come to perfection is to observe the order which Christ established in the Church when He gave pastors, cursed be the extravagance and presumption of those who would leap into the air, and pretend to mount to heaven by their speculations, despising both sermons and the use of the sacraments, as if they were external things, and not very requisite! Observe, brethren, of what people I speak. I acknowledge that God guards His own people under the captivity of Antichrist, although they are destitute of the aids which are free to us here. The Word of God is not preached to them, they have no place where it is permitted them to make confession of their faith, the sacraments are taken from them; but because in separating themselves from the abominations of Antichrist, they sigh and regret that they have not that which would be of so much advantage, God works in them by the energy of His Spirit, and supplies what is wanting.

But there are persons who, being for the most part in such desolate circumstances, nevertheless take pleasure in it, and though famished have no appetite. I mean the persons who counterfeit philosophers; persons who, contenting themselves with three or four pages on a subject, say that they know everything about it that is necessary to be known! Such persons (so it seems to them) have no need of being preached to. As to the Supper, it is all one whether they ever approach it. As to the external order of the Church, they leave it to little children, as a thing far beneath them!

I ask, must not such persons be more than blind? And yet they will blame us for exhorting those to whom our Lord has manifested His truth, to use means which God ordains for the increase, preservation, and perseverance of our faith. And why so, but just because they are annoyed at being awakened to a sense of their own destitution? Assuming that they do not commit idolatry with the Papists, is it not an accursed bondage not to be able to confess the name of God and of Jesus Christ? The Holy Spirit, wishing to prick the hearts of the faithful who were captives in Babylon, puts the following words into their mouths: "How shall we sing the praises of the Lord in a strange land?" I admit that, in the present day, the kingdom of God is everywhere, and that there is no longer any distinction between Judea and other countries: still, however, I hold that the country in which the service of God is abolished, and religion annihilated, well deserves to be regarded as strange and profane. Those, then, who feel no regret at not daring to make profession of their faith, and celebrate the name of God, must be devoid of feeling. Let the children of God be warned by this remonstrance, not to fall, of their own accord, into the same state.

As to the jeering prattle of those who, making a mock of us, say that "No man can get to Paradise without going the way of Geneva!" I answer, that would to God they had the courage to assemble themselves in the name of Jesus Christ, wherever they may be, and set up some form of church, as well in their own houses as in those of their neighbors, in order to do in their own place what we do here in our churches! But what? Not deigning to use means which God gives them, they wish to be saved. It is therefore just the same as if they were to ask, whether they may not reach the harbor by sailing in an opposite course; and whether, while tempting God, they cannot enjoy His grace. Now, let them make themselves as great and strong as they will to break their own necks, but let all believers beware of climbing up along with them, and whoever has not the means of being in the Christian Church, where God is purely worshipped, let him at least groan out day and night, "Thy altars, O Lord! nothing but Thy altars do I desire, my God and King!" Let this fire remain always kindled in all good hearts; in order that, whatever happens, they may not weary of being thus treated, nor be cooled by length of time, nor cease from always desiring to be brought into the fold. Moreover, let each be on the alert quickly to avail himself of instruction the moment our Lord may furnish the means; for this is the way to show that we are not feigning when we request to dwell in the house of the Lord.

It remains now, in conclusion, to attend to what David adds, viz., that he will see the beauty of the Lord, and behold His temple; for we do not at all exercise ourselves with the faithful, in all the external order of the Church, if we do not make it our constant aim to know God better and better. Here, two things are requisite,—the one is, that we be diligent in our attendance on the public sermons and prayers; the second is, that we know why; for there are many who come with a foolish devotion, imagining that they have acquitted themselves well by merely shewing their faces in the church. Let us be on our guard, then, brethren, for there is a danger that the majority may find themselves condemned in regard to both.

How many are there who shun sermons, and would be very glad never to have mention made of them! But I pass by those who shew themselves out-and-out despisers of God. I speak only of the contempt or indifference which many shew who would never think of coming to sermon, if it were not Sunday; and yet it is only by way of acquittance, as if they had a running account with God! The bell tolls every day, but it is enough for them to appear every eight days. The Sunday summons them to church four times; but they think they do well if they appear only once, as there are some who deem every second Sunday sufficient. In short the great body verify the old proverb, "Near the church and far from God I" Of those, even, who have forsaken their country to come hither and serve God, there are some whose conduct is abundantly lax.

How, then, are we to act? Since God manifests Himself to us, let us contemplate His beauty. But let us not lose sight of the proper mode of contemplating. We must be enraptured with admiration of it, and transformed into its likeness, as St. Paul says. And to be so it behooves us to be more attentive than we are, or have been accustomed to be, in considering what God sets before us in His temple. For why is it that we derive so little benefit from sermons and sacraments, but just that we give no attentive heed to what is said and done? Thus our ears are beaten, but our hearts are no way touched. Moreover, there are many who do not listen to a sermon out and out, but only to bits of it, in passing, here and there.

Wherefore, it is not without cause that David speaks of being attentive in visiting the temple of the Lord. And, in fact, the great treasures of divine wisdom which are there set before us well deserve to fix and engage our attention. Now, as I have already hinted, God does not wish us to look and then come away empty. Let us know, then, that we have profited by the doctrine when we are duly trained to serve God. This is what David means in the eighty-fourth Psalm, in the passage already quoted, "Those who dwell in the house of God will praise Him." For what purpose do we assemble? Why is the Gospel preached to us? Why have we Baptism and the Supper, but just that the Lord may be magnified in us? Now, this magnifying or praise does not lie merely at the tip of the tongue, but extends over the whole life; and hence it is said in another passage, "I will wash my hands in integrity, O Lord; then will I go to thy altar."

We now see the true use of the whole order of the Church; it is, that we may serve God purely. In the time of the law, those who came to worship in the temple, and the priests who entered to perform their office, washed themselves. The ceremony is abolished, but we ought to retain the reality. Inasmuch as we have the means of going in to the service of God, we ought to walk with more integrity than others; for the more the assistance which God gives us, the less is our excuse if we do not make it available. If we stumble, it is not from not seeing the road before us; if we go astray, it is not because God does not give us sufficient light; if we forget our duty, it is not for want of being urged to it. In short, God omits no method of advancing our salvation.

Let us, therefore, fear the reproach which God utters by His prophet Isaiah, "All day have I stretched out my hands to this rebellious people." If those who are wandering in the deserts of the Papacy will not be spared when they do not walk aright, what, I ask, will become of us who are brought up as it were in the house, under the eye of our heavenly Father? Some have quitted the land of their nativity to form themselves into a Christian Church; others have been more favorably dealt with, in that God has come and visited them in their own home. How, if those who are natives of the place do not in acknowledgment of the great privilege dedicate themselves entirely to God, who has thus drawn near to them, will such ingratitude remain unpunished? Rather let them say, "Lord, Thou hast built Thy temple and dressed Thy altar in the midst of us; be graciously pleased, then, to purify us, that we may not by our defilements pollute Thy holy gifts, and that we may not turn the glory of Thy benefits into a reproach."

As to those who have come from distant lands, let them take heed to conduct themselves holily, as in the house of God. It had been easy for them to lead a life of dissipation elsewhere, and they had no occasion to move one foot from the Papacy if their object was to follow a dissolute course. And in fact there are some who had far better have had a millstone about their necks than have set foot in this Church to behave so ill as they do! Some connect themselves with scoffers to harden them in their wickedness; others will be gluttons and drunkards; others seditious and noisy. There are households where husbands and wives live like dogs and cats. There are some who swell out their means; and counterfeiting lords, without any ground for it, give themselves up to worldly pomp and luxury. Others become so delicate that they no longer know what work is, and there is no satisfying of them with provision. There are evil-speakers and slanderers, who would find something to say against the angels of heaven; and while besmeared with their own vices make all their holiness consist in throwing out scandal against their neighbors. Meanwhile, they all seem to think that God is under great obligation to them, because "they have made the journey to Geneva!" as if it would not have been far better had they remained where they were, instead of coming to cause such scandal in the Church of God.

Now, in so far as there had been anything wrong before, let every one in his own particular case endeavor to amend it; and if there are some persons altogether incorrigible, let the children of God provide themselves with this doctrine, so as not to be infected by their bad lives. We cannot help feeling angry when we see the Church of God thus profaned. But since we must be like good grain amongst chaff, let us exercise patience till such time as God shall separate us from the counsel of the ungodly. There also can be no doubt that our Church here is a kind of touchstone by which many are to be proved. Be this as it may, let us strive, since God has been pleased to gather us into His family, to conduct ourselves with all purity, renouncing all worldly pollution, in order that the Lord Jesus may acknowledge us on the great day, and count us in the number of those who have borne His name unfeignedly.

HUGH LATIMER

Hugh Latimer was born in Thurcaston, Leicestershire, in the year 1490, where his father was a yeoman, but possessed no land of his own. Young Latimer's education was begun early, for the yeoman at that time enjoyed considerable prosperity. About 1505 he was sent to Cambridge and was elected a fellow of Clare Hall. He took his Master's degree in 1514, having been already ordained priest. Latimer was for a long time unmoved by the new ideas that were continually being introduced, but he could not always resist their influence. He seems to have been won to the Reformation, not so much on grounds of doctrine, as from a deep yearning to improve the moral condition of the people. He attacked the clergy, but generally in a way that was so well justified that Wolsey, when complaint was made to him against Latimer's preaching, granted him permission to preach anywhere in the kingdom. He soon attracted the attention of the King, and in 1530 was invited to preach before him, but Latimer soon wearied of the life in the court and accepted the living of West Kington, Wiltshire. After Cranmer had become Archbishop in 1533, and the breach with Rome had taken place in the following year, Latimer was brought into close relations with Henry, and took an active part in the changes in the Church that ensued. It should be remembered that the Reformation in England proceeded on entirely different lines from those followed on the Continent. The Church organization remained, with the exception of the relation to Rome. The doctrinal and liturgical changes were very gradual, and followed no clearly defined plan. In these circumstances the preaching of Latimer was especially valuable as winning men over to the new order, by pointing out the need of reform in morals. In September, 1535, Latimer was consecrated Bishop of Worcester, but resigned his see in 1339, and seems to have fallen into disfavor, and on the death of Henry he was in the Tower of London awaiting trial. Under Edward VII. he was liberated and began to preach with great effect, declining to resume the charge of his see. On the accession of

Mary he was arrested, and after a long imprisonment was, with Ridley, burnt at Oxford, October 16, 1555.

As a preacher Latimer was a man of great power, not from his rhetorical eloquence,—for in this respect he is far from impressive,—but from his eminently clear and forcible form and statement. He was practical, earnest, and on the whole undoctrinal. He aimed to make religion a reality. He looked at life in a thoroughly unconventional way, and consequently unconventional people listened to him. But there was a heartiness about the man that made him popular with the highest classes as well. Latimer's best sermons are those On the Card, On the Plough, and the seven sermons preached before Edward VI. All of these are found in the first volume of his works (Parker Society Edition).

The works of Latimer have been frequently published. The best edition is that of the Parker Society, in two volumes, Oxford, 1844-45. For an account of Latimer fuller than the notices of the Church Histories, see the preface to the Oxford edition of his works, the Life by Demaus, and the contemporary works of Foxe and Strype. *Leaders of the Reformation*, by John Tulloch, is especially good. His own sermons are full of biographical details.

SECOND SERMON ON THE CARD

by Hugh Latimer

The two famous sermons On the Card were preached at Cambridge in the year 1529. Of these the second is here given. It is a good illustration of the homely manner which Latimer, after the fashion of the times, sometimes employed in his preaching. The time was near Christmas, as he says in his first sermon, and the idea of the card is quaintly brought out in a passage in the opening of that sermon. "Because I cannot declare Christ's rule unto you at one time, as it ought to be done, I will apply myself according to your custom at this time of Christmas: I will, as I said, declare unto you Christ's rule, but that shall be in Christ's cards. And whereas you are wont to celebrate Christmas in playing cards, I intend, by God's grace, to deal unto you Christ's cards, wherein ye shall perceive Christ's rule. The game that we shall play at shall be called the triumph" (see Singer: *Researches into the History of Playing Cards*, pp. 269, 270), "which if it be well played, he that dealeth shall win; the players shall likewise win; and the standers and lookers upon shall do the same; insomuch that there is no man that is willing to play at this triumph with these cards but they shall all be winners and not losers." This whimsical and, to some minds, shocking idea is kept up throughout the sermons. It was, however, quite in keeping with a custom prevalent before and after the Reformation and lasting nearly into this century in some parts of Europe. The last great example of this style of preaching was the noted preacher of Vienna, Ulrich Megerle, known as Abraham de St. Clara.

NOW you have heard what is meant by this first card, and how you ought to play it, I purpose again to deal unto you another card, almost of the same suit; for they be of so nigh affinity, that one cannot well be played without the other. The first card declared that you should not kill, which might be done in divers ways: as being angry with your neighbor, in mind, in countenance, in word, or deed; it declared also, how you should subdue the passions of ire, and so clear evermore yourselves from them. And whereas this first card doth kill in you these stubborn Turks of ire, this second card will not only they should be mortified in you, but that you yourselves shall cause them to be likewise mortified in your neighbor, if that your said neighbor hath been through your occasion moved unto ire, either in countenance, word, or deed. Now let us hear therefore the tenor of this card: "When thou makest thine oblation at Mine altar, and there dost remember that thy neighbor hath anything against thee, lay down there thine oblation, and go first and reconcile thy neighbor, and then come and offer thine oblation."

This card was spoken by Christ, as testifieth St. Matthew in his fifth chapter, against all such as do presume to come unto the church to make oblation unto God, either by prayer, or any other deed of charity, not having their neighbors reconciled. Reconciling is as much to say as to restore thy neighbor unto charity, which by thy words or deeds is moved against thee; then, if so be that thou hast spoken to or by thy neighbor, whereby he is moved to ire or wrath, thou must lay down thine oblation. Oblations be prayers, alms-deeds, or any work of charity; these be all called oblations to God. Lay down therefore thine oblation; begin to do none of these foresaid works before thou goest unto thy neighbor and confessest thy fault unto him; declaring thy mind, that if thou hast offended him, thou art glad and willing to make him amends, as far forth as thy words and substance will extend, requiring him not to take it at the worst; thou art sorry in thy mind that thou shouldest be occasion of his offending.

"What manner of card is this?" will some say: "Why, what have I to do with my neighbor's or brother's malice?" As Cain said: "Have I the keeping of my brother? or shall I answer for him and for his faults? This were no reason. As for myself, I thank God I owe no man malice or displeasure; if others owe me any, at their own peril be it. Let every man answer for himself!" Nay, sir, not so, as you may understand by this card; for it saith: "If thy neighbor hath anything, any malice against thee, through thine occasion, lay even down, saith Christ, thine oblation; pray not to Me; do no good deeds for Me; but go first unto thy neighbor and bring him again unto My flock, which hath forsaken the same through thy naughty words, mocks, scorns, or disdainous countenance, and so forth; and then come and offer thine oblation; then do thy devotion; then do thine alms-deeds; then pray, if thou wilt have Me hear thee."

"O good Lord, this is a hard reckoning, that I must go and seek out him that is offended with me before I pray or do any good deed. I cannot go unto him. Peradventure he is a hundred miles from me, beyond the seas; or else I cannot tell where; if he were here nigh, I would with all my heart go unto him." This is a lawful excuse before God on this fashion, that thou wouldest in thy heart be glad to reconcile thy neighbor, if he were present; and that thou thinkest in thy heart, whensoever thou shalt meet him, to go unto him and require him charitably to forgive thee; and so never intend to come from him, until the time that you both depart one from the other, true brethren in Christ.

Yet, peradventure, there be some in the world that be so devilish and hard-hearted that they will not apply in any condition unto charity. For all that, do what lieth in thee by all charitable means to bring him to unity. If he will in no wise apply thereunto, thou mayest be sorrowful in thy heart that by thine occasion that man or woman continueth in such a damnable state. This notwithstanding, if thou do the best that lieth in thee to reconcile him, according to some doctors' minds, thou art discharged towards God. Nevertheless St. Augustine doubteth in this case, whether thine oblations, prayers, or good deeds shall avail thee before God or no, until thy neighbor come again to good state, whom thou hast brought out of the way. Doth this noble doctor doubt therein? What aileth us to be so bold, and count it but a small fault, or none, to bring our neighbor out of patience for every trifle that standeth not with our mind? You may see what a grievous thing this is, to bring another man out of patience, that peradventure you cannot bring in again with all the goods that you have; for surely, after the opinion of great wise men, friendship once broken will be never well made whole again. Wherefore you shall hear what Christ saith unto such persons. Saith Christ: "I came down into this world, and so took on Me bitter passion for man's sake, by the merits whereof I intended to make unity and peace in mankind, to make man brother unto Me, and so to expel the dominion of Satan, the devil, which worketh nothing else but dissension; and yet now there be a great number of you, that have professed My name and say you be Christian men, which do rebel against My purpose and mind. I go about to make My fold; you go about to break the same and kill My flock." "How darest thou," saith Christ, "presume to come unto Mine altar, unto My church, or into My presence, to make oblation unto Me, that takest on thee to spoil My lambs? I go about like a good shepherd to gather them together, and thou dost the contrary, evermore ready to divide and lose them. Who made thee so bold to meddle with My silly beasts, which I bought so dearly with My precious blood? I warn thee out of My sight, come not in My presence; I refuse thee and all thy works, except thou go and bring home again My lambs which thou hast lost. Wherefore, if thou thyself intend to be one of Mine, lay even down by and bye thine oblation, and come no farther toward Mine altar; but go and seek them without any questions, as it becometh a true and faithful servant."

A true and faithful servant, whensoever his master commandeth him to do anything, he maketh no stops nor questions, but goeth forth with a good mind; and it is not unlike he, continuing in such a good mind and will, shall well overcome all dangers and stops, whatsoever betide him in his journey, and bring to pass effectually his master's will and pleasure. On the contrary, a slothful servant, when his master commandeth him to do anything, by and bye he will ask questions, "Where?" "When?" "Which way?" and so forth; and so he putteth everything in doubt, that although both his errand and way be never so plain, yet by his untoward and slothful behavior his master's commandment is either undone quite, or else so done that it shall stand to no good purpose. Go now forth with the good servant, and ask no such questions, and put no doubts. Be not ashamed to do thy Master's and Lord's will and commandment. Go, as I said, unto thy neighbor that is offended by thee, and reconcile him, as is aforesaid, whom thou hast lost by thine unkind words, by thy scorns, mocks, and other disdainous words and behaviors; and be not nice to ask of him the cause why he is displeased with thee; require of him charitably to remit; and cease not till you both depart one from the other, true brethren in Christ.

Do not, like the slothful servant, thy master's message with cautels and doubts; come not to thy neighbor whom thou hast offended, and give him a pennyworth of ale, or a banquet, and so make him a fair countenance, thinking that by thy drink or dinner he will show thee like countenance. I grant you may both laugh and make good cheer, and yet there may remain a bag of rusty malice, twenty years old, in thy neighbor's bosom. When he departeth from thee with a good countenance, thou thinkest all is well then. But now, I tell thee, it is worse than it was, for by such cloaked charity, where thou dost offend before Christ but once, thou hast offended twice herein; for now thou goest about to give Christ a mock, if He would take it of thee. Thou thinkest to blind thy master Christ's commandment. Beware, do not so, for at length He will overmatch thee and take thee tardy whatsoever thou be; and so, as I said, it should be better for thee not to do His message on this fashion, for it will stand thee in no purpose. "What?" some will say, "lam sure he loveth me well enough; he speaketh fair to my face." Yet for all that thou mayest be deceived. It proveth not true love in a man, to speak fair. If he love thee with his mind and heart, he loveth thee with his eyes, with his tongue, with his feet, with his hands and his body; for all these parts of a man's body be obedient to the will and mind. He loveth thee with his eyes, that looketh cheerfully on thee when thou meetest with him, and is glad to see thee prosper and do well. He loveth thee with his tongue, that speaketh well by thee behind thy back, or giveth thee good counsel. He loveth thee with his hands, that will help thee in time of necessity, by giving some alms-deeds or with any other occupation of the hand. He loveth thee with his body, that will labor with his body, or put his body in danger to do good for thee, or to deliver thee from adversity; and so forth, with the other members of his body. And if thy neighbor will do according to these sayings, then thou mayest think that he loveth thee well; and thou, in like wise, oughtest to declare and open thy love unto thy neighbor in like fashion, or else you be bound one to reconcile the other, till this perfect love be engendered amongst you.

It may fortune thou wilt say: "I am content to do the best for my neighbor that I can, saving myself harmless." I promise thee, Christ will not hear this excuse; for He Himself suffered harm for our sakes, and for our salvation was put to extreme death. I wis, if it had pleased Him, He might have saved us and never felt pain; but in suffering pains and death He did give us example and teach us how we should do one for another, as He did for us all; for, as He saith Himself, "He that will be Mine, let him deny himself, and follow Me, in bearing My cross and suffering My pains." Wherefore we must needs suffer pain with Christ to do our neighbor good, as well with the body and all its members as with heart and mind.

Now I trust you what your card meaneth; let us see how that we can play with the same. Whensoever it shall happen you to go and make your oblation unto God, ask of yourselves this question, "Who art thou?" The answer, as you know, is, "I am a Christian man." Then you must again ask unto yourself, what Christ requireth of a Christian man. By and bye cast down your trump, your heart, and look first of one card, then of another. The first card telleth thee thou shalt not kill, thou shalt not be angry, thou shalt not be out of patience. This done, thou shalt look if there be any more cards to take up; and if thou look well, thou shalt see another card of the same suit, wherein thou shalt know that thou art bound to reconcile thy neighbor. Then cast thy trump upon them both, and gather them all three together, and do according to the virtue of thy cards; and surely thou shalt not lose. Thou shalt first kill the great Turks, and discomfort and thrust them down. Thou shalt again fetch home Christ's sheep that thou hast lost; whereby thou mayest go both patiently and with a quiet mind unto the church and make thine oblation unto God; and then, without doubt, He will hear thee.

But yet Christ will not accept our oblation, although we be in patience and have reconciled our neighbor, if that our oblation be made of another man's substance; but it must be our own. See therefore that thou hast gotten thy goods according to the laws of God and of thy prince. For if thou gettest thy goods by polling and extortion, or by any other unlawful ways, then, if thou offer a thousand pounds of it, it will stand thee in no good effect; for it is not thine. In this point a great number of executors do offend; for when they be made rich by other men's goods, then they will take upon them to build churches, to give ornaments to God and His altar, to gild saints, and to do many good works therewith; but it shall be all in their own name and for their own glory. Wherefore, saith Christ, they have in this world their reward; and so their oblations be not their own, nor be they acceptable before God.

Another way God will refuse thy voluntary oblation, as thus: if so be it that thou hast gotten never so truly thy goods, according both to the laws of God and man, and hast with the same goods not relieved thy poor neighbor when thou hast seen him hungry, thirsty, and naked, He will not take thine oblation when thou shalt offer the same, because He will say unto thee, "When I was hungry, thou gavest Me no meat; when I was thirsty, thou gavest no drink; and when I was naked, thou didst not clothe Me. Wherefore I will not take thine oblation, because it is none of thine. I left it thee to relieve thy poor neighbors, and thou hast not therein done according unto this My commandment, *Misericordiam volo, et non sacrificium*: I had rather have mercy done than sacrifice or oblation. Wherefore until thou hast done the one more than the other, I will not accept thine oblation."

Evermore bestow the greatest part of thy goods in works of mercy, and the less parts in voluntary works. Voluntary works be called all manner of offering in the Church, except your four offering days and your tithes; setting up candles, gilding and painting, building of churches, giving of ornaments, going on pilgrimages, making of highways, and such other be called voluntary works; which works be of themselves marvellous good, and convenient to be done. Necessary works, and works of mercy, are called the Commandments, the four offering-days, your tithes, and such other that belong to the Commandments; and works of mercy consist in relieving and visiting thy poor neighbors. Now, then, if men be so foolish of themselves, that they will bestow the most part of their goods in voluntary works, which they be not bound to keep, but willingly and by their devotion, and leave the necessary works undone, which they are bound to do, they and all their voluntary works are like to go unto everlasting damnation. And I promise you, if you build a hundred churches, give as much as you can make to gilding of saints and honoring of the Church, and if thou go as many pilgrimages as thy body can well suffer, and offer as great candles as oaks; if thou leave the works of mercy and the Commandments undone, these works shall nothing avail thee. No doubt the voluntary works be good and ought to be done; but yet they must be so done, that by their occasion the necessary works and the works of mercy be not decayed and forgotten. If you will build a glorious church unto God, see first yourselves to be in charity with your neighbors, and suffer not them to be offended by your works. Then, when ye come into your parish-church, you bring with you the holy temple of God; as St. Paul saith, "You yourselves be the very holy temples of God"; and Christ saith by His prophet, "In you will I rest, and intend to make My mansion and abiding-place." Again, if you list to gild and paint Christ in your churches and honor Him in vestments, see that before your eyes the poor people die not for lack of meat, drink, and clothing. Then do you deck the very true temple of God, and honor Him in rich vestures that will never be worn, and so forth use yourselves according to the Commandments; and then, finally, set up your candles, and they will report what a glorious light remaineth in your hearts; for it is not fitting to see a dead man light candles. Then, I say, go your pilgrimages, build your material churches, do all your voluntary works; and they will then represent you unto God, and testify with you that you have provided Him a glorious place in your hearts. But beware, I say again, that you do not run so far in your voluntary works that ye do quite forget your necessary works of mercy, which you are bound to keep; you must have ever a good respect unto the best and worthiest works toward God to be done first and with more efficacy, and the other to be done secondarily. Thus if you do, with the other that I have spoken of before, ye may come according to the tenor of your cards, and offer your oblations and prayers to our Lord Jesus Christ, who will both hear and accept them to your everlasting joy and glory; to the which He bring us, and all those whom He suffered death for. Amen.

RICHARD HOOKER

Richard Hooker was born at Heavitree, near Exeter, in March, 1553. His father was a man of respectable position but limited means, and the education of the boy was undertaken by a wealthy uncle. He was sent to the grammar school at Exeter, whence he passed to Corpus Christi College, Oxford. He here enjoyed the patronage of Bishop Jewel. In 1577 he took his Master's degree in arts, and for a little while acted as lecturer in Hebrew. After filling for a short time the benefice of Drayton Beauchamp, he was, in 1586, instituted Master of the Temple on the recommendation of Sandys, Archbishop of York, whose son he had tutored at Oxford. Here Hooker began the great controversy with the Puritans, Travers and Cartwright, which influenced the rest of his life and turned his thoughts in the direction of the fundamental principles on which Church government rested. These he determined to expound in an elaborate treatise, and in order to obtain more leisure for his work he resigned his Mastership and retired to the living of Boscombe, where he spent the remainder of his life. The first four books of his great work, which may be justly described as the first English philosophical work of first-rate importance, appeared in 1594. The fifth book—the most remarkable of all—appeared three years later. The remaining books of *The Laws of Ecclesiastical Polity* seem to have been much mutilated by those who were intrusted with their publication after Hooker's death in 1600.

Hooker deserves a place among the great preachers, not because he was able to stir the enthusiasm that rewarded the efforts of Latimer, for the Master of the Temple was not in the position to do that, but because his sermons are really fine productions. They are filled with thought expressed in a language that was, without question, the finest prose of the century in which they were written. Hooker's style has always been greatly admired, and the magnificent passage on law in the first book of his *Ecclesiastical Polity* is a familiar selection. In the sermons there is much of the same lofty grandeur. Owing to his nearsightedness and his habit of reading his sermons, Hooker was not an attractive speaker, and he had few graces in his delivery.

The works of Hooker have been very often printed. The best edition is that of John Keble, Oxford, 1836, and since then frequently reprinted, as the *Ecclesiastical Polity* has for many years been used as a theological text-book. The best life of Hooker is that by Izaak Walton, first published in 1652, and to be found prefixed to nearly all the modern editions of Hooker's works.

SERMON ON THE NATURE OF JUSTICE

by Richard Hooker

The following example of the style of Hooker as a preacher is taken from a discourse entitled A Learned Sermon on the Nature of Pride. The connection of titles might seem strange, but is explained by the text taken from the prophet Habakkuk, "His mind swelleth, and is not right in him, but the just by his faith shall live." Hooker proceeds in his usual manner to examine the whole subject and to reduce it to fundamental principles. In the course of his argument he is brought face to face with the question: What is justice as opposed to that attitude toward men which is the root of the sin of pride? He must find this justice in some supreme and divine cause and constitution of things. The discussion is especially interesting as anticipating, in some degree, the famous first book of the Polity. The sermon is very long, as are all of Hooker's, and an extract has therefore been made, but it is a continuous section of the sermon. Hooker's careful analysis of his matter and orderly arrangement of his thought renders selection quite easy and satisfactory, though the massive method of the writer can only be appreciated in the examination of his works as a whole.

THERE never was that man so carelessly affected towards the safety of his own soul, but knowing what salvation and life doth mean, though his own ways were the very paths of endless destruction, yet his secret natural desire must needs be not to perish but to live. "What man is he," saith the prophet David, "which desireth, or rather what man is there which doth not desire life, and delight in days wherein he may see everlasting good? Let that man keep his tongue from harm, his lips from guile; let him shun evil, embrace good, pursue peace and follow after it. For the eyes of the Lord are upon the righteous, and His ears unto their cry. Their cry He heareth, and delivereth them from all their troubles: near He is unto them that are contrite in heart: men afflicted in spirit He will save: the troubles of the righteous are great, but He delivereth out of all: their very bones [are] so charily kept that not as much as one of them [is] broken: such as hate them malice shall slay: the Lord redeemeth the souls of His servants, and none that trust in Him shall perish." What the prophet David largely unfoldeth, the same we have here by way of abridgement comprehended in small room. So that hearing how the just shall live, you hear no less in weight, though in sound much less to be spoken. For whatsoever the watchful eye of God, whatsoever His attentive ear; whatsoever deliverance out of trouble; whatsoever, in trouble, nearness of ghostly assistance; whatsoever salvation, custody, redemption, safe preservation of their souls and bodies and very bones from perishing, doth import: the promise of life includeth all. And those sundry rehearsed specialities, harmlessness and sincerity in speech, averseness from evil, inclination unto good things, pursuit of peace, continuance in prayer, contrition of heart, humility of spirit, integrity, obedience, trust and affiance in God; what import they more than this one only name of Justice doth insinuate? which name expresseth fully their quality unto whom God doth promise life.

Slightly to touch a thing so needful most exactly to be known, were towards justice itself to be unjust. Wherefore I cannot let slip so fit an occasion to wade herein somewhat further than perhaps were expedient, unless both the weightiness and the hardness of the matter itself did urgently press thereunto. Justice, that which flourishing upholdeth, and not prevailing disturbed, shaketh, threateneth with utter desolation and ruin the whole world: justice, that whereby the poor have their succor, the rich their ease, the potent their honor, the living their peace, the souls of the righteous departed their endless rest and quietness: justice, that which God and angels and men are principally exalted by: justice, the chiefest matter contended for this day in the Christian world: in a word, justice, that whereon not only all our present happiness, but in the kingdom of God our future joy dependeth. So that, whether we be in love with the one or with the other, with things present or things to come, with earth or with heaven; in that which is so greatly available to both, none can but wish to be instructed. Wherein the first thing to be inquired of is, the nature of justice in general: the second, that justice which is in God: the last, that whereby we ourselves being just are in expectancy of life here promised in this sentence of the prophet: "By faith the just shall live."

God hath created nothing simply for itself; but each thing in all things, and of every thing each part in other hath such interest, that in the whole world nothing is found whereunto any thing created can say: "I need thee not." The prophet Osee, to express this, maketh by a singular grace of speech the people of Israel suitors unto corn and wine and oil, as men are unto men which have power to do them good; corn and wine and oil supplicants unto the earth; the earth to the heavens; the heavens to God. "In that day, saith the Lord, I will hear the heavens, and the heavens shall hear the earth, and the earth shall hear the corn and wine and oil, and the corn and wine and oil shall hear Israel." They are said to hear that which we ask, and we to ask the thing which we want, and wish to have. So hath that Supreme Commander disposed it, that each creature should have some peculiar task and charge, reaching further than only unto its own preservation. What good the sun doth, by heat and light: the moon and stars, by their secret influence: the air, and wind, and water, by their several qualities: what commodity the earth, receiving their services, yieldeth again unto her inhabitants: how beneficial by nature the operations of all things are: how far the use and profit of them is ex-tended: somewhat the greatness of the works of God, but much more our own inadvertency and carelessness, doth disable us to conceive. Only this, because we see, we cannot be ignorant of, that whatsoever doth in dignity and preeminence of nature most excel, by it other things receive most benefit and commodity. Which should be a motive unto the children of men to delight by so much more in imparting that good which they may, by how much their natural excellency hath made them more to abound with ability and store of such good as may be imparted. Those good things therefore which be communicable: those which they that have do know they have them, and do likewise know that they may be derived unto others: those which may be wanting in one, and yet not without possibility to be had from some other: such are matter for exercise of justice.

And such things are of two kinds: good and desirable either simply unto him which receiveth them, as counsel in perplexity, succor in our need, comfort when we are in sorrow or grief; or, though not desired where they are bestowed, yet good in respect of a further end; so punishments, trembled at by such as suffer them, yet in public nothing more needful.

Now forasmuch as God hath so furnished the world, that there is no good thing needful but the same is also possible to be had, justice is the virtue whereby that good which wanteth in ourselves we receive inoffensively at the hands of others. I say inoffensively: for we must note, that although the want of any be a token of some defect in that mutual assistance which should be, yet howsoever to have such want supplied were far from equity and justice. If it be so, then must we find out some rule which determineth what every one's due is, from whom, and how it must be had.

For this cause justice is defined, a virtue whereby we have our own in such sort as law prescribeth. So that neither God, nor angels, nor men, could in any sense be termed just, were it not for that which is due from one to another in regard of some received law between them; some law either natural and immutable, or else subject unto change, otherwise called positive law. The difference between which two undiscerned hath not a little obscured justice. It is no small perplexity which this one thing hath bred in the minds of many, who, beholding the laws which God Himself hath given abrogated and disannulled by human authority, imagine that justice is hereby conculcated, that men take upon them to be wiser than God Himself, that unto their devices His ordinances are constrained to give place; which popular discourses, when they are polished with such art and cunning as some men's wits are well acquainted with, it is no hard matter with such tunes to enchant most religiously affected souls. The root of which error is a misconceit that all laws are positive which men establish, and all laws which God delivereth immutable. No, it is not the author which maketh, but the matter whereon they are made, that causeth laws to be thus distinguished. Those Roman laws, "Hominem indemnatum ne occidito"; "Patronus si clienti fraudem fecerit, sacer esto," were laws unchangeable, though by men established. All those Jewish ordinances for civil punishment of malefactors, "the prophet that enticeth unto idolatory shall be slain," a false witness shall suffer the same hurt which his testimony might have brought upon another, life for life, eye for eye, tooth for tooth; all canons apostolical touching the form of Church government, though received from God Himself, yet [were] positive laws and therefore alterable. Herein therefore they differ: a positive law is that which bindeth them that receive it in such things as might before have been either done or not done without offence, but not after, during the time it standeth in force. Such were those Church constitutions concerning strangled and blood. But there is no person whom, nor time wherein, a law natural doth not bind. If God had never spoken word unto men concerning the duty which children owe unto their parents, yet from the first-born of Adam unto the last of us, "Honor thy father and thy mother" could not but have tied all. For this cause, to dispense with the one can never possibly be justice; nor other than injustice sometimes not to dispense with the other. These things therefore justice evermore doth imply: first, some good thing which is from one person due to another; secondly, a law either natural or positive which maketh it due; thirdly, in him from whom it is due a right and constant will of doing it as law prescribeth.

The several kinds of justice, distributive, commutative, and corrective, I mean not presently to dwell upon. Only before we come to speak of the justice of God, this one thing generally I note concerning justice among men. Almost the only complaint in all men's mouths, and that not without great cause, is: "There is no justice." The cure of which evil, because all men do even give over in utter despair that ever any remedy can be devised to help a sore so far gone—seeing there is no hope that men will cease to offer, it remaineth that we study with patience how to suffer wrongs and injuries being offered.

And although the fault of injustice be too general, yet whom particularly we do charge with so heavy a crime, it standeth us upon to be wary and circumspect, lest our reproving do make us reprovable. What more injurious than undeservedly to accuse of injury? It cannot be denied but that cause on all sides hath been and is daily given, for each to blame other in this respect. Howbeit, patience, quietness, contentment, wise and considerate meditation, might surely cut off much from those scandalous accusations which are so often and so grievously, without regard what beseemeth either place or person, poured out in the ears of men. Wherein perhaps our kindled affection were better slaked with sober advice, than overmuch liberty taken to feed our displeased minds. No man thinketh the injuries light which himself receiveth. But first, when we seem to receive injury, how do we know that injury is done us? Whereby discern we that we have not the thing which is due? Doth not every man measure his due for the most part by his own desire? When we have not what we would, we think we should have that which we have not, and that therefore we are wronged. Might not Daniel be thus condemned for being unjust to the Babylonian? the Jew towards the Persian? our Lord and Savior Christ Himself towards the high-priest Annas, before whom He stood in judgment? No man can be a competent judge of his own right. Wherefore upon our own only bare conceit to say of any man, we find him unjust, must needs be rashness; which being abated, many accusations of injustice would be answered before they be made. Again: be it that we claim nothing as to ourselves or to others due more than by law we seem to have warrant for, and that in the judgment of more than one besides ourselves. Do we think it so easy for men to define what law doth warrant?

One example I will propose to you instead of many, to the end it may appear that there are now and then great likelihoods inducing to think that in equity warrantable which in the end proveth otherwise. A law there was sometime among the Grecians, that whosoever did kill a tyrant should appoint his own reward, and demanding, receive it at the hands of the chief magistrate. Another law, that a tyrant being slain, his five nearest in blood should also be put to death. Alexander Phereus, exercising tyranny, was by his own wife treacherously murdered. In lieu of this act she requireth the life of a son both hers and his, which son the same law commandeth to be executed because of his father's tyranny, and not executed by reason of his mother's request. The question is, whether the grant or denial of her demand, being such, were justice. On the one side, since all commonwealths do stand no less by performance of promised rewards than by taking appointed revenge, let their hope, who in such cases hazard themselves, be once defrauded, and who will undertake so dangerous attempts? Again, if in this case law have provided that none might revenge the death of tyrants, by appointing so many of their nearest to die, how much more likely that such a benefit should make the son to his country ever afterwards dutiful, than his father's deserved punishment kindle in him a desire of revenge? Besides that punishments, are, if anything, to be abridged, rewards always to be received with largest extent, what if the son had done this which the mother did, should his act, by law rewardable, be punished because of his near conjunction in blood? And that the father's offence should more disadvantage the son than his mother's deserts profit him, it seemeth hard. A bridle undoubtedly it would be to stay men from affecting tyranny forever, if they might see that enmity with them could not in any case go unrewarded. On the contrary side there is either greater or no less appearance of justice. For first, when two laws do by an unexpected casualty each control other, so that both cannot possibly be kept, what remaineth but to keep that which cannot but with most public harm be broken? which in this case seemeth not greatly hard to discern; the one being needful unto the common safety of all, the other one body's only benefit. Secondly, fathers being often much more careful of their children than of themselves, more afraid of the overthrow of their progeny than of their own estate and condition, they could not but be the bolder to tyrannize if they did hope that their offspring any way might wind itself out of the evil which law inflicteth. Thirdly, were it not a thing intolerable, that so monstrous an act as a woman to murder her husband unto whom she is so nearly linked should not only not receive punishment, but receive what reward soever she will herself? Finally, the law bidding first generally anything that should be demanded in way of reward to be granted, and afterwards commanding the death of the five next in blood, doth by this specialty abridge, as it seemeth, the former generality, and grant anything but so this thing be not demanded. Otherwise, what letteth but that license to exercise tyranny might be required as a reward for taking tyrants out of the way? Not therefore simply what men will ask, but what they ask with reason and without contradiction to law, that only by law doth seem granted.

This may suffice to show how hard it is oftentimes even for the wisest and skilfullest to see what is justice and what is not. So that not only to ourselves but to others we may seem to take injury when we do not. Howbeit, even when we have not the thing which in truth and in right we should have, it may be notwithstanding that they who do us hurt, do us not that injury for which we may blame them as unjust. There is no injustice but where wrong is wilfully offered. Is it not a rule of equity and justice, "Nullum crimen patitur is qui non prohibet quod prohibere non potest"?—"we are towards them unjust, whose injustice we make complaint of for not doing that which to do they want not will but ability." And when we do not receive as we should at the hands of men, it may be so much even against their wills whom in such cases we think most hardly of, that their infelicity is rather to be sorrowed for than their iniquity to be accused.

But let it be that men of very set purpose and malice bend themselves against us; in this case to abate the keen edge of our indignation at wrong which we suffer, it were nothing if we did consider the wrong which we do. God we are not able to answer one of a thousand; and of a thousand, if but one be unanswered us by men, we are unable to bear it.

To conclude: though we had ourselves never injured God or man, the patience and meekness of Christ in putting up with injuries were worthy our imitation. His meekness were sufficient to meeken us, were the wrongs which be offered us never so grievous and unsufferable. If therefore men will not be persuaded not to do, let these persuasions induce us to take wrong with all patience, and to show ourselves just men in bearing the cross which men's injustice doth lay upon us. Which wisdom the Father for His Son's sake grant; unto whom, with the Holy Ghost, three Persons, one eternal and ever-living God, be honor, glory, and praise, forever.

JOHN KNOX

John Knox was born in 1505 near Haddington. His earliest education was at the grammar school at Haddington. He subsequently attended the University of Glasgow, where he studied for the Church. During his university course the reformed doctrine was introduced into Scotland by Patrick Hamilton, who died when Knox was twenty-three. Knox was ordained about 1530 and removed to St. Andrews, where he taught. In 1543 he appeared as a reformer and a follower of George Wishart, and after the death of Wishart he continued the latter's work. He was soon forced to take refuge in the castle of St. Andrews, which became, for a time, the centre of the reform movement. After the capitulation of the castle when attacked by the French fleet, Knox was carried prisoner to France and sent to the galleys. He was released after two years and at once went to England, where he remained for five years in close intercourse with Cranmer and Latimer. On the accession of Mary, Knox was obliged to leave England, and after some wanderings he settled in Geneva, where he enjoyed the friendship of Calvin, then in the height of his power. The influence of Calvin upon the Scotch reformer is difficult to estimate. Knox's mind was not such as was likely to be influenced by doctrinal subtleties; but, on the other hand, Knox saw in Geneva a theocratic system opposed to the episcopacy to which he was hostile, but for which he could find no adequate substitute. It is probable that in this second respect the influence of Calvin was stronger, though the doctrinal system that subsequently prevailed in Scotland was moulded closely upon the system of the Geneva autocrat. Knox was like all the other great reformers, with the exception of Calvin, in that he was in the first instance a reformer of morals and manners and of Christian religious feeling, and left to others the formulation of a system. Knox returned to Scotland in May, 1559, and though he was at once proclaimed an outlaw he set about preaching the Reformation. His success was so great that, in the year following, the Parliament formally adopted the Protestant faith as the established religion. Knox now came in conflict with the queen, who was unable to win him by her tears or ruin him by her plots. For a time he was inhibited from preaching on account of a sermon in which he had offended Damley. Knox returned to Edinburgh in 1572,after the defeat and withdrawal of the queen's party. He was able, however, to preach but two sermons, one of these being on the massacre of St Bartholomew, which had just taken place. Knox died November 24,1572.

Knox published very few of his speeches or sermons, and the impressions of those who heard him, and his characteristics as revealed in his other works, must supplement what can be gathered from the little he published. Of his sermons we have only a long homily on Isaiah 26:13-21, an explanation of Psalm 6 and of St Matthew 4, a speech against the Mass, and a few minor pieces. Knox was no learned disputant He does not attempt to expound theological questions. His nature was not in sympathy with such. He was too much a man of the people to take an interest in what, in his opinion, was not essential to the moral and religious life. He was, however, a man of great logical acumen. He was resolute and intensely in earnest, without being the gloomy fanatic he is so often depicted. The testimony of one of Knox's auditors is that by his preaching Knox put more life into him than could six hundred trumpets.

The best edition of the works of Knox was published under the editorship of David Laing in six volumes, Edinburgh, 1846-1864. The standard life of Knox is that by McCrie. See also Lorimer, *John Knox and the Church of England*; Carlyle, *Heroes and Hero Worship*; Hill Burton, *History of Scotland*; Tulloch, *Leaders of the Reformation*.

HOMILY ON ISAIAH 26:13-21

by John Knox

The long homily from which the following extract has been taken was preached in Edinburgh, August 19, 1565. In an earlier portion Knox had presumed to define the limitations of the royal prerogative in such a way as to give offence. He was brought before the Council and forbidden to preach in Edinburgh as long as the King and Queen were in the town. He had preached without a written copy, and on account of the offence and misunderstanding caused in many quarters, he wrote the sermon out in full. In this way the sermon has been preserved; but, as in almost all cases when the sermon is written after delivery, much, if not all, the freshness and glow of the spoken discourse is lost.

"Come, thou My people, enter within thy chamber , shut thy door after thee, hide thyself a very little while, until the indignation pass over."

HERE the prophet brings in God amiably, calling upon His people to come to Himself, and to rest with Him, until such time as the fury and sharp plagues should be executed upon the wicked and disobedient. It may appear at the first sight, that all these words of the prophet, in the person of God, calling the people unto rest, are spoken in vain; for we neither find chambers nor rest more prepared for the dearest children of God, so far as man's judgment can discern, than for the rebellious and disobedient; for such as fell not by the edge of the sword, or died not of pestilence, or by hunger, were either carried captives into Babylon, or else departed afterward into Egypt, so that none of Abraham's seed had either chamber or quiet place to remain in within the land of Canaan. For the resolution hereof, we must understand, that albeit the chambers whereunto God has called His chosen be not visible, yet notwithstanding they are certain, and offer unto God's children a quiet habitation in spirit, howsoever the flesh be travailed or tormented.

The chambers, then, are God's sure promise, unto which God's people are commanded to resort; yea, within which they are commanded to close themselves in the time of greatest adversity. The manner of speaking is borrowed from that judgment and foresight which God has printed in this our nature; for when men espy great tempests appearing to come, they will not willingly remain uncovered in the fields, but straightway they will draw them to their houses or holds, that they may escape the vehemence of the same; and if they fear any enemy pursues them, they will shut their doors, to the end that the enemy should not suddenly have entry.

After this manner God speaks to His people; as if He should say, "The tempest that shall come upon the whole nation shall be so terrible, that nothing but extermination shall appear to come upon the whole body. But thou My people, that hearest My word, believest the same, and tremblest at the threatenings of My prophets, now, when the world does insolently resist—let such, I say, enter within the secret chamber of My promise, let them contain themselves quietly there; yea, let them shut the door upon them, and suffer not infidelity, the mortal enemy of My truth and of My people that depend thereupon, to have free entry to trouble them, yea, further to murder, in My promise; and so shall they perceive that My indignation shall pass, and that such as depend upon Me shall be saved."

Thus we may perceive the meaning of the prophet; whereof we have first to observe that God acknowledges them for His people who are in the greatest affliction; yea, such as are reputed unworthy of men's presence are yet admitted within the secret chamber of God. Let no man think that flesh and blood can suddenly attain to that comfort; and therefore most expedient it is, that we be frequently exercised in meditation of the same. Easy it is, I grant, in time of prosperity, to say and to think that God is our God, and that we are His people; but when He has given us over into the hands of our enemies, and turned, as it were, His back unto us, then, I say, still to proclaim Him to be our God, and to have this assurance, that we are His people, proceeds wholly from the Holy Spirit of God, as it is the great victory of faith, which overcomes the world; for increase whereof we ought continually to pray.

This doctrine we shall not think strange, if we consider how suddenly our spirits are carried away from our God, and from believing His promise. So soon as any great temptation apprehends us, then we begin to doubt if ever we believed God's promises, if God will fulfil them to us, if we abide in His favor, if He regards and looks upon the violence and injury that is done unto us; and a multitude of such cogitations, which before lurked quietly in our corrupted hearts, burst violently forth when we are oppressed with any desperate calamity. Against which this is the remedy: once to apprehend, and still to retain God to be our God, and firmly to believe that we are His people whom He loves, and will defend, not only in affliction, but even in the midst of death itself.

Again, let us observe, that the judgments of our God never were, nor yet shall be, so vehement upon the face of the earth, but that there has been, and shall be, some secret habitation prepared in the sanctuary of God, for some of His chosen, where they shall be preserved until the indignation pass by; and that God prepares a time, that they may glorify Him again, before the face of the world, which once despised them. And this ought to be unto us no small comfort in these appearing dangers, namely, that we are surely persuaded that how vehement soever the tempest shall be, it yet shall pass over, and some of us shall be preserved to glorify the name of our God, as is aforesaid.

Two vices lurk in this our nature: the one is, that we cannot tremble at God's threatenings, before the plagues apprehend us, albeit we see cause most just why His fierce wrath should bum as a devouring fire; and the other is, that when calamities before pronounced fall upon us, then we begin to sink down in despair, so that we never look for any comfortable end of the same.

To correct this our mortal infirmity, in time of quietness we ought to consider what is the justice of our God, and how odious sin is; and, above all, how odious idolatry is in His presence, who has forbidden it, and who has so severely punished it in all ages from the beginning: and in the time of our affliction we ought to consider, what have been the wondrous works of our God, in the preservation of His Church when it hath been in uttermost extremity. For never shall we find the Church humbled under the hands of traitors, and cruelly tormented by them, but we shall find God's just vengeance full upon the cruel persecutors, and His merciful deliverance showed to the afflicted. And, in talking of this trial, we should not only call to mind the histories of ancient times, but also we should diligently mark what notable works God hath wrought, even in this our age, as well upon the one as upon the other. We ought not to think that our God bears less love to His Church this day, than what He does from the beginning; for as our God in His own nature is immutable, so His love toward His elect remains always unchangeable. For as in Christ Jesus He hath chosen His Church, before the beginning of all ages; so by Him will He maintain and preserve the same unto the end. Yea, He will quiet the storm, and cause the earth to open her mouth and receive the raging floods of violent waters, cast out by the dragon to drown and carry away the woman, which is the spouse of Jesus Christ, unto whom God for His own name's sake will be the perpetual Protector.

This saw that notable servant of Jesus Christ, Athanasius, who being exiled from Alexandria by that blasphemous apostate, Julian the Emperor, said unto his flock, who bitterly wept for his envious banishment, "Weep not, but be of good comfort, for this little cloud will suddenly vanish." He called both the Emperor himself and his cruel tyranny a little cloud; and albeit there was small appearance of any deliverance to the Church of God, or of any punishment to have apprehended the proud tyrant, when the man of God pronounced these words, yet shortly after God did give witness that those words did not proceed from flesh nor blood, but from God's very spirit. For not long after, being in warfare, Julian received a deadly wound, whether by his own hand, or by one of his own soldiers, the writers clearly conclude not; but, casting his own blood against the heaven, he said, "At last Thou hast overcome, Thou Galilean": so in despite he termed the Lord Jesus. And so perished that tyrant in his own iniquity; the storm ceased, and the Church of God received new comfort.

Such shall be the end of all cruel persecutions; their reign shall be short, their end miserable, and their name shall be left in execration to God's people; and yet shall the Church of God remain to God's glory, after all storms. But now shortly, let us come to the last point:

"For behold," saith the prophet, "the Lord will come out of His place, to visit the iniquity of the inhabitants of the earth upon them; and the earth shall disclose her blood, and shall no more hide her slain." Because that the final end of the troubles of God's chosen shall not be, before the Lord Jesus shall return to restore all things to their full perfection.

The prophet brings forth the eternal God, as it were, from His own place and habitation, and therewith shows the cause of His coming to be, that He might take account of all such as have wrought wickedly; for that He means, where He saith, "He will visit the iniquity of the inhabitants of the earth upon them." And lest any should think the wrong-doers are so many that they cannot be called to an account, he gives unto the earth as it were an office and charge, to bear witness against all those that have wrought wickedly, and chiefly against those that have shed innocent blood from the beginning; and saith, "That the earth shall disclose her blood, and shall no more hide her slain men."

If tyrants of the earth, and such as delight in the shedding of blood, should be persuaded that this sentence is true, they would not so furiously come to their destruction; for what man can be so enraged that he would willingly do, even before the eyes of God, that which might provoke His majesty to anger, yea, provoke Him to become his enemy forever, if he understood how fearful a thing it is to fall into the hands of a living God?

The cause, then, of this blind fury of the world is the ignorance of God, and that men think that God is but an idol and that there is no knowledge above that beholds their tyranny; nor yet justice that will, nor power that can, repress their impiety. But the Spirit of truth witnesses the contrary, affirming that as the eyes of the Lord are upon the just, and as His ears are ready to receive their sobbing and prayers, so is His visage angry against such as work iniquity; He hateth and holdeth in abomination every deceitful and bloodthirsty man, whereof He has given sufficient document from age to age, in preserving the one, or at least in avenging their cause, and in punishing the other.

Where it is said, "That the Lord will come from His place, and that He will visit the iniquity of the inhabitants of the earth upon them, and that the earth shall disclose her blood," we have to consider what most commonly has been, and what shall be, the condition of the Church of God, namely, that it is not only hated, mocked, and despised, but that it is exposed as a prey unto the fury of the wicked; so that the blood of the children of God is spilled like unto water upon the face of the earth.

The understanding whereof, albeit it is unpleasant to the flesh, yet to us it is most profitable, lest that we, seeing the cruel treatment of God's servants, begin to forsake the spouse of Jesus Christ, because she is not to be dealt with in this unthankful world as the just and upright dealings of God's children do deserve. But contrariwise, for mercy they receive cruelty, for doing good to many, of all the reprobate they receive evil; and this is decreed in God's eternal counsel, that the members may follow the trace of the Head; to the end that God in His just judgment should finally condemn the wicked. For how should He punish the inhabitants of the earth, if their iniquity deserve it not? How should the earth disclose our blood, if it should not be unjustly spilled? We must then commit ourselves into the hands of our God, and lay down our necks; yea, and patiently suffer our blood to be shed, that the righteous Judge may require account, as most assuredly He will, of all the blood that hath been shed, from the blood of Abel the just, till the day that the earth shall disclose the same. I say, every one that sheds, or consents to shed the blood of God's children, shall be guilty of the whole; so that all the blood of God's children shall cry vengeance, not only in general, but also in particular, upon every one that has shed the blood of any that unjustly suffered.

And if any think it strange that such as live this day can be guilty of the blood that was shed in the days of the Apostles, let them consider that the Verity itself pronounced, That all the blood that was shed from the days of Abel, unto the days of Zacharias, should come upon the unthankful generation that heard His doctrine and refused it.

The reason is evident; for as there are two heads and captains that rule over the whole world, namely, Jesus Christ, the Prince of justice and peace, and Satan, called the prince of the world, so there are but two armies that have continued battle from the beginning, and shall fight unto the end. The quarrel which the army of Jesus Christ sustains, and which the reprobate persecute, is the same, namely, the eternal truth of the eternal God, and the image of Jesus Christ printed in His elect—so that whosoever, in any age, persecutes any one member of Jesus Christ for His truth's sake, subscribes, as it were with his hand, to the persecution of all that have passed before him.

And this ought the tyrants of this age deeply to consider; for they shall be guilty, not only of the blood shed by themselves, but of all, as is said, that has been shed for the cause of Jesus Christ from the beginning of the world.

Let the faithful not be discouraged, although they be appointed to be sheep to the slaughterhouse; for He, for whose sake they suffer, shall not forget to avenge their cause. I am not ignorant that flesh and blood will think that kind of support too late; for we had rather be preserved still alive, than have our blood avenged after our death. And truly, if our felicity stood in this life, or if temporal death should bring unto us any damage, our desire in that behalf were not to be disallowed or condemned; but seeing that death is common to all, and that this temporal life is nothing but misery, and that death fully joins us with our God, and gives unto us the possession of our inheritance, why should we think it strange to leave this world, and go to our Head and sovereign Captain, Jesus Christ?

Lastly, we have to observe this manner of speaking, where the prophet saith that "the earth shall disclose her blood": in which words the prophet would accuse the cruelty of those that dare to unmercifully and violently force, from the breasts of the earth, the dearest children of God, and cruelly cut their throats in her bosom, who is by God appointed mother of mankind, so that she unwillingly is compelled to open her mouth and receive their blood.

If such tyranny were used against any woman, as violently to pull her infant from her breast, cut the throat of it on her own bosom, and compel her to receive the blood of her dear child in her own mouth, all nations would hold that act so abominable that the like had never been done in the course of nature. No less wickedness commit they that shed the blood of God's children upon the face of their common mother, the earth, as I said before. But be of good courage, O little and despised flock of Christ Jesus! for He that seeth your grief hath power to revenge it; He will not suffer one tear of yours to fall, but it shall be kept and reserved in His bottle, till the fulness thereof be poured down from heaven upon those that caused you to weep and mourn. This your merciful God, I say, will not suffer your blood for ever to be covered with the earth; nay, the flaming fires that have licked up the blood of any of our brethren, the earth that has been defiled with it, I say, with the blood of God's children (for otherwise, to shed the blood of the cruel blood-shedders is to purge the land from blood, and as it were to sanctify it)—the earth, I say, shall purge herself of it, and show it before the face of God. Yea, the beasts, fowls, and other creatures whatsoever, shall be compelled to render that which they have received, be it flesh, blood, or bones, that appertained to Thy children, O Lord! which altogether Thou shalt . glorify, according to Thy promise, made to us in our Lord and Savior Jesus Christ, Thy well-beloved Son; to whom, with Thee, and the Holy Ghost, be honor, praise, and glory for ever and ever. Amen.

Let us now humble ourselves in the presence of our God, and from the bottom of our hearts let us desire Him to assist us with the power of His Holy Spirit; that albeit, for our former negligence, God gives us over into the hands of others than such as rule in His fear; and yet He let us forget His mercy, and the glorious name that hath been proclaimed among us; but that we may look through the dolorous storm of His present displeasure, and see as well what punishment He has appointed for the cruel tyrants, as what reward He has laid in store for such as continue in His fear to the end.

That it would further please Him to assist, that albeit we see His Church so diminished that it appears to be brought, as it were, to utter extermination, we may be assured that in our God there is great power and will, to increase the number of His chosen, until they are enlarged to the uttermost parts of the earth. Give us, O Lord! hearts to visit Thee in time of affliction; and albeit we see no end of our dolors, yet our faith and hope may conduct us to the assured hope of that joyful resurrection, in which we shall possess the fruit of that for which we now labor. In the meantime, grant unto us, O Lord! to repose ourselves in the sanctuary of Thy promise, that in Thee we may find comfort, till this Thy great indignation, begun among us, may pass over, and Thou Thyself appear to the comfort of Thine afflicted, and to the terror of Thine and our enemies.

Let us pray with heart and mouth,

Almighty God, and merciful Father, etc. Lord, unto Thy hands I commend my spirit; for the terrible roaring of guns, and the noise of armor, do so pierce my heart, that my soul thirsteth to depart.

FRANCIS DE SALES

Francis de Sales was born in the Chateau de Sales near Annecy in Savoy, August 27, 1567. His family was of noble rank and his mother had inherited great wealth. He was educated in Annecy and at the Jesuit college in Paris. His studies were pursued with the object of becoming a jurist; he was admitted to the bar and even practised with some success. He had, nevertheless, strong leanings towards an ecclesiastical career, in which desire he had been much opposed by his father. But, in spite of parental opposition, he was ordained priest in 1593, and at once became Provost of Geneva, the city with which his name is associated. The new office did not bring him into relations with the city, which was held by the Calvinists, but it greatly stimulated his missionary zeal in converting the Protestants back to the Catholic faith. He labored among the inhabitants of Chablis from 1594 to 1598 with such success that many of the rude inhabitants returned to the faith of their fathers. In 1598 he was appointed and consecrated bishop of Geneva, although he never resided in the city or performed any duties there. He had, however, several colloquies with Beza, whom he aspired to convert. In 1602 he went to Paris and soon acquired great fame as a preacher at the court of Henry IV. In 1608 he published the best known of his books, *The Devout Life*, which has enjoyed a reputation and extensive popularity second only to the *Imitation of Christ*. His *Treatise on the Love of God*, published in 1614, has been nearly as popular. Francis died November 22, 1622, at Lyons, and was canonized as a saint in 1665.

St. Francis was one of the most successful preachers of modern times. He has been likened, not without reason, to his contemporary, Montaigne, on account of his originality of style and charm of diction. In his preaching he was extremely simple and studied brevity and clearness. There are few or no bursts of eloquence in his writings. He attempts neither display of learning nor subtle arguments. To quote his own words in setting his standard, "My test of the worth of a preacher is, when his congregation go away for them to say, not 'What a beautiful sermon,' but 'I will do something.'" One feature of the style of St. Francis, which might be called "sweetness," has greatly influenced all devotional literature since his time.

The works of St. Francis have been published several times. A good edition is that in seventeen volumes, Paris, 1835. The principal devotional works have been translated and are easily accessible. Good lives have been written of this saint by the Abbé Marsolier, and by Loyau d'Amboise, both in French, and by Sidney Lear in English.

SERMON FOR THE FEAST OF PENTECOST

by Francis de Sales

There are several sermons for the feast of Pentecost among the sermons of St. Francis de Sales; of these the following is probably the most successful. He takes the well-known thought of the sevenfold gifts of the Holy Ghost, and shows the order and importance of these gifts. The sermon retains much of the flavor of the mediaeval sermons, not only in the simplicity of its arrangement, but in the mystical application of texts and allegorical exegesis. This was to be expected, as the modern style of preaching in the Roman Church may be said to have come in only with the great French preachers. The great charm of the sermon, furthermore, is the same as in the mediaeval sermons, an attempt to bring the historical event into the present life of Christians, and to make them, as members of the same body as that which received the Holy Ghost on Pentecost, profit by that gift which they had all received.

"And there appeared unto them cloven tongues like as of fire, and it sat upon each of them . And they were all filled with the Holy Ghost, and began to speak with other tongues, as the Spirit gave them utterance."—Acts 2:3,4.

WE celebrate today the feast of the Divine Presence and the greatest of all gifts, the gift of the Holy Ghost, who was sent from the Father and the Son, under the form and figure of tongues of fire, upon the Apostles and upon those assembled with them in the chamber. But in this incomparable gift are contained seven other gifts, which we call the gifts of the Holy Ghost. It was certainly a very great gift that the eternal Father made to the world, when He gave His own Son, as our Lord Himself says: "God so loved the world that He gave His only begotten Son." Ah I as the great Apostle St. Paul says, what would he be willing to exchange for that gift?

You remember well, I am sure, the beautiful story of the patriarch Joseph, which has been so often related, but which cannot be too much considered. You remember that when he was viceroy of Egypt his brothers who were in Mesopotamia came several times to him to be helped by him in their extreme necessity, when their good father Jacob and they were reduced by the famine in their country. You know that they returned each time to their father laden with corn. But when they brought little Benjamin they did not return as at other times laden merely with corn and such things given solely by measure, but with rich gifts and with chariots of all that could be desired. From this let us see what the eternal Father does in our day; for although the ancient law bestowed many great benefits upon its people, it was always by measure. But on the other hand, in the new law, when He saw the dear Benjamin, that is, when our Lord entered into His glory, He opened His generous hand most liberally to scatter gifts and graces on His faithful, as He said by the prophet Joel, that He would pour out His Spirit upon all flesh, that is, upon all men and not merely upon the Apostles.

You know also what Isaiah said of our Lord, that He received infinite grace and the gifts of the Spirit rested upon His head. The Spirit of the Lord, said he, would rest upon Him, the spirit of wisdom and of understanding, the spirit of counsel and strength, the spirit of knowledge and of piety, and He would be filled with the fear of the Lord. But wherefore did the prophet say that all these gifts would rest upon our Lord, when He could have had no need of them, seeing that He Himself was the Source of all grace? It was not otherwise than for us, to cause us to understand that all graces and heavenly blessings must be given to us by Him who is our Head, who distributes them to us who are His members, that is, children of the holy Church of which He is the Head.

And as a proof of this truth hear what He said in the Song of Songs to His well-beloved: "Open to Me, My spouse, My sister." He called her spouse, because of the greatness of His love, and His sister, as an evidence of the purity and chasteness of that love. "Open to Me," He said, "open to Me quickly, for My head is filled with dew and My locks with the drops of the night." Now the dew and the drops of the night are one and the same thing. What do you think that that well-beloved of the soul meant by these words but that He desired ardently that His well-beloved might open to Him promptly the door of her heart, that He might be able to bestow there those sacred gifts and those graces which He had received so abundantly from His eternal Father, as a dew and a very precious liquor which He wished to present to her?

See then when He sends His Holy Ghost upon the Apostles, and upon all the others assembled in the chamber with them, what He does for them. And this is the meaning of the words of St. Luke in saying that they spoke as the Spirit gave them utterance. But you tell me that the Apostles had already received the Holy Ghost, that is, when our Lord breathed upon them after His resurrection and said to them: "Receive ye the Holy Ghost; whosesoever sins ye remit, they are remitted unto them, and whosesoever sins ye retain, they are retained"; and He thereby constituted them prelates in His Church and gave them the power of remitting sins and of binding and loosing souls. It is true that they received the Holy Ghost at that time, but it was not with such abundance, nor with such glory and magnificence, as when they received it today, nor did it produce in them such effects as today. From the same eternal Father there was that great gift to the world when He gave His only Son; but it was a gift that was hidden, concealed in our humanity and mortal nature. That was by no means such a gift as that He gives today to His Church, for that ought to be regarded as the more excellent gift which had never before been given to men, especially since it was by the Father and the Son that it was sent; and we know well that gifts are regarded great according to the love that prompts them. We can therefore conjecture the excellence of that gift, because it is not only made with great love but it is love itself that gives itself and is given. For we all know that the Holy Ghost is the love of the Father and the Son, and that when we say that the Holy Ghost was given us by the Father and the Son, we do not mean that He should be separated from one or the other, for that could not be, since He is true God, indivisible from the Father and the Son. But we mean that God has given us His divinity, although it was in the person of the Holy Ghost, and of that it is necessary to speak little, but to believe much.

Let us now consider the greatness of the gift of the Holy Ghost with all its effects, inasmuch as He was sent by the Father and by our Lord Jesus Christ to His Church; or as He has been sent to each one of us. For it is true that we cannot thank God too much that He has made this singular gift to the Church, on account of the benefits which result to us from it. It was certainly very appropriate that the Holy Ghost was sent under the form and figure of tongues of fire, because it is in the tongue that the power of the Church resides. Who does not know that all the greatest mysteries are performed by the tongue? Preaching is performed by the tongue; in Holy Baptism, without which no one can be saved, it is necessary that the tongue intervene to give the power to the water to wash us from our sins and iniquities, by the sacred words that are pronounced upon it; in the same way, the most holy sacrifice of the Mass could not be celebrated without the ministry of the tongue, and likewise many other mysteries.

But consider, I pray you, this sacred and precious gift of the Holy Ghost, especially as it was made to each one of us as individuals. We have already said that there were seven other gifts included in it, namely those that the prophet Isaiah enumerated: the spirit of wisdom and understanding, of counsel and strength, of knowledge, piety, and fear. We have, accordingly, in these seven gifts a mystical ladder whereby we may know whether we have received the Holy Ghost, because He is accustomed to communicate with souls in which these gifts have descended and which he finds ready to receive Him.

Let us commence with the gift of fear because the prophet names that last. The gift of fear is the most common gift of all, because we see that even the wicked have fear and dread, when they hear death, judgment, and the eternal suffering of hell spoken of; but, nevertheless, that fear does not at all drive out of them their sin and iniquity, because they have not received it of the Holy Ghost. For the fear which is called the gift of the Holy Ghost not only makes us fear the divine judgment, death, and the pains of hell, but it makes us fear God, as our sovereign Judge; consequently that fear drives out of us our sin and all that we know to be offensive to God.

Notice, I beg of you, what Isaiah says, that all the gifts of the Holy Ghost, which he enumerates, as we have said, rest upon the head of our divine Savior, and thereupon concludes that He was filled with the fear of the Lord. But what do these words mean? For it is certain that our Lord had no reason to fear, for He was sinless on account of the hypostatic union of His soul and His human nature with His divinity. We ought to understand that our Lord was filled with fear only for Him to bestow it upon all men, the perfect as well as the imperfect, because all have need of fear—those who are perfect need to fear lest they might forfeit their perfection, and the imperfect need to fear on account of their failure to attain perfection. And as we see that a bottle may be filled with water without any need of the water, and that the bottle is so hard that it is not at all moistened by it, so our blessed Lord was filled with fear, not at all for Himself, because it could not aid Him, but because He received it to give to His brethren, that is to say, to men.

Let us pass to the other gifts, for it is not necessary to say much about fear, especially in the place in which I am, because we ought to use it only as an aid to love when it is needed. And it is not necessary to be held in fear in order to pain or restrain one, because such fear is servile and harmful. But we ought to have that fear which is filial, we ought to retain it in our hearts in order that it may be quick to aid love, when love needs it, as I have said.

Let us now come to the gift of piety, which is the second gift. Piety is nothing else than a fear that is not servile as is the fear that many have, but it is filial and loving, that which makes us regard God, not as our Judge but as our loving Father, whom we do not merely dread to displease, but whom we desire to please.

But it will help us very little to have the desire to please God and the fear of displeasing Him, if the Holy Ghost does not give us the third gift, which is that of knowledge, by which we are able to know and distinguish virtue from vice, that which is pleasing to God from that which is displeasing to Him. Many of the ancient philosophers knew well how to make this distinction. Aristotle has treated admirably of virtue; nevertheless that did not leave the doctors of the Church in doubt as to his salvation, because, having recognized the pathway of virtue, he did not walk in it. But the gift of knowledge which is given us by the Holy Ghost causes us to embrace the practice of the virtue which we recognize and makes us shun vice.

After these first three gifts it is very necessary that the Holy Ghost give us the fourth, which is that of strength. For otherwise it is likely that the others would in no respect help us, because it does not suffice to fear God and to have the desire to quit vice and to do good, and still less to know one from the other, if we do not proceed to practise the good, and therefore we have great need of the gift of strength; it is needful, however, for us to know in what it consists.

The gift of strength will not make us as Alexander, whom the worldlings call great. He conquered, indeed, nearly the whole earth with his arms, but, for all that, he did not have the gift of strength,—although one may vainly attribute it to him on account of his conquests which he made of the world,—since his strength consisted only in the great number of his soldiers and in the instruments of war which he used. With these he beat down the walls of cities and destroyed castles, to subject all races to his empire. Nevertheless he ought not to be praised for his strength, and still less for his courage, because, according to those who have written of him and those who have mentioned him in their histories, he did not have sufficient power over himself to abstain from a glass of wine, and was very often intoxicated. And as an evidence of his weakness, see him weep as a child, when a certain complimentary philosopher had just said to him that there were still many other worlds beyond that which he had conquered and subjected to his dominion. He had so great regret at not being able to conquer all that no one could console him: so great was his ambition.

Now, I pray you, make a slight comparison between the courage and bravery of such an one as St. Paul, the first hermit, or, still better, the great Apostle St. Paul, with the courage and bravery of Alexander, and you will see that the latter, having ruined cities, destroyed castles, and subjected the whole world to the strength of his arms, allowed himself finally to be conquered by himself. But on the other hand, our great Apostle was full of the strength of the Holy Ghost and seemed anxious to overrun and subjugate the whole world, not to throw down the walls of cities, but the hearts of men, until by his preaching he should subject the whole world to the service of the divine Master. Not content with that, see the power, I pray you, which he had over himself, carrying on a continual warfare against his flesh, subjecting all his affections, emotions, passions and inclinations to the rule of reason, and all to the most holy will of the divine Majesty. And it is in this that the gift of strength consists and the greatness of courage: in the overcoming oneself to subject oneself to God; in mortifying and cutting off from our souls all those superfluities and imperfections which produce self-love, without any reserve of even the little things, whatsoever they may be, undertaking courageously to attain the highest perfection without fearing the difficulties there may be in acquiring it.

But when we are so well resolved and strengthened as to undertake the true practice of virtue, it is very needful that we should have the gift of counsel, to choose what is most necessary, according to our vocation: for although it might always be good to practise all virtues, it is especially needful to know how to practise them in order and with discretion. How do I know but that someone will say that on this or that occasion it would not be more useful, or more expedient for me or for others, that I should practise the virtue of patience, either internally or externally, or else whether I ought not to join the one virtue with the other. To understand this it is necessary to have the gift of counsel in order to pursue that exercise which the gift of strength has made us undertake; and that we may not deceive ourselves by choosing the exercises of virtue according to our inclinations and not according to our needs, having regard only to the appearance of things and not to the true essence of virtue.

Now after the gift of counsel comes that of understanding, whereby we are filled with a sense of the goodness and beauty of the mysteries of our holy faith by means of meditation, and made to choose the precepts of internal perfection in the profound mysteries of the same. But note, dear friends, I pray you, that I spoke of meditation and prayer, and not of reasoning and mere speculation of the understanding, as do the theologians of the schools, for that would not be meditation and prayer, but study, inasmuch as it is necessary that meditation have for its end the love of God, and for that neither natural or acquired knowledge is at all needful. For a poor and simple woman, provided she is humble and holds the faith, would be better able to perform a meditation than the greatest doctors who have less piety. So that with neither knowledge nor instruction she would at once see in regard to the cross of the Savior, that precept of Christian perfection: "Blessed are the poor in spirit," even in the heart of God; and in the mystery of the Incarnation she would see the same precept and still more of that humility and love of self-abnegation.

You see well what are the effects of the gift of understanding, which in addition to what we have already said enables us to penetrate and comprehend the truth of the mysteries of our faith, and that it is necessary for us to regard the true essence of the virtues and not the external appearances only; and as it is useful for us to follow these true essences we are enabled to discern them by the gift of counsel.

But the Holy Ghost is not accustomed, when once He has been willing to bestow the six gifts which we have mentioned, to leave the soul without adding to the others the seventh gift, that of wisdom. This is that satisfying knowledge of the things of God that gives to the soul a taste, a savor, an appreciation of, and an unspeakable satisfaction in, the practice of the counsels of Christian perfection, which it has recognized by the gift of understanding. This wisdom bears the soul in a direction entirely different from that of worldly persons, who, contrary to the precepts of the Savior, esteem as happy only those who are rich and honored, or who live luxuriously. But when men have received the gift of understanding they regard as happy only the humble in heart, and those who show outwardly that mortification that proceeds from an inward renunciation and contempt of themselves and of all that the world esteems, since it finds the precepts in the heart itself of our Lord. For in reality wisdom is nothing else than love, which causes us to taste and perceive how sweet and gracious the Lord is. As the prophet says: "O taste and see how gracious the Lord is."

Now that last gift of the Holy Ghost represents to us the last step of that mysterious ladder which Jacob saw and at the summit of which is God, who is ever ready to give to our souls the blessing of peace and make us taste the sweetness of His sacred breast, better a thousand times than the finest earthly wine.

I finish in considering that portion of the passage which I have selected for our instruction from the Acts of the Apostles, in which St. Luke says that all those who were in the chamber received the Holy Ghost and spake divers languages as the Spirit gave them utterance. But they did not all speak after one fashion, because all men were not commissioned to preach the Gospel, as were St. Peter and the other Apostles; for we cannot deny that there were women there, since St. Luke says that there were about six score assembled in the chamber, and that assembled in prayer there was Mary, the mother of Jesus, with the other women; and nevertheless they all spoke as the Spirit gave them utterance; that is to say that they who did not preach publicly encouraged one another in praising and magnifying God. But in addition to that, we should know that there is a certain kind of speaking that is of great effect but which takes place without words, and this is none other than the good example that we give our neighbors.

David says that the heavens declare the glory of God. And how do they do that? for the heavens do not speak. It is the beauty of the heavens and the firmament, for they invite men to admire the greatness of God and preach His wonderful works. That is what he would have us understand when in the same psalm he says that the days and nights commit to each other the duty of telling the glory of God. For who imagines that when we regard the beauty of the sky on a night that is serene, we are not in the least excited to admire and adore Him who made so many beautiful stars, or that when we see a fine day in the clear light of the sun, or even when our Lord sends us the showers to fertilize the earth so that it may bring forth plants, we are not likewise affected? What conclusion ought we to draw from this, my dear friends, if not that we who are much more than the heavens and all else that has been created, because all else has been made for us and not for themselves, that we, by the good example which we give our neighbor, are much more capable of pro-claiming the glory of God than are the heavens and the stars? A good example is a sort of silent preaching that has great force. And although all have not received the gift of languages for preaching, yet all are able to do this most usefully. For is it not a greater marvel to see a soul adorned with many noble virtues than to see the heavens decorated with so many beautiful stars? The days give each other the duty of proclaiming the glory of God, says the prophet, and who does not see that the saints have done the same and resigned to each other that duty? Do we not see that to St. Anthony Hilarion succeeds, and to Hilarion another? And so from one to another the report goes on from century to century, to bless, love, praise, and magnify that infinite goodness of our Lord, whom, with the Father, I pray to give you abundantly the grace of the Holy Ghost in this life and the joy of everlasting felicity in the other life. May it be so.

JACQUES BÉNIGNE BOSSUET

Jacques Bénigne Bossuet was born September 27, 1627, at Dijon, where his father held a place in the government of the city. He was educated at the Jesuit college at Dijon, where he distinguished himself as a classical scholar. In 1642 he was sent to Paris and entered the College of Navarre in the University. He at once became famous for his extraordinary talents, and, encouraged by his friends, he took every opportunity to improve his oratorical gifts. To this end he frequented the theatres and studied attentively the elocution and gestures of the best actors. He was ordained in 1632, and returned to Metz, where he spent his time in the study of the Fathers and the duties of his cure. In 1659, and in the years following, he was often in Paris and preached frequently before the King and the court. In 1669 he was appointed instructor to the Dauphin. Bossuet was indefatigable in his efforts to train his charge in every virtue, and composed for his instruction his celebrated treatise on universal history and other works of no less merit. In 1679 his duties in the education of the Dauphin ceased, and two years later he was made Bishop of Meaux. From this time he was rarely in Paris except to deliver one or another of his funeral orations. But he was by no means inactive. He took a prominent part in the controversy connected with what has been known as the Gallican liberties, and founded a party opposed to "Ultra-montanism" which survived many years. He also composed his famous work on the variations of the Protestant churches, in which he showed the endless fluctuations of the Protestants in matters of faith as opposed to the stability of the Roman Church. He was also concerned in the attack upon the movement known as Quietism, of which Fénelon was the most distinguished representative. In this he was able to bring about the condemnation by Rome of the whole line of suspected doctrine, though it must be confessed that Bossuet here showed too much personal animosity toward one whom the world recognizes as a holy and just man. Bossuet died at Paris, April 12, 1704.

Bossuet was an orator of the first rank. Whether he was the greatest of the French ecclesiastical orators it would be difficult to say. He had everything to make his oratory effective,—a strong and pleasing voice, a commanding and beautiful personal appearance, perfect grace of manner, and complete control of himself and all his powers at every moment. His literary style, moreover, is of the highest order of excellence. He had a wonderful skill in attracting and holding the attention by a judicious blending of passion and repose, of vivid description and clear detail. He is at his best in his funeral orations, in which line of oratory he has certainly never been surpassed and perhaps never equalled. The masterpieces of Bossuet are his orations on the death of Henrietta of England, of her daughter the Duchess of Orleans, and of Prince Condé.

The best edition of Bossuet's works is that of Lachat, thirty-one volumes, Paris. Another, almost equally good, is that of Didot, Paris, 1841. The best life of Bossuet in English is that by the author of the life of St Francis de Sales, London, 1874. See also *Life of Bossuet*, by Cardinal de Bossuet, and *Memoirs of Bossuet*, by l'Abbé le Dieu.

FUNERAL ORATION ON THE PRINCE OF CONDÉ

by Jacques Bénigne Bossuet

The following oration was delivered in the Church of Notre Dame in Paris, March 10, 1687, in the presence of the son of the deceased, to whom reference is made. It is considered the masterpiece of its illustrious author. It was furthermore the last oration Bossuet delivered, as he intimates in the closing passage. Though he lived for some time after this, his career as an orator may be said to culminate and end with this oration.

Louis II. of Bourbon, Prince of Condé, was born at Paris, September 8, 1621. He was the son of Henry II. of Bourbon and Charlotte Marguerite de Montmorency. As an instance of his courage and valor, his exploit at Freiburg has been often mentioned. He threw his baton into the midst of the enemy and then at the head of his troops plunged into the thick of the fight and rescued it. By this act he obtained the victory. At Seneffe he had four horses shot under him. He passed his last years at Chantilly, and died at Fontainebleau, December 11, 1686.

"The Lord is with thee, thou mighty man of valor. Go in this thy might. Surely I will be with thee."

AT the moment that I open my lips to celebrate the immortal glory of Louis Bourbon, Prince of Condé, I find myself equally overwhelmed by the greatness of the subject, and, if permitted to avow it, by the uselessness of the task. What part of the habitable world has not heard of the victories of the Prince of Condé and the wonders of his life? Everywhere they are rehearsed. The Frenchman, in extolling them, can give no information to the stranger. And although I may remind you of them today, yet, always anticipated by your thoughts, I shall have to suffer your secret reproach for falling so far below them. We feeble orators can add nothing to the glory of extraordinary souls. Well has the sage remarked that their actions alone praise them; all other praise languishes by the side of their great names. The simplicity of a faithful narrative alone can sustain the glory of the Prince of Condé. But awaiting the time when history, which owes such a narrative to future ages, will make this appear, we must satisfy, as we can, the gratitude of the public, and the commands of the greatest of kings. What does the empire not owe to a prince who has honored the house of France, the whole French name, and, so to speak, mankind at large? Louis the Great himself has entertained these sentiments. After having mourned that great man, and given by his tears, in the presence of his whole court, the most glorious eulogy which he could receive, he gathers together in this illustrious temple whatever is most august in his kingdom, to render public acknowledgments to the memory of the Prince; and he desires that my feeble voice should animate all these mournful signs—all this funeral array. Let us then subdue our grief and make the effort.

But here a greater object, and one more worthy of the pulpit, presents itself to my thoughts, for it is God who makes warriors and conquerors. "Thou," said David, "hast taught my hands to war, and my fingers to fight." If He inspires courage, He gives no less other great qualities, natural and supernatural, both of the heart and mind. Everything comes from His powerful hand; it is He who sends from heaven all generous sentiments, wise counsels, and good thoughts. But He would have us distinguish between the gifts which He permits to fall to His enemies and those which He reserves for His servants. What distinguishes His friends from all others is piety; until that gift of heaven is received, all others are not only useless, but aid the ruin of those whom they adorn. Without this inestimable gift of piety, what were the Prince of Condé, with all his great heart and lofty genius? No, my brethren, if piety had not consecrated his other virtues, neither would these princes have found any solace for their grief, nor that venerable pontiff any confidence in his prayers, nor myself any support for the praises which are due to so great a man. Under the influence of such an example, let us lose sight of all human glory! Let us destroy the idol of the ambitious! Let it fall prostrate before these altars! On this occasion, let us group together (for we can do it with propriety) the highest qualities of an excellent nature, and, to the glory of truth, let us exhibit in a Prince admired by the whole world whatever constitutes the hero and carries the glory of the world to the loftiest eminence, valor, magnanimity, and natural goodness—qualities of the heart; vivacity and penetration, grandeur of thought and sublimity of genius—qualities of the intellect; all these would be only an illusion if piety were not added, for piety is, indeed, the whole of man! This it is, gentlemen, which you see in the life, eternally memorable, of the high and illustrious Prince Louis Bourbon, Prince of Condé, First Prince of the blood!

God has revealed to us that He alone makes conquerors, that He alone causes them to subserve His designs. Who else made Cyrus but God, who, in the prophecies of Isaiah, named him two hundred years before his birth? "Thou hast not known Me," said He to him, "but I have even called thee by thy name, and surnamed thee. I will go before thee and make the crooked places straight; I will break in pieces the gates of brass, and cut in sunder the bars of iron. I am the Lord, and there is none else, there is no God beside Me. I form the light and create darkness"; as if He had said, "It is I that made everything, and from eternity know everything that I do." Who else could have formed an Alexander but the same God who made him visible from afar to the prophet Daniel, and revealed by such vivid images his unconquerable ardor? "See," said He, "that conqueror, with what rapidity he advances from the west, as it were by bounds and without touching the earth." Resembling, in his bold movements and rapid march, certain vigorous and bounding animals, he advances only by quick and impetuous attacks, and is arrested neither by mountains nor precipices. Already the King of Persia is in his power. "At sight of him, he is moved with anger," says the prophet,—"rushes upon him, stamps him under his feet; none can defend him from his attacks, or deliver him out of his hand." Listening only to these words of Daniel, whom do you expect to see under that image—Alexander or the Prince of Condé?

God had given him that indomitable valor for the salvation of France during the minority of a King of four years of age. But let that King, cherished of Heaven, advance in life, everything will yield to his exploits. Equally superior to his friends and his enemies, he will hasten now to employ, now to surpass, his most distinguished generals; and under the hand of God, who will ever befriend him, he will be acknowledged the firm bulwark of his kingdom. But God had chosen the Duke d'Enghien [Condé] to defend him in his childhood. Thus, during the first years of his reign, the Duke conceived a design which the most experienced veterans could not work out; but victory justified it before Rocroi. True, the hostile army is the stronger. It is composed of those old bands of Valonnaise, Italians, and Spaniards, which never till then were broken. But how much could be trusted to the courage which inspired our troops, the pressing necessity of the State, past advantages, and a Prince of the blood who carried victory in his eyes! Don Francisco de Mellos steadily waits his approach; and, without the possibility of retreating, the two generals and their armies had chosen to shut themselves in by woods and marshes, in order to decide their quarrels like two warriors, in close combat. Then, what was seen? The young Prince appeared another man! Moved by so great an object, his mighty soul revealed itself entirely; his courage increased with his peril, his sagacity with his ardor. During the night, which must be spent in presence of the enemy, like a vigilant general, he was the last to retire; yet never did he repose more peacefully. In the prospect of so great a day, and his first battle, he is tranquil, so thoroughly is he in his element; for well is it known that on the morrow, at the appointed time, he must awake from his profound slumber as another Alexander!

See him, as he rushes either to victory or to death. As soon as he has spread from rank to rank the ardor which animates himself, he is seen, almost at the same time, attacking the right wing of the enemy; sustaining ours about to give way; rallying the half-subdued Frenchmen; putting to flight the victorious Spaniard; carrying terror everywhere, and confounding with his lightning glance those who had escaped his blows. But that formidable infantry of the Spanish army, whose heavy and wedged battalions, resembling so many towers,—towers which had succeeded in repairing their breaches,—remained immovable in the midst of all others in disorder, and from all sides kept up a steady fire. Thrice the young conqueror attempted to break these intrepid warriors; thrice was he repulsed by the valorous Count de Fontaine, who was borne in his carriage, and, notwithstanding his infirmities, proved that the warrior spirit is master of the body which it animates. In vain does Bek, with his fresh cavalry, endeavor to rush through the wood to fall on our exhausted soldiers; the Prince has prevented him; the routed battalions demand quarter: but the victory was nearly to be more disastrous to the Duke d'Enghien than conflict itself. As he advances with an assured air to receive the surrender of those brave men, they, ever on their guard, are seized with the fear of being surprised by a new attack;—their terrible volley renders our army furious; nothing is seen but carnage; blood maddens the soldiers; until that great Prince, who could not slaughter those lions like timid sheep, calmed their excited courage, and joined to the pleasure of conquering that of pardoning his enemies.

What then was the astonishment of those veteran troops and their brave officers, when they saw that there was no safety but in the arms of the conqueror! With what wonder did they look upon that young Prince, whose victory had enhanced his lofty bearing, and whose clemency added to it a new charm! Ah, how willingly would he have saved the life of the brave Duke de Fontaine! But he was found on the ground among thousands of the dead, of whom Spain yet feels the loss. She knew not that the Prince who had destroyed so many of her veteran regiments on the field of Rocroi, would complete their subjugation on the plains of Lens. Thus the first victory was the pledge of many more. The Prince bends the knee, and on the battle-field renders back to the God of armies the glory which He had conferred. There they celebrated Rocroi delivered, the threatenings of a formidable army turned to shame, the regency established, France in repose, and a reign, destined to such prosperity, begun by an omen so happy. The army commenced the thanksgiving; all France followed. The first achievement of the Duke d' Enghien was extolled to the skies. Such an event was enough to render illustrious any other life; but in his case, it was but the first step in his career.

From that first campaign, after the taking of Thionville, noble fruit of the victory at Rocroi, he passed for a general equally invincible in sieges and battles. But observe in this young Prince what is not less beautiful than victory. The court, which had prepared for him the applause which he merited, was astonished at the manner in which he received it. The Queen-regent testified to him that the King was satisfied with his services. In the mouth of the sovereign, that was a recompense worthy of his toils. But if others ventured to praise him, he rejected their praises as offensive. Invincible to flattery, he dreaded its very appearance. Such was the delicacy, or rather such was the good sense, of the Prince. His maxim was (and note that it is maxims which make great men) that in great actions our only care ought to be to perform well our part, and let glory follow virtue. This he inspired in others, this he followed himself, so that he was never tempted by false glory; everything in him tended to truth and greatness. Thence it followed that he placed his glory in the service of the King and the prosperity of the State. Here was the fundamental principle of his life; here were his first and most cherished feelings.

The court could scarcely retain him, though he was the object of its admiration. He must show himself everywhere, to Germany as to Flanders, as the intrepid defender given us by God. Here direct your special attention! A contest awaits the Prince more formidable than Rocroi: to prove his virtue, war is about to exhaust all its inventions, all its efforts. What object presents itself to my eyes? Not only men to combat, but inaccessible mountains, ravines, and precipices on one side; on the other an impenetrable wood, the bottom of which is a marsh; behind, streams, and prodigious intrenchments; everywhere lofty forts, and levelled forests traversed by frightful roads; in the midst Merci with his brave Bavarians, flushed with distinguished success and the capture of Fribourg;—Merci, whom the Prince of Condé and the vigilant Turenne had never surprised in an irregular movement, and to whom they rendered the distinguished testimony that he never lost a favorable opportunity, and never failed to foresee their plans as if he had assisted at their councils.

Here, during eight days, and in four different attacks, was seen all that could be endured and undertaken in war. Our troops seemed disheartened as much by the resistance of the enemy as by the frightful character of the ground; and the Prince at times saw himself almost abandoned. But like another Maccabasus, "his own arm never failed him; and his courage, excited by so many perils, brought him succor." No sooner was he seen on foot to be the first to force those inaccessible heights, than his ardor drew all others after him. Merci sees his destruction certain: his best regiments are defeated; the night saves the remnant of his army. But what excessive rains also come to the enemy's aid, so that we have at once not only all courage and all art, but all nature to contend with! What advantage is taken of this by a bold and dexterous enemy, and in what frightful mountains does he intrench himself anew! Beaten on all sides, he must leave as booty to the Duke d'Enghien, not only his cannon and baggage, but also all the country bordering on the Rhine. See how the whole gives way. In ten days Philipsbourg is reduced, notwithstanding the approach of winter,—Philipsbourg, which so long held the Rhine captive under our laws, and whose loss the most illustrious of kings has so gloriously repaired. Worms, Spire, Mayence, Landau, and twenty other places of note open their gates. Merci cannot defend them, and no longer appears before his conqueror. But this is not enough; he must fall at his feet, a victim worthy of his valor: Nordlingen shall see his fall;—then shall it be decided that their enemies cannot stand before the French, either in Germany or Flanders; and there shall it be seen that to the Prince all these advantages are due. God, the Protector of France and of a King whom He has destined for His mighty works, ordains it thus.

By such arrangements, everything appeared safe under the conduct of the Duke d'Enghien; and without wishing to spend the day in recounting his other exploits, you know that among so many places attacked not one escaped his hands; and thus the glory of the Prince continued to rise. Europe, which admired the noble ardor by which he was animated in his battles, was astonished to perceive that he was master of himself; and that at the age of twenty-six years he was as capable of managing his troops, as of urging them into perils; of yielding to fortune, as of causing it to subserve his designs. In all situations we see in him one of those extraordinary men who force all obstacles. The promptitude of his action leaves no time for its contravention. Such is the character of conquerors. When David, himself a great warrior, deplored the death of two captains, he gave them this eulogy: "They were swifter than eagles, they were stronger than lions." Such is the very image of the Prince whom we mourn. Like lightning, he appeared in the most remote countries. He was seen at the same time in all attacks, in all quarters. When occupied on one side, he sends to reconnoitre the other; the active officer who conveys his orders is, to his astonishment, anticipated, and finds that already all are reanimated by the presence of the Prince. He seems to multiply himself in action; neither fire nor steel stops him. No need has he to arm his head, exposed to so many perils; God is his assured armor; blows lose their force as they approach him, and leave upon him the tokens of his courage and of the protection only of Heaven. Tell him not that the life of the first Prince of the blood, so necessary to the State, ought to be spared; he answers that such a prince, more interested by his birth in the glory of the King and crown, ought, in the extremity of the State, more readily than all others to devote himself to its recovery.

After having made his enemies, during so many years, feel the invincible power of the King, were it asked, What did he do to sustain it at home? I would answer, in a word, he made the Regent respected. And since it is necessary to speak once of those things respecting which I would be glad to be forever silent, let me say that up to the time of that unfortunate imprisonment, he had never dreamed that it was possible for him to attempt anything against the State; and to his honor be it said, if he desired to secure a recompense, he desired still more to merit it. It was this which caused him to say (and here I can confidently repeat before these altars his words, which I received from his own lips, and which so strikingly indicate his true disposition): that caused him to say, in speaking of that unhappy prison, that he had entered it the most innocent of men, and had issued from it the most culpable. "Alas!" said he, "I lived only for the service of the King, and the honor of the State." We perceive in these words a sincere regret for having been carried so far by his misfortunes. But without excusing what he himself so strongly condemned, let us say, so that it may never again be mentioned, that as in celestial glory the faults of holy penitents,covered by what they have done to repair them, and the infinite glory of the compassion of God, never more appear, so in the faults so sincerely acknowledged, and in the end so gloriously atoned for by faithful services, nothing ought to be remembered but the penitence of the Prince, and the clemency of his sovereign who has forgotten them.

However much he was involved in those unfortunate wars, he has at least this glory, never to have permitted the grandeur of his house to be tarnished among strangers. Notwithstanding the majesty of the empire, the pride of Austria, and the hereditary crowns attached to that house, particularly in the branch which reigns in Germany; even when a refugee at Namur, and sustained only by his courage and reputation, he urged the claims of a Prince of France and of the first family in the world so far that all that could be obtained from him was his consent to treat upon equality with the Archduke, although a brother of the Emperor, and the descendant of so many emperors, on condition that the Prince in the third degree should wear the honors of the Low Countries. The same treatment was secured to the Duke d'Enghien; and even in Brussels the house of France maintained its rank over that of Austria. But mark what constitutes true courage. While the Prince bore himself so loftily with the Archduke who governed, he rendered to the King of England and the Duke of York, now so great a monarch, but then unfortunate, all the honors which were their due; and finally he taught Spain, too disdainful, what was that majesty which misfortune could not tear from princes. The rest of his conduct was not less distinguished. Amid the difficulties which his interests introduced into the Treaty of the Pyrenees, hear what were his orders, and see whether any one ever acted so nobly, with reference to his own interests. He wrote to his agents in the conference, that it was not right that the peace of Christendom should be postponed for his sake; that they might take care of his friends, but must leave him to his fate.

Ah, what a noble victim thus sacrificed himself for the public good! But when things changed, and Spain was willing to give him either Cambray and its environs, or Luxembourg in full sovereignty, he declared that to these advantages, and all others, however great, which they could give him, he preferred—what? His duty and the good will of the King! This formed the passion of his heart. This he was incessantly repeating to the Duke d'Enghien, his son. Thus did he appear himself! France beheld him, in these last deeds, returning to her bosom with a character ennobled by suffering, and more than ever devoted to his King and country. But in those first wars he had but one life to offer; now he has another which is dearer to him than his own. After having, under his father's example, nobly finished his studies, the Duke d'Enghien is ready to follow him to the battle-field. Not content with teaching him the art of war by his instructions, he conducts him to living lessons and actual practice. Let us leave aside the passage of the Rhine, the wonder of our age and the life of Louis the Great. In the field of Seneffe, although the youth commanded, as he had already done in other campaigns, he learned war by the side of his father, in the most terrible conflicts. In the midst of so many perils, he sees the great Prince thrown down in a trench under a horse, covered with blood. While offering him his own horse and raising the fallen Prince, he is wounded in the arms of his affectionate father, but he does not discontinue his kind offices. He is delighted with the opportunity of satisfying at once his filial piety and love of glory. How could the Prince fail to think that nothing was wanting to that noble son but opportunities, to achieve the greatest things? Moreover his tenderness increased with his esteem.

But not only for his son and his family did he cherish such tender sentiments. I have seen him (and do not think that I here exaggerate) deeply moved with the perils of his friends; I have seen him, simple and natural, change color at the recital of their misfortunes, entering into their minutest as well as most important affairs, reconciling contending parties and calming angry spirits with a patience and gentleness which could never have been expected from a temper so sensitive, and a rank so high. Far from us be heroes without humanity! As in the case of all extraordinary things, they might force our respect and seduce our admiration, but they could never win our love. When God formed the heart and affections of man, He planted goodness there, as the proper characteristic of the divine nature and the mark of that beneficent hand from which we sprang. Goodness, then, ought to be the principal element of our character and the great means of attracting the affection of others. Greatness, which supervenes upon this, so far from diminishing goodness, ought only to enable it, like a public fountain, to diffuse itself more extensively. This is the price of hearts! For the great whose goodness is not diffusive, as a just punishment of their haughty indifference remain forever deprived of the greatest good of life, the joys of fellowship. Never did man enjoy this joy more than the Prince of whom we are speaking. Never did one less fear that familiarity would diminish respect. Is this the man who stormed cities and gained battles? What! he seems to have forgotten the high rank he knew so well how to defend! Let us recognize the hero, who, always equal to himself, without rising to appear great, or descending to be civil and kind, naturally appeared everything that he ought to be toward all men, like a majestic and beneficent river, which peacefully conveys to the cities the abundance which it has spread through the countries which it waters; which gives itself to all, and rises and swells only when some violent opposition is made to the gentle current which bears it on its tranquil course. Such was the gentleness and such the energy of the Prince of Condé. Have you an important secret? Confide it freely to that noble heart; your affair becomes his by that confidence. Nothing was more inviolable to that Prince than the rights of friendship. When a favor was asked of him, it was he that appeared obliged; and never was his joy so natural or lively, as when he conferred pleasure upon others. The first money which, by the permission of the King, he received from Spain, notwithstanding the necessities of his exhausted house was given to his friends, although after the peace he had nothing to hope from their friendship. Four hundred thousand crowns, distributed by his orders (rare instance in human life), showed that gratitude was as powerful in the Prince of Condé as hope is in most men. With him virtue was ever its own reward. He praised it even in his enemies. Whenever he had occasion to speak of his actions, and even in the communications which he sent to the court, he extolled the wise counsels of one, and the courage of another; each one received his proper rank in his reports; and in what he gave to every one he never seemed to find a place for what he had done himself.

Without envy, without disguise or pretension, always great, in action as well as in repose, he appeared at Chantilly as he did at the head of his troops. Whether he embellished that magnificent and charming residence, whether he planted his camp or fortified a place in the midst of a hostile country, whether he marched with an army amid perils or conducted his friends through superb paths to the noise of falling fountains silent neither by day nor night, he was al-ways the same man; his glory followed him everywhere. How delightful, after the contest and tumult of arms, to be able to relish those peaceful virtues and that tranquil glory which none can share with the soldier more than with fortune; where one can pursue the great end of life without being stunned with the noise of trumpets, the roar of cannons, or the cries of the wounded; and when in solitude, man appears as great, and as worthy of respect, as when he gives the word of command, and whole armies do his bidding.

Come, ye people, come now—or rather ye princes and lords, ye judges of the earth, and ye who open to man the portals of heaven; and more than all others, ye princes and princesses, nobles descended from a long line of kings, lights of France, but today in gloom, and covered with your grief as with a cloud;—come and see how little remains of a birth so august, a grandeur so high, a glory so dazzling. Cast your eyes around you; see all that magnificence and devotion can do to honor so great a hero: titles and inscriptions, vain signs of that which is no more; forms which seem to weep around a tomb, fragile images of a grief which time sweeps away with everything else; columns which appear as if they would bear to heaven the magnificent evidence of our emptiness; nothing, indeed, is wanting in all these honors but he to whom they are rendered! Weep then over these feeble remains of human life; weep over that mournful immortality we give to heroes.

But draw near especially ye who run, with such ardor, the career of glory, intrepid and warrior spirits! Who was more worthy to command you? and in whom did ye find command more honorable? Mourn then that great Captain, and weeping, say: "Here is the man who led us through all hazards, under whom were formed so many renowned captains, raised by his example to the highest honors of war; his shadow might yet gain battles, and lo! in his silence, his very name animates us, and at the same time warns us, that to find, at death, some rest from our toils, and not arrive unprepared at our eternal dwelling, we must, with an earthly king, yet serve the King of Heaven." Serve then that immortal and ever merciful King, who will value a sigh or a cup of cold water, given in His name, more than all others will value the shedding of your blood. And begin to reckon the time of your useful services from the day on which you gave yourselves to so beneficent a Master. Will ye not too come, ye, I say, whom he was pleased to count among his friends? To whatever extent you enjoyed his confidence, come all of you and surround this tomb. Mingle your prayers with your tears; and while admiring, in so great a Prince, a friendship so excellent, and intercourse so sweet, preserve the remembrance of a hero whose goodness equalled his courage. Thus may he ever prove your cherished instructor; thus may you profit by his virtues; and may his death, which you deplore, serve you at once for consolation and example.

For myself, if permitted, after all others, to render the last offices at this tomb, O Prince, the worthy subject of our praises and regrets, thou wilt live forever in my memory. There will thy image be traced, but not with that bold aspect which promises victory. No, I would see in you nothing which death can efface. You will have in that image only immortal traits. I shall behold you such as you were in your last hours, under the hand of God, when His glory began to dawn upon you. There shall I see you more triumphant than at Fribourg and at Rocroi; and ravished by so glorious a triumph, I shall give thanks in the beautiful words of the well-beloved disciple, "This is the victory that overcometh the world, even our faith." Enjoy, O Prince, this victory, enjoy it forever, through the everlasting efficacy of that sacrifice. Accept these last efforts of a voice once familiar to you. With you these discourses shall end. Instead of deploring the death of others, great Prince, I would henceforth learn from you to render my own holy; happy if, reminded by these white locks of the account which I must give of my ministry, I reserve for the flock which I have to feed with the word of life, the remnants of a voice which falters, and an ardor which is fading away.

ESPRIT FLÉCHIER

Esprit Fléchier was born June 10, 1632, at Pernes in the department of Vaucluse. He was educated at the college at Tarascon-sur-Rhône, belonging to the congregation of Christian Doctrine, of which his uncle, Father Audifret, was the General. He subsequently entered the congregation and began to teach. In 1659 he was appointed professor of rhetoric at Narbonne, where he pronounced the funeral oration on M. de Rebe, Archbishop of Narbonne. He soon removed to Paris, where he became an obscure catechist He was able, after a time, to attract the attention of Colbert, the minister of Louis XIV., and was appointed preceptor in the family of De Caumartin. Soon after this he was appointed reader to the Dauphin, on the recommendation of the Duke de Montausier, the Dauphin's governor. Meanwhile his reputation as a preacher was constantly increasing. In 167a he delivered the funeral oration on the death of the wife of his patron, M. de Montausier, and was made a member of the Academy. Two other masterpieces were delivered soon after, the oration on the death of the Duchess d'Aiguillon in 1675, and on Turenne in 1676. He received from the King the Abbey of St Leverin, and in 1685 the see of Lavaur, from which he was promoted to the more important see of Nismes. The administration of his diocese was unexceptionable. He was not only mild and successful in his dealings with the many religious dissensions which confronted him, but was able to correct many abuses which had given offence and occasion to the Protestant party. Fléchier died at Montpellier, February 16, 1710.

The masterpieces of Fléchier have been already mentioned. He is at his best in his funeral orations. He does not possess the grandeur of Bossuet, nor his magnificent sweep of imagination. Neither does he equal Massillon in his passionate earnestness. He has, however, special merits, which were in his lifetime, perhaps, overrated, and have since been too little appreciated. His style is at once clear and ornate. He is never dull or prosy. His language is carefully chosen and his thought arranged with exquisite symmetry. Every passage is eminently adapted to oral delivery and must be spoken to be appreciated. In this he was unexcelled. If at times his thought is less antithetical than his language, this defect is more apparent in reading than in listening to his superb diction. In the grand style of the French preachers, in which the highest art is employed to enhance the effect of the sermon or oration, the form has a value which it does not have in ordinary prose. In this respect oratory approaches poetry.

The collected works of Fléchier have been published by the Abbé Ducreux in ten volumes, Nismes, 1782. There is an inferior edition, published at Paris, 1825. The funeral orations have often been reprinted, and may be found in a convenient edition, with those of Massillon and Mascaron, published by Didot, Paris. Notices of Fléchier are to be found in the various histories of French literature and biographical dictionaries, but his life does not seem to have been adequately treated. There are two old accounts of him, by L. Juillard du Jarry, *Oraison Funèbre d' E. Fléchier, evêque de Nismes*; and by Trinquelague, *Éloge d' E. Fléchier, evêque de Nismes*; but they are by no means generally accessible.

FUNERAL ORATION ON MARSHAL TURENNE

by Esprit Fléchier

The following oration was delivered in Paris, January 10, 1676, at the Church of St Eustache. It may be regarded as the most finished expression of the rhetorical school of French oratory. In the lifetime of Fléchier this speech was regarded as the equal of anything produced by Bossuet, but however much opinions may vary as to the comparative merits of the two men, it is clear that for sublime eloquence the oration on the Prince of Condé by Bossuet is the greater work. The extremely ornate rhetoric of Fléchier and his expressions of grief do not appear to advantage in comparison with the manly sorrow of the Bishop of Meaux. Fléchier combined with his polished diction a remarkable degree of skill in the effective delivery of his orations. When, for instance, he delivered the passage, "Turenne is dying," the audience were so affected by the pathos of his tone and manner that many present burst into sobs.

Turenne was born at Sedan, November 11, 1611. He became Marshal in 1644, and was sent to Germany with Condé. In 1648, in the civil war of the Fronde, he joined the forces of the malcontents, but soon deserted their ranks. In 1659 he succeeded in defeating the Spanish forces and in effecting the Peace of the Pyrenees. Louis XIV employed him in subsequent wars in Holland and the Palatinate. Turenne was killed in crossing the Rhine, July 27, 1675. He was originally a Protestant. Reference is made to this in a portion of the oration here presented. He embraced the Catholic faith in 1668.

"Moreover they bewailed him and all Israel made great lamentation for him, and mourned many days, saying, How is the valiant man fallen that delivered Israel!"—1 Macc. 9:20, 21.

I CANNOT, gentlemen, at the outset, give you a higher idea of the mournful subject with which I am about to occupy your attention, than by citing the noble and expressive terms used by Holy Scripture to praise the life and deplore the death of the sage and valiant Maccabaeus, the man who spread the glory of his nation to the ends of the earth; who covered his camp with a buckler, and forced that of the enemy with the sword; who gave mortal grief to the kings leagued against him, and rejoiced Jacob with those virtues and exploits, the memory of which shall endure forever.

This man, who defended the cities of Judah, who subdued the pride of the children of Ammon and Esau, and returned loaded with the spoils of Samaria, after having burned upon their own altars the gods of foreign nations; this man, whom God had thrown around Israel like a wall of iron, against which all the hordes of Asia had so frequently dashed themselves to pieces; who, after he had defeated numerous armies, and disconcerted the proudest and most accomplished generals of the King of Syria, came annually like the least of the Israelites, to repair, with his own triumphant hands, the ruins of the sanctuary, and desired no other recompense for the services he had rendered his country, than the honor of having served it; this valiant man, while driving before him, with invincible courage, the enemies whom he had reduced to a shameful flight, at last received a mortal wound, and remained buried, as it were, in his own triumph. At the first report of this disaster, all the cities of Judah were moved, and floods of tears ran from the eyes of all the inhabitants. For a time they were confounded, dumb, and motionless. At length breaking the long and mournful silence, in a voice interrupted by sobs, they gave . utterance to the grief, the pity and fear, which oppressed their hearts, and exclaimed: "Why is that great man dead, who saved the people of Israel?" At this cry, Jerusalem redoubled its weeping; the arches of the temple trembled; Jordan was troubled, and all its banks reechoed the sound of those mournful words: "Why is that great man dead, who saved the people of Israel?"

Christians, whom a mournful ceremony has assembled in this place, do you not call to mind what you saw and felt five months ago? Do you not recognize yourselves in the affliction which I have described, and in your minds substitute for the hero spoken of in Scripture him of whom I purpose to speak? The virtues and the fate of the one resemble those of the other, and to the latter nothing is wanting today but a eulogy worthy of him. Oh, if the Spirit divine, Spirit of power and truth, should enrich my discourse with those natural and vivid images which represent virtue, and, at the same time, persuade to its practice, with what lofty conceptions should I fill your minds, and what noble impressions should I communicate to your hearts, by the recital of so many edifying and glorious actions!

What subject was ever better fitted to receive all the ornaments of a grave and solemn eloquence than the life and death of the high and mighty Prince Henry de la Tour d'Auvergne, Viscount Turenne, Marshal-general of the Camps and Armies of the King, and Colonel-general of the Light Cavalry? Where else shine with such lustre the glorious results of military virtue, the conduct of armies, sieges of castles, storming of cities, passages of rivers, bold attacks, honorable retreats, well-ordered encampments, vigorous combats, battles gained, enemies vanquished by force, scattered by address, or worn out and consumed by a sage and lofty prudence? Where else can be found such numerous and striking examples, than in the action of a man wise, modest, liberal, disinterested, devoted to the service of his king and country, great in adversity by his fortitude, in prosperity by his moderation, in difficulties by his prudence, in danger by his valor, in religion by his piety?

What subject can inspire sentiments more just and affecting than a death so sudden and surprising; a death which suspended the course of our victories, and dissipated the fondest hopes of peace? Powerful enemies of France, ye live, and the spirit of Christian charity forbids me to cherish a wish for your death. Only may ye recognize the justice of our arms, accept the peace which, in spite of your losses, ye have so often refused, and in the abundance of your tears extinguish the fires of a war which ye have unfortunately kindled. God forbid that I should extend my wishes further. In-scrutable are the judgments of God! But ye live; and I mourn in this pulpit, a wise and virtuous

General, whose intentions were pure, and whose virtue seemed to merit a longer life and a more extended career.

But let us suppress our complaints; it is time to commence his eulogy, and to show how that powerful man triumphed over the enemies of the State by his bravery, over the passions of his soul by his wisdom, over the errors and vanities of the world by his piety. If I interrupt the order of my discourse, pardon a little confusion in a subject which has caused us so much grief. I may sometimes confound the general of the army with the sage and the Christian. I shall praise now his victories, and now the virtues which gained them. If I cannot rehearse all his actions, I shall discover them in their principles; I shall adore the God of armies, I shall invoke the God of peace, I shall bless the God of mercy, and through the whole I shall win your attention, not by the force of eloquence, but by the reality and greatness of the virtues about which I shall speak.

Do not suppose, gentlemen, that I shall follow the custom of orators, and praise M. de Turenne as ordinary men are praised. If his life had less of glory, I should dwell upon the grandeur and nobility of his house; and if his portrait were less beautiful, would discover those of his ancestors. But the glory of his actions effaces that of his birth, and the smallest praise that can be given him is, that he sprang from the ancient and illustrious house of Tour d'Auvergne, which has mingled its blood with that of kings and emperors, has given rulers to Aquitaine, princes to all the courts of Europe, and queens even to that of France. But what do I say? It is not for me to praise him in this respect; it is for me to mourn him. How glorious was the source from which he took his rise! The heresy of recent times had, however, infected it, and he received with noble blood principles of error and falsehood, and even among the members of his household he found some ignoring and some combating the truth. Let us not make the matter of his eulogy that which was for him an occasion for penitence; let us see the paths of glory and honor which the providence of God opened to him in the world before His mercy recalled him from the ways of perdition and the mistakes of his fathers.

Before his fourteenth year he began to carry arms. Sieges and battles were the exercises of his youth, and his first amusements were victories. Under the discipline of his maternal uncle, the Prince of Orange, he learned the art of war, in the quality of a simple soldier, and neither pride nor indolence restrained him from one of the employments which required labor and obedience. He was seen in this lowest rank of military service, neither refusing any labor, nor dreading any peril; doing from a sense of honor what others did from necessity, and distinguishing himself from them only by a greater attachment to fatigue and a nobler application to all his duties.

Then commenced a life whose career was yet to become so glorious, like those rivers which deepen and expand the farther they extend from their source, and which carry wealth and prosperity to all the regions through which they flow. From that time, he lived only for the glory and welfare of his country. He performed all the services which could be expected from a mind firm and active, lodged in a robust and healthy frame. In his youth he had all the prudence of mature age, and in his mature age all the vigor of youth. His days were full, to use the language of Scripture; and as he did not lose his early years in luxury and pleasure, he was not compelled to spend his last in weakness and inactivity.

What enemy of France has not felt the effects of his valor, and what part of our frontier has not served as the theatre of his glory? He crosses the Alps, and in the famous actions of Casal, of Turin, and of the rout of Quiers, he signalizes himself by his courage and prudence. Italy regards him as one of the principal instruments of those great and prodigious successes which posterity will scarcely credit. He passes from the Alps to the Pyrenees, to aid in the conquest of two important places, which puts one of our finest provinces under protection from all the efforts of Spain. He goes to collect, beyond the Rhine, the remnants of a defeated army; he takes cities, and assists in gaining battles. Thus by degrees, and by his own merit, he rises to supreme command, and shows, during the whole course of his life, what can be done for the defence of a kingdom by a general who is rendered worthy to command by obeying, and who joins to courage and genius application and experience.

Then it was that his mind and heart displayed all their energies. Whether called to prepare matters, or to decide them; to pursue victory with ardor, or wait for it with patience; whether to counteract the designs of the enemy by bravery, or dissipate the fears and jealousies of his allies by wisdom; whether to control himself amid the successes or sustain himself amid the reverses, of war;—his soul was always equal to the occasion. He had only to change virtues when fortune changed her face; elated, but without pride; depressed, but with dignity; almost equally admirable when, with judgment and boldness, he saved the remains of his troops beaten at Mariandel, as when he himself beat the Imperials and the Bavarians; or when, with triumphant troops, he forced all Germany to ask peace from France. . . .

Let us follow this prince in his last campaigns, during which so many difficult enterprises, so many glorious successes, are to be regarded as proofs of his courage, and rewards of his piety. To commence his marches with prayer, to repress impiety and blasphemy, to protect sacred persons and property against the insolence and avarice of the soldiers, to invoke in every danger the God of armies, is the common care and duty of all generals. But he goes far beyond this. Even while commanding the army, he regards himself as a simple soldier of Jesus Christ. He sanctifies wars by the purity of his intentions, by the desire of a happy peace, and by the laws of Christian discipline. He looks upon his soldiers as his brethren, and believes himself under obligation to exercise Christian charity in a cruel profession, wherein general humanity itself is lost. Animated by these lofty motives, he surpasses himself, and proves that courage becomes firmer when sustained by the principles of religion, that there is a pious magnanimity which wins success in spite of perils and obstacles, and that a warrior is invincible when he combats with faith and stretches forth pure hands to the God of armies, who protects him.

As from God he derives all his glory, so to Him he returns it all, and cherishes no other confidence than that which is founded on the divine approbation. Here let us set before you one of those critical occasions, when he attacks with a small number of troops the entire forces of Germany! He marches three days, crosses three rivers, meets the enemy, and gives them battle. With numbers on one side, and valor on the other, fortune is long doubtful. At last courage fires the multitude; the enemy is confused, and begins to yield. "Victory!" shouts a voice. At once the General checks all emotion which gives ardor to battle, and in a severe tone says: "Silence! Our fate is not in our own hands, and we ourselves will be vanquished, if God does not succor us!" With these words, he raises his hands to heaven, whence cometh help, and continuing to give his orders, he waits, with submission between hope and fear, for the execution of heaven's will.

How difficult it is to be at once victorious and humble! Military success leaves in the mind I know not what exquisite pleasure, which fills and absorbs it. In such circumstances one attributes to himself a superiority of force and capacity. He crowns himself with his own hands; he decrees to himself a secret triumph; he regards as his own the laurels which he gathers with infinite toil and frequently moistens with his blood; and even when he renders to God solemn thanks and hangs in His temples the torn and blood-stained trophies which he has taken from the enemy, is not vanity liable to stifle a portion of his gratitude, and mingle with the vows which he pays to God applauses which he thinks due to himself; at least does he not retain some grains of the incense which he burns upon His altars?

It was on such occasions that Marshal Turenne, renouncing all pretensions, returned all the glory to Him to whom it legitimately belongs. If he marches, he acknowledges that it is God who protects and guides him; if he defends fortresses, he knows that he defends them in vain if God does not guard them; if he makes an intrenchment, he feels that it is God who forms a rampart around him to defend him from every attack; if he fights, he knows whence to draw all his force; and if he triumphs, he thinks that he sees an invisible hand crowning him from heaven. Referring thus all the favors he receives to their origin, he thence derives new blessings. No longer does he fear the enemies by whom he is surrounded; without being surprised at their numbers or strength, he exclaims with the prophet: "Some trust in their horses and chariots, but we will trust in the Almighty." In this steadfast and just confidence he redoubles his ardor, forms great designs, executes great things, and begins a campaign which appears as if it must prove fatal to the empire.

He passes the Rhine, and eludes the vigilance of an accomplished and prudent general. He observes the movements of the enemy. He raises the courage of the allies, and controls the suspicions and vacillating faith of neighboring powers. He takes away from the one the will, from the other the means, of injuring him; and profiting by all those important conjunctures which prepare the way for great and glorious events, he leaves to fortune nothing which human skill and counsel can take from it. Already the enemy tremble in their camp, confused and disconcerted. Already has that eagle whose bold approach once alarmed our provinces, taken its flight to the mountains. Those brazen mouths, invented by hell for the destruction of men, thunder on all sides, to favor and precipitate the retreat; and France in suspense awaits the success of an enterprise which, according to all the rules of war, must be infallible.

Alas! we knew all that we might hope, but we knew not all that we might fear. Divine Providence concealed from us a calamity greater than the loss of a battle. It was to cost a life which each of us would have been willing to redeem with his own: and all that we could gain was of less value than what we were to lose. O God I terrible but just in Thy counsels toward the children of men, Thou disposest of victors and victories! To fulfil Thy pleasure, and cause us to fear Thy judgments, Thy power casts down those whom it has lifted up. Thou sacrificest to Thy Sovereign Majesty the noblest victims, and strikest, at Thy pleasure, those illustrious heads which Thou hast so often crowned 1

Do not suppose, gentlemen, that I am about to open here a tragic scene: to represent that great man stretched upon his own trophies; to uncover that body, blood-stained and ghastly, over which still lingers the smoke of the thunder which struck it; to cause his blood, like that of Abel's, to cry from the ground, or expose to your eyes the mournful images of your country and religion in tears! In slight losses, we may thus surprise the pity of our auditors, and by studied efforts draw from their eyes a few forced and useless tears. But we describe without art a death which we mourn without deceit. Every one finds in himself the source of his grief, and reopens his own wound; and it is not necessary to excite the imagination in order to affect the heart.

Here I am almost forced to interrupt my discourse. I am troubled, gentlemen! Turenne dies! All is confusion; fortune vacillates; victory leaves us; peace takes its flight; the good intentions of the allies relax; the courage of the troops anon fails with grief, anon burns with vengeance; the whole army remains motionless. The wounded think of the loss which they have suffered, and not of the wounds which they have received. Dying fathers see their sons weeping over their dead General. The army, in mourning, is engaged in rendering him funeral honors, and Fame, which delights to spread through the world extraordinary events, goes to make known through Europe the glorious history of the Prince's life, and the mournful regrets occasioned by his death.

What sighs then, what lamentations, what praises reecho through the cities and the country! One, looking upon his growing crops, blesses the memory of him to whom he owes the hope of gathering them. Another, who enjoys in repose the heritage which he received from his fathers, prays that eternal peace may be his who saved him from the horrors and cruelties of war. Here, they offer the adorable Sacrifice of Jesus Christ for the soul of him who sacrificed his life and his blood for the public good. There, others prepare for him a funeral service, where they expected to prepare a triumph. Each selects for praise that point in his glorious life which appears the most illustrious. All unite in his eulogy. And each interrupts the other by his sobs; with tears they admire the past, regret the present, and tremble for the future. Thus the whole empire mourns the death of its defender. The loss of a single man is felt to be a public calamity.

Wherefore, my God,—if I may presume to pour out my heart in Thy presence, and speak to Thee, I who am but dust and ashes,—wherefore did we lose him in our most pressing necessity, in the midst of his greatest achievements, at the highest point of his valor, and in the maturity of his wisdom? Was it that, after so many actions worthy of immortality, he had nothing further of a mortal nature to perform? Had the time arrived when he was to enjoy the reward of so many virtues, and receive from Thee the crown of righteousness which Thou reservest for such as have finished a glorious career? Perhaps we placed too much confidence in him, for Thou forbiddest us in the sacred Scriptures to trust in an arm of flesh or put confidence in the children of men. Perhaps it was a punishment of our pride, ambition, and injustice. As the gross vapors ascend from the depths of the valleys and form themselves into thunder which falls upon the mountains, so rises from the hearts of the people those iniquities, the punishment of which falls upon the heads of such as govern and defend them. I presume not, O Lord, to sound the depths of Thy judgments, nor to discover the secret and inscrutable causes from which Thy justice or Thy mercy acts. It is my duty and desire only to adore! But Thou art just, and Thou hast afflicted us. And in an age so corrupt as ours, we need not seek the causes of our calamities elsewhere than in the evil of our ways.

Let us then, gentlemen, derive from our sorrows motives for penitence, and seek only true and substantial consolation in the piety of that great man. Citizens, strangers, enemies, nations, kings, and emperors, mourn and revere him. Yet what can all this contribute to his real happiness? His King even—and such a King!—honors him with his regrets and tears: a noble and precious mark of affection and esteem for a subject, but useless to a Christian. He shall live, I acknowledge, in the minds and memories of men; but the Scripture teaches me that the thoughts of man, and man himself, are but vanity. A magnificent tomb may enclose his piteous remains; but he shall rise again from that superb monument, not to be praised for his heroic exploits, but to be judged according to his works, whether good or bad. His ashes shall mingle with those of the numerous kings who governed the kingdom which he so generously defended; but, after all, what remains under those precious marbles, any more to those kings than to him, of human applause, the pomp of courts, or the splendor of fortune, except an eternal silence, a frightful solitude, and a terrible expectation of the judgment of God? Let the world, then, honor as it will the glory of man, God only is the recompense of faithful Christians.

O death, too sudden! nevertheless, through the mercy of God, long anticipated: of how many edifying words and holy examples hast thou deprived us! We might have seen him, sublime spectacle! a Christian, dying humbly in the midst of triumphs and victories. With what profound sincerity would he have mourned his past errors, abasing himself before the majesty of God, and imploring the succor of His arm, no longer against visible enemies, but against the enemies of his salvation! His living faith and fervent charity, doubtless, would have deeply affected our hearts; and he might have remained to us a model of confidence without presumption, of fear without feebleness, of penitence without artifice, of constancy without affectation, and of a death precious in the sight both of God and man.

Are not these conjectures just? They were involved in his character. They were his cherished designs. He had resolved to live in a manner so holy that it is presumed he would have died in the same way. Ready to cast all his crowns at the feet of Jesus Christ like the conquerors in the Apocalypse, ready to gather together all his honors and dispossess himself of them by a voluntary renunciation, he was no longer of the world, though Providence retained him in it. In the tumult of armies, he solaced himself with the sweet and secret aspirations of solitude. With one hand he smote the Amalekites, and with the other, stretched out to heaven, he drew down the blessing of God. This Joshua, in battle, already performed the functions of Moses upon the Mount, and under the arms of a warrior bore the heart and will of a penitent.

O God! who piercest the profoundest depths of our conscience, and seest the most secret intentions of our hearts, even before they are formed, receive into the bosom of Thy glory that soul, ever occupied with thoughts of Thine eternity! Honor those desires which Thou Thyself didst inspire. Time failed him, but not the courage to fulfil them. If Thou requirest works with desires, behold the charities which he made or destined for the comfort and salvation of his brethren; behold the misled souls which, by his assistance, his counsel, and by his example, he brought back to Thee; behold the blood of Thy people which he so frequently spared; behold his own blood which he so generously shed on our behalf; and yet more than all, behold the blood shed for him by Jesus Christ.

Ministers of God, complete the holy Sacrifice! Christians, redouble your vows and prayers, that God, as a recompense of his toils, may admit his spirit to the place of everlasting repose, and give him an infinite peace in heaven, who three times procured for us a peace on earth, evanescent it is true, yet ever delightful, ever desirable 1

FRANCOIS FÉNELON

Francois de Salignac de Lamothe Fénelon was born August 6, 1651, at the Chateau de Fénelon in Perigord. His family was of noble rank, and he was educated in his boyhood in his father's house. Later he passed to the Jesuit college of Du Plesgis at Paris. On the death of his father he was removed to the seminary of St. Sulpice. It was his first intention to devote himself to the cause of foreign missions, especially in Canada, but he was dissuaded from this, and in 1675 was put at the head of the community of Nouvelles Catholiques, where he remained until 1685. On the revocation of the Edict of Nantes and the commencement of a new policy towards the Protestants, Fénelon was given charge of the missions among the Protestants of Poitou and Saintonge. Here he labored for several years endeavoring to allay the irritation caused by the revocation of the edict of toleration. On his return to Paris he was about to resume his former work when he was called to be the preceptor of the Duke of Burgundy, the son of the Dauphin. Here he was employed for several years in a task that was thoroughly congenial and eminently successful. His educational principles were carried out with admirable results, and Fénelon's fame as a leader in the art of pedagogy is hardly less than as a leader in the Church. In 1695 he was nominated by the King as Archbishop of Cambray and duly consecrated. At this time the controversies concerning the teachings of Mme. Guyon and Quietism broke out, and in them Fénelon became involved. He did not at first assume the defence of the objectionable doctrines, but later in the controversy he became a bold champion of them. This roused the indignation of Bossuet, who had hitherto been his friend. So fierce and active was Bossuet that he was able to procure Fénelon's condemnation at Rome and his banishment from the court. Fénelon retired to Cambray, where he spent the rest of his life in the administration of his diocese and in deeds of charity. Apart from the unfortunate connection with the Quietistic controversy the life of Fénelon is open to no reproach. His profound piety and his genuine devotion to the duties of his sacred calling mark him as one of the most saintly men of modern times. He died January 17, 1713.

Fénelon as an orator does not occupy the same distinguished place as the four great preachers of the court of Louis XIV., but his oratorical gifts were of a high order. He always spoke without notes, and severely condemned the practice of Bourdaloue and others in committing to memory compositions which they afterwards recited with dramatic art. He has, accordingly, left but very few specimens of his oratorical style, and these seem to have been written in early life, so that any representation of his style as a preacher must be very imperfect. In this way the world has lost that which might have been worthy to put beside the masterpieces of Massillon and Bossuet. But the impression that is gained from his prose works, in which his remarkably pure style and fine and tender sentiment are brought out can be used to supplement the imperfect sermons that we have from his hand.

The works of Fénelon have been collected and frequently published. The edition by Leclerc, Paris, 1827-1830, is perhaps the best. Many of his works have appeared separately, and some have been translated into English and other languages, as he enjoys a high reputation as a devotional writer. There is an excellent life of Fénelon in English by Sidney Lear.

SERMON ON PRAYER

by Francois Fénelon

The following is one of the very few specimens that have been preserved of the preaching of Fénelon. It belongs to an early period in his career, and therefore does not reveal him in the maturity of his powers. But there runs throughout it the same intensely devout and pious feeling that is so marked in all of Fénelon's writings. No details have been preserved of the date of the delivery of the sermon, or the place of its composition.

OF all the duties enjoined by Christianity none is more essential, and yet none more neglected, than prayer. Most people consider this exercise a wearisome ceremony, which they are justified in abridging as much as possible. Even those whose profession or fears lead them to pray, do it with such languor and wanderings of mind that their prayers, far from drawing down blessings, only increase their condemnation. I wish in this discourse to show first, the general necessity of prayer; secondly, its peculiar duty; thirdly, the manner in which we ought to pray.

First: God alone can instruct us in our duty. The teachings of men, however wise and well disposed they may be, are still ineffectual, if God does not shed on the soul that light which opens the mind to truth. The imperfections of our fellow-creatures cast a shade over the truths that we learn from them. Such is our weakness that we do not receive, with sufficient docility, the instructions of those who are as imperfect as ourselves. A thousand suspicions, jealousies, fears, and prejudices prevent us from profiting, as we might, by what we hear from men; and though they announce the most serious truths, yet what they do weakens the effect of what they say. In a word, it is God alone who can perfectly teach us.

St. Bernard said, in writing to a pious friend: "If you are seeking less to satisfy a vain curiosity than to get true wisdom, you will sooner find it in deserts than in books. The silence of the rocks and the pathless forests will teach you better than the eloquence of the most gifted men." "All," says St. Augustine, "that we possess of truth and wisdom is a borrowed good, flowing from that fountain for which we ought to thirst in the fearful desert of this world, that, being refreshed and invigorated by these dews from heaven, we may not faint upon the road that conducts us to a better country. Every attempt to satisfy the cravings of our hearts at other sources only increases the void. You will always be poor, if you do not possess the only true riches." All light that does not proceed from God, is false; it only dazzles us; it sheds no illumination upon the difficult paths in which we must walk, or along the precipices that are about us.

Our experience and our reflections cannot, on all occasions, give us just and certain rules of conduct. The advice of our wisest and most sincere friends is not always sufficient; many things escape their observation, and many that do not are too painful to be mentioned. They suppress much from delicacy, or sometimes from fear of transgressing the bounds that our friendship and confidence in them will allow. The animadversions of our enemies, however severe or vigilant they may be, fail to enlighten us with regard to ourselves. Their malignity furnishes our self-love with a pretext for the indulgence of the greatest faults. The blindness of our self-love is so great that we find reasons for being satisfied with ourselves, while all the world condemns us. What must we learn from all this darkness? That it is God alone who can dissipate it; that it is He alone whom we can never doubt; that He alone is true, and knoweth all things; that if we go to Him in sincerity, He will teach us what men dare not, what books cannot tell us, all that is essential for us to know.

Be assured that the greatest obstacle to true wisdom is the self-confidence inspired by that which is false. The first step toward this precious knowledge is, earnestly to desire it, to feel the want of it, and to be convinced that they who seek it must address themselves to the Father of lights, who freely gives to him who asks in faith. But if it be true that God alone can enlighten us, it is not the less true that He will do this simply in answer to our prayers. Are we not happy, indeed, in being able to obtain so great a blessing by merely asking for it? No part of the effort that we make to acquire the transient enjoyments of this life is necessary to obtain these heavenly blessings. What are we not willing to do, what are we not willing to suffer, to possess dangerous and contemptible things, and often without any success? It is not thus with heavenly things. God is always ready to grant them to those who make the request in sincerity and truth. The Christian life is a long and continual movement of our hearts toward that eternal goodness which we desire on earth. All our happiness consists in thirsting for it. Now this thirst is prayer. Ever desire to approach your Creator, and you will never cease to pray.

Do not think that it is necessary to pronounce many words. To pray is to say: Thy will be done. It is to form a good purpose; to raise your heart to God; to lament your weakness; to sigh at the recollection of your frequent disobedience. This prayer demands neither method, nor science, nor reasoning; it is not essential to quit one's employment; it is a simple movement of the heart toward the Creator, and a desire that whatever you are doing, you may do it to His glory. The best of all prayers is to act with a pure intention, and with a continual reference to the will of God. It depends much upon ourselves whether our prayers be efficacious. It is not by a miracle, but by a movement of the heart, by a submissive spirit, that we are benefited. Let us believe, let us trust, let us hope, and God will never reject our prayer. Yet how many Christians do we see strangers to the privilege, aliens from God, who seldom think of Him, who never open their hearts to Him; who seek elsewhere the counsels of a false wisdom, and vain and dangerous consolations; who cannot resolve to seek, in humble, fervent prayer to God, a remedy for their griefs and a true knowledge of their defects, the necessary power to conquer their vicious and perverse inclinations, and the consolations and assistance they require, so as not to be discouraged in a virtuous life.

But some will say, "I take no interest in prayer; it wearies me; my imagination is excited by sensible and more agreeable objects, and wanders in spite of me."

If neither your reverence for the great truths of religion, nor the majesty of the ever-present Deity, nor the interest of your eternal salvation, have power to arrest your mind and engage it in prayer, at least mourn with me for your infidelity; be ashamed of your weakness, and wish that your thoughts were more under your control; and desire to become less frivolous and inconstant. Make an effort to subject your mind to this discipline. You will gradually acquire habit and facility. What is now tedious will become delightful; and you will then feel, with a peace that the world cannot give nor take away, that God is good. Make a courageous effort to overcome yourself. There can be no occasion that more demands it.

Secondly: The peculiar obligation of prayer. Were I to give all the proofs that the subject affords, I should describe every condition of life, that I might point out its dangers and the necessity of recourse to God in prayer. But I will simply state that under all circumstances we have need of prayer. There is no situation in which it is possible to be placed, where we have not many virtues to acquire, and many faults to correct. We find in our temperament, in our habits, or in the peculiar character of our minds, qualities that do not suit our occupations, and that oppose our duties. One person is connected by marriage with another whose temper is so unequal that life becomes a perpetual warfare. Some, who are exposed to the contagious atmosphere of the world, find themselves so susceptible to the vanity which they inhale that all their pure desires vanish. Others have solemnly promised to renounce their resentments, to conquer their aversions, to suffer with patience certain crosses, and to repress their eagerness for wealth; but nature prevails, and they are vindictive, violent, impatient, and avaricious.

Whence comes it that these resolutions are so frail? that all these people wish to improve, desire to perform their duty toward God and man better, and yet fail? It is because our own strength and wisdom alone are not enough. We undertake to do everything without God; therefore we do not succeed. It is at the foot of the altar that we must seek for counsel which will aid us. It is with God that we must lay our plan of virtue and usefulness; it is He alone that can render them successful. Without Him all our designs, however good they may appear, are only temerity and delusion. Let us then pray that we may learn what we are and what we ought to be. By this means we shall not only learn the number and the evil effects of our peculiar faults, but we shall also learn to what virtues we are called, and in what we should practise them. The rays of that pure and heavenly light that visits the humble soul will beam on us; and we shall feel and understand that everything is possible to those who put their whole trust in God. Thus, not only to those who live in retirement, but to those who are exposed to the agitations of the world and the excitements of business it is peculiarly necessary, by contemplation and fervent prayer, to restore their souls to that serenity which the dissipations of life and intercourse with men have disturbed. To those who are engaged in business, contemplation and prayer are much more difficult than to those who live in retirement; but it is far more necessary for them to have frequent recourse to God in fervent prayer. In the most holy occupation, a certain degree of precaution is necessary.

Do not devote all your time to action, but reserve a certain portion of it for meditation upon eternity. We see Jesus Christ inviting His disciples to go apart, in a desert place, and rest awhile, after their return from the cities, where they had been to announce His religion. How much more necessary, is it for us to approach the source of all virtue, that we may revive our declining faith and charity, when we return from the busy scenes of life, where men speak and act as if they had never known that there is a God! We should look upon prayer as the remedy for our weaknesses, the rectifier of our faults. He who was without sin prayed constantly; how much more ought we, who are sinners, to be faithful in prayer!

Even the exercise of charity is often a snare to us. It calls us to certain occupations that dissipate the mind, and that may degenerate into mere amusement. It is for this reason that St. Chrysostom says that nothing is so important as to keep an exact proportion between the interior source of virtue and the external practice of it; else, like the foolish virgins, we shall find that the oil in our lamps is exhausted when the bridegroom comes.

The necessity we feel that God should bless our labors is another powerful motive to prayer. It often happens that all human help is vain. It is God alone who can aid us, and it does not require much faith to believe that it is less our exertions, our foresight, and our industry, than the blessing of the Almighty, that gives success to our wishes.

Thirdly: Of the manner in which we ought to pray. We must pray with attention. God listens to the voice of the heart, not to that of the lips. Our whole heart must be engaged in prayer. It must be concentrated upon what it prays for; and every human object must disappear from our minds. To whom should we speak with attention, if not to God? Can He demand less of us than that we should think of what we say to Him? Dare we hope that He will listen to us and think of us, when we forget ourselves in the midst of our prayers? This attention to prayer, which it is so just to exact from Christians, may be practised with less difficulty than we imagine. It is true that the most faithful souls suffer from occasional involuntary distractions. They cannot always control their imaginations, and, in the silence of their spirits, enter into the presence of God. But these unbidden wanderings of the mind ought not to trouble us; and they may conduce to our perfection even more than the most sublime and affecting prayers, if we earnestly strive to overcome them, and submit with humility to this experience of our infirmity. But to dwell willingly on frivolous and worldly things during prayer, to make no effort to check the vain thoughts that intrude upon this sacred employment and come between us and the Father of our spirits—is not this choosing to live the sport of our senses, and separated from God?

We must also ask with faith,—a faith so firm that it never falters. He who prays without confidence cannot hope that his prayer will be granted. Will not God love the heart that trusts in Him? Will He reject those who bring all their treasures to Him, and repose everything upon His goodness? "When we pray to God," says St. Cyprian, "with entire assurance, it is Himself who has given us the spirit of our prayer." Then it is the Father listening to the words of His child; it is He who dwells in our hearts, teaching us to pray. But must we not confess that this filial confidence is wanting in all our prayers? Is not prayer our resource only when all others have failed us? If we look into our hearts, shall we not find that we ask of God as if we had never before received benefits from Him? Shall we not discover there a secret infidelity that renders us unworthy of His goodness? Let us tremble, lest, when Jesus Christ shall judge us, He pronounces the same reproach that He did to Peter, "O thou of little faith, wherefore didst thou doubt?"

We must join humility with trust. "Great God," said Daniel, "when we prostrate ourselves at Thy feet, we do not place our hopes for the success of our prayers upon our righteousness, but upon Thy mercy." Without this disposition in our hearts, all others, however pious they may be, cannot please God. St. Augustine observes that the failure of Peter should not be attributed to in-sincerity in his zeal for Jesus Christ. He loved his Master in good faith; in good faith he would rather have died than have forsaken Him; but his fault lay in trusting to his own strength to do what his own heart dictated.

It is not enough to possess a right spirit, an exact knowledge of duty, a sincere desire to perform it. We must continually renew this desire, and enkindle this flame within us, at the fountain of pure and eternal light.

It is the humble and contrite heart that God will not despise. Note the difference which the Evangelist has pointed out between the prayer of the proud and presumptuous Pharisee and the humble and penitent Publican. The one relates his virtues, the other deplores his sins. The good works of the one shall be set aside, while the penitence of the other shall be accepted. It will be thus with many Christians. Sinners, vile in their own eyes, will be objects of the mercy of God; while some who have made professions of piety will be condemned on account of the pride and arrogance that have contaminated their good works. It will be so, because these have said in their hearts, "Lord, I thank Thee that I am not as other men are." They imagine themselves privileged souls; they pretend that they alone have penetrated the mysteries of the kingdom of God; they have a language and science of their own; they believe that their zeal can accomplish everything. Their regular lives favor their vanity; but in truth they are incapable of self-sacrifice, and they go to their devotions with their hearts full of pride and presumption. Unhappy are those who pray in this manner! Unhappy are they whose prayers do not render them more humble, more submissive, more watchful over their faults, and more willing to live in obscurity!

We must pray with love. It is love, says St. Augustine, that asks, that seeks, that knocks, that finds, and that is faithful to what it finds. We cease to pray to God as soon as we cease to love Him, as soon as we cease to thirst for His perfections. The coldness of our love is the silence of our hearts toward God. Without this, we may pronounce prayers, but we do not pray; for what shall lead us to meditate upon the laws of God, if it be not the love of Him who has made these laws? Let our hearts be full of love, then, and they will pray. Happy are they who think seriously of the truths of religion; but far more happy are they who feel and love them! We must ardently desire that God will grant us spiritual blessings; and the ardor of our wishes must render us fit to receive the blessings. For if we pray only from custom, from fear, in the time of tribulation; if we honor God only with our lips, while our hearts are far from Him; if we do not feel a strong desire for the success of our prayers; if we feel a chilling indifference in approaching Him who is a consuming fire; if we have no zeal for His glory; if we do not feel hatred for sin and a thirst for perfection, we cannot hope for a blessing upon such heartless prayers.

We must pray with perseverance. The perfect heart is never weary of seeking God. Ought we to complain if God sometimes leaves us to obscurity, and doubt, and temptation? Trials purify humble souls, and they serve to expiate the faults of the unfaithful. They confound those who, even in their prayers, have flattered their cowardice and pride. If an innocent soul, devoted to God, suffer from any secret disturbance, it should be humble, adore the designs of God, and redouble its prayers and its fervor. How often do we hear those who every day have to reproach themselves with unfaithfulness toward God, complain that He refuses to answer their prayers! Ought they not to acknowledge that it is their sins which have formed a thick cloud between heaven and them, and that God has justly hidden Himself from them? How often has He recalled us from our wanderings! How often, ungrateful as we are, have we been deaf to His voice, and insensible to His goodness! He would make us feel that we are blind and miserable when we forsake Him. He would teach us, by privation, the value of the blessings that we have slighted. And shall we not bear our punishment with patience? Who can boast of having done all that he ought to have done; of having repaired all his past errors; of having purified his heart, so that he may claim as a right that God should listen to his prayer? Most truly, all our pride, great as it is, would not be sufficient to inspire such presumption! If, then, the Almighty does not grant our petitions, let us adore His justice, let us be silent, let us humble ourselves, and let us pray without ceasing. This humble perseverance will obtain from Him what we should never obtain by our own merit. It will make us pass happily from darkness to light; for know, says St. Augustine, that God is near to us, even when He appears far from us.

We should pray with a pure intention. We should not mingle in our prayers what is false with what is real; what is perishable with what is eternal; low and temporal interests with what concerns our salvation. Do not seek to render God the protector of your self-love and ambition, but the promoter of your good desires. You ask for the gratification of your passions, or to be delivered from the cross of which He knows you have need, Carry not to the foot of the altar irregular desires and indiscreet prayers. Sigh not there for vain and fleeting pleasures. Open your heart to your Father in Heaven that His Spirit may enable you to ask for the true riches. How can He grant you, says St. Augustine, what you do not yourself desire to receive? You pray every day that His will may be done, and that His kingdom may come. How can you utter this prayer with sincerity when you prefer your own will to His, and make His law yield to the vain pretexts with which your self-love seeks to elude it? Can you make this prayer, you who disturb His reign in your heart by so many impure and vain desires? you, in fine, who fear the coming of His reign, and do not desire that God should grant what you seem to pray for? No! if He at this moment were to offer to give you a new heart, and render you humble and meek, and self-denying, and willing to bear the cross, your pride would revolt, and you would not accept the offer; or you would make a reservation in favor of your ruling passion, and try to accommodate your piety to your humor and fancies!

LOUIS BOURDALOUE

Louis Bourdaloue was born August 20, 1632, at Bourges, France. He was educated by the Jesuits, and at an early age entered that order. The course of preparation which he, with all other aspirants for membership, was obliged to undergo had a marked and beneficial effect upon his style. The practice in clear exposition and argument required by his years spent in teaching made his sermons masterpieces of logical discourse. The members of the order soon perceived the unusual oratorical talent of the novice, and he was employed in preaching. At first he worked in the country, but after 1669 the field of his labors was chiefly in Paris, where he often preached before the court in Advent and Lent. After the revocation of the Edict of Nantes in 1685, he was sent to Languedoc to convert the Protestants. In this work he achieved some success and was noted for his moderation in dealing with theological opponents, a virtue at that time very unusual in either party. .In his closing years he was busy in Paris, spending his time in the hospitals, among the poor, and in the prisons. He died May 13, 1704.

Bourdaloue was a man of the purest character. His perfect frankness and fairness won him friends even among the enemies of his religion and his order. He was, as might be expected, an orator who sought to convince. -He appeals first of all to the intellect. He aims to make the truth entirely clear and self-evident. The strongest point, therefore, in his sermons is their remarkable clearness and their logical force. But he is by no means a mere logician. He appeals to the conscience, but by the presentation of truth rather than by appeals to the passions and emotions. He never spares vice, whether on the throne or in the gutter. His boldness in denunciation of those vices to which the King was especially addicted startled the courtiers, but the King recognized the right and duty of the preacher to rebuke sin wherever it was to be found. It is said that Bourdaloue, in the height of his fame, surprised by the great simplicity of his style the congregations of country churches where he sometimes preached. It is more than possible that this simplicity and clearness was the result of the many years spent in teaching. Bourdaloue was weak in that in which Bossuet was strongest. His funeral orations by no means take the same rank as his other sermons. There was not that opportunity for appeal to reason and conscience. Imagination and pathos, elements in which Bourdaloue did not excel, were needed here.

The works of Bourdaloue, consisting entirely of sermons, were edited and published after his death by P. Bretonneau, in fourteen volumes, Paris, 1707. See Feugere, *Bourdaloue, Sa Prédication et son Temps*, Paris, 1874; Lauras, Bourdaloue, *Sa Vie et ses OEuvres*, Paris, 1881.

SERMON ON THE PASSION OF JESUS CHRIST

by Louis Bourdaloue

The sermon on the Passion of Christ, of which the exordium and concluding part are here given, is one of several on the same topic preached by Bourdaloue before the King. This sermon is by common consent the finest of the series, and is a noble specimen of the pulpit eloquence of the day. As in all Bourdaloue's sermons, the understanding is addressed rather than the imagination or heart; yet the style is frequently impassioned, and is always dignified and chaste, while there is in it a pathos which was one of the most marked characteristics of the great preacher.

YOUR Majesty: Is it then true that the Passion of Jesus Christ—of which we celebrate today the august but sorrowful mystery, some idea of which faith gives us—is not the most touching object which can occupy our minds and excite our grief? Is it true that our tears can be more holily and more suitably employed than in weeping over the death of the God-man; and that another duty more pressing and more necessary suspends, so to speak, the obligation which so just a gratitude imposes upon us in another place, to sympathize by sentiments of tenderness in the sufferings of our Divine Redeemer? Never could we have supposed it, Christians; and yet it is Jesus Christ who speaks to us; and who, as the last proof of His love, the most generous and the most disinterested that ever existed, on His way to

Calvary, where He must die for us, warns us not to weep at His death, and to weep for every other thing rather than His death. "Weep not for Me, but weep for yourselves." St. Ambrose, delivering the funeral oration of the Emperor Valentinian the Younger, in the presence of all the people of Milan, thought that he had sufficiently executed his ministry, and had fully answered the expectations of his auditors, when he exhorted them to confess by the tribute of their tears how much they were indebted to the memory of that incomparable prince, who had exposed his life, and had, as it were, immolated himself, for them. But I, engaged to address you in this discourse on the bloody death of the Savior of men, I behold myself reduced to the necessity of employing a language widely different; since, instead of borrowing the words of St. Ambrose, which seemed naturally to agree with my subject, I must, on the contrary, say to you—Give not to this dying Redeemer tears, which He demands not from you: the tears which you shed are precious tears; do not waste them; they are required for a subject more important than you imagine. Jesus Christ not only refuses to accept your tears for His death, but He even expressly forbids them; because to weep for it might prevent you from weeping for another evil, which much more nearly affects you, and which indeed is more deplorable than even the death of the Son of God. I know that all creatures are or seem sensible of it; that the sun is eclipsed, that the earth trembles, that the veil of the temple is rent, that the rocks are torn asunder, that the tombs are opened, that the ashes of the dead revive, that all nature is moved at it: man only is for once freed from this duty, provided he acquits himself in a manner less tender in appearance, but more solid in reality. Let us then leave to the heavenly bodies and to the elements, or, if you will associate with them intelligent creatures, let us leave to the blessed angels the care of honoring the funeral of Jesus Christ by the marks of their sorrow; "these ambassadors of peace," says Isaiah, "have wept bitterly." But as for us, upon whom God has other designs, instead of weeping for Jesus Christ, let us weep for that which made Jesus Christ weep: thus we shall consecrate our tears, and render them beneficial.

An evil greater in the idea of God than even the death of Christ; an evil more worthy of being deplored than all that the only Son of God has suffered; an evil to which our tears are more legitimately due than to the Passion of the God-man;—this, you are too much enlightened, Christians, not to comprehend at one glance, is sin. There has never been among all created beings anything but sin which could predominate over the sufferings of Jesus Christ, and justify the words of this Savior God, when He commands us, with as much propriety as affection, "Weep not for Me, but for yourselves." To obey, Christians, this commandment, which our Divine Master gives us, and to profit by such important advice, let us consider today the mystery of the holy Passion, only that we may weep over the devastation of our sins; and let us not weep over the devastation of our sins but in sight of the mystery of the holy Passion. Indeed, if Jesus Christ had suffered independently of our sin, His Passion, however severe it might be for Him, would have nothing in it so frightful to us; and if our sin had no connection with the sufferings of Christ, exceedingly sinful as it is, it would be less odious to us. It is then by sin that we must measure the inestimable benefit of the Passion of the Son of God, that we must measure the enormity of sin: of sin, I say—observe well these three propositions which I advance, and which will divide this discourse—of sin, which is a continual renewal of the Passion of Jesus Christ caused by sin; the Passion of Jesus Christ renewed by sin; the Passion of Jesus Christ rendered useless and even prejudicial by sin. Behold what it is that claims our tears and demands our attention.

•••••••

That there are men, and Christian men, to whom, by a secret judgment of God, the Passion of Jesus Christ, salutary as it is, may become useless, is a truth too essential in our religion to be unknown, and too sorrowful not to be the subject of our grief. When the Savior from the height of His cross, ready to give up His Spirit, raised this cry toward heaven, "My God, my God, why hast Thou forsaken Me?" there was no one who did not suppose but that the violence of His torments forced from Him this complaint, and perhaps we ourselves yet believe it. But the great Bishop Amauld de Chartres, penetrating deeper into the thoughts and affections of this dying Savior, says, with much more reason, that the complaint of Jesus Christ to His Father proceeded from the sentiment with which He was affected, in representing to Himself the little fruit which His death would produce; in considering the small number of the elect who would profit by it; in foreseeing with horror the infinite number of the reprobate, for whom it would be useless: as if He had wished to proclaim that His merits were not fully enough, nor worthily enough, remunerated; and that after having done so much work, He had a right to promise to Himself a different success in behalf of men. The words of this author are admirable: Jesus Christ complains, says the learned prelate, but of what does He complain? That the wickedness of sinners makes Him lose what ought to be the reward of the conflicts which He has maintained. That millions of the human race for whom He suffers will nevertheless be excluded from the benefit of redemption. And because He regards Himself in them as their Head, and themselves, in spite of their worthlessness, as the members of His mystical body, seeing them abandoned by God, He complains of being abandoned Himself: "My God, my God, why hast Thou forsaken Me!" He complains of what made St. Paul groan, when, transported with an apostolic zeal, he said to the Galatians, "What, my brethren, is Jesus Christ then dead in vain? Is the mystery of the cross then nothing to you? Will not this blood which He has so abundantly shed have the virtue to sanctify you?"

But here, Christians, I feel myself affected with a thought which, contrary as it appears to that of the Apostle, only serves to strengthen and confirm it. For it appears that St. Paul is grieved because Jesus Christ has suffered in vain; but I, I should almost console myself if He had only suffered in vain, and if His Passion was only rendered useless to us. That which fills me with consternation is, that at the same time that we render it useless to ourselves, by an inevitable necessity it must become pernicious: for this Passion, says St. Gregory of Nazianzus, "partakes of the nature of those remedies which kill if they do not heal, and of which the effect is either to give life, or to convert itself into poison: lose nothing of this, I beseech you." Remember then, Christians, what happened during judgment, and at the moment of the condemnation of the Son of God.

When Pilate washed his hands before the Jews, and declared to them that there was nothing worthy of death in this righteous Man, but that the crime from which he freed himself rested upon them, and that they would have to answer for it, they all cried with one voice that they consented to it and that they readily agreed that the blood of this just Man should fall upon them and upon their children. You know what this cry has cost them. You know the curses which one such imprecation has drawn upon them: the anger of Heaven which began from that time to burst upon this nation, the ruin of

Jerusalem which followed soon after, the carnage of their citizens, the profanation of their temple, the destruction of their republic, the visible character of their reprobation which their unhappy posterity bear to this day, that universal banishment, that exile of sixteen hundred years, that slavery through all the earth—and all in consequence of the authentic prediction which Jesus Christ made to them of it when going to Calvary, and with circumstances which incontestably prove that a punishment as exemplary as this cannot be imputed but to the deicide which they had committed in the person of the Savior; since it is evident, says St. Augustine, that the Jews were never further from idolatry nor more religious observers of their law than they were then, and that, excepting the crime of the death of Jesus Christ, God, very far from punishing them, would, it seems, rather have loaded them with His blessings. You know all this, I say; and all this is a convincing proof that the blood of this God-man is virtually fallen upon these sacrilegious men, and that God, in condemning them by their own mouth, although in spite of Himself, employs to destroy them that which was designed for their salvation.

But, Christians, to speak with the Holy Spirit, this has happened to the Jews only as a figure; it is only the shadow of the fearful curses of which the abuse of the merits and Passion of the Son of God must be to us the source and the measure. I will explain myself. What is it we do, my dear hearers, when borne away by the immoderate desires of our hearts to a sin against which our consciences protest? And what is it we do, when, possessed of the spirit of the world, we resist a grace which solicits us, which presses us to obey God? Without thinking upon it, and without wishing it, we secretly pronounce the same sentence of death which the Jews pronounced against themselves before Pilate, when they said to him, "His blood be upon us." For this grace which we despise is the price of the blood of Jesus Christ; and the sin which we commit is an actual profanation of this very blood. It is, then, as if we were to say to God: "Lord, I clearly see what engagement I make, and I know what risk I run, but rather than not satisfy my own desires, I consent that the blood of Thy Son shall fall upon me. This will be to bear the chastisement of it; but I will indulge my passion; Thou hast a right to draw forth from it a just indignation, but nevertheless I will complete my undertaking."

Thus we condemn ourselves. And here, Christians, is one of the essential foundations of this terrible mystery of the eternity of the punishments with which faith threatens us, and against which our reason revolts. We suppose that we cannot have any knowledge of it in this life, and we are not aware, says St. Chrysostom, that we find it completely in the blood of the Savior, or rather in our profanation of it every day. For this blood, my brethren, adds this holy doctor, is enough to make eternity not less frightful, but less incredible. And behold the reason. This blood is of an infinite dignity; it can therefore be avenged only by an infinite punishment. This blood, if we destroy ourselves, will cry eternally against us at the tribunal of God. It will eternally excite the wrath of God against us. This blood, falling upon our lost souls, will fix a stain upon them which shall never be effaced. This torment must consequently never end. A reprobate in hell will always appear in the eyes of God stained with that blood which he has so basely treated. God will then always abhor him; and, as the aversion of God from His creatures is that which makes hell, it must be inferred that hell will be eternal. And in this, O my God, Thou art sovereignly just, sovereignly holy, and worthy of our praise and adoration. It is in this way that the beloved disciple declared it even to God Himself in the Apocalypse. Men, said he, have shed the blood of Thy servants and of Thy prophets; therefore they deserve to drink it, and to drink it from the cup of Thine indignation. "For they have shed the blood of saints and prophets, and Thou hast given them blood to drink"—an expression which the Scripture employs to describe the extreme infliction of divine vengeance. Ah! if the blood of the prophets has drawn down the scourge of God upon men, what may we not expect from the blood of Jesus Christ? If the blood of the martyrs is heard crying out in heaven against the persecutors of the faith, how much more will the blood of the Redeemer be heard!

Then once more, Christians, behold the deplorable necessity to which we are reduced. This blood which flows from Calvary either demands grace for us or justice against us. When we apply ourselves to it by a lively faith and a sincere repentance, it demands grace; but when by our disorders and impieties we check its salutary virtue, it demands justice, and it infallibly obtains it. It is in this blood, says St. Bernard, that all righteous souls are purified; but by a prodigy exactly opposite, it is also in this same blood that all sinners of the land defile themselves, and render themselves, if I may use the expression, more hideous in the sight of God.

Ah, my God! shall I eternally appear in Thine eyes polluted with that blood which washes away the crimes of others? If I had simply to bear my own sins, I might promise myself a punishment less rigorous, considering my sins as my misfortune, my weakness, my ignorance. Then, perhaps, Thou wouldest be less offended on account of them. But when these sins with which I shall be covered shall present themselves before me as so many sacrileges with respect to the blood of Thy Son; when the abuse of this blood shall be mixed and confounded with all the disorders of my life; when there shall not be one of them against which this blood shall not cry louder than the blood of Abel against Cain;—then, O God of my soul! what will become of me in Thy presence? No, Lord, cries the same St. Bernard, affectionately, suffer not the blood of my Savior to fall upon me in this manner. Let it fall upon me to sanctify, but let it not fall upon me to destroy! Let it fall upon me in a right use of the favors which are the divine overflowings of it, and not through the blindness of mind and hardness of heart which are the most terrible punishments of it. Let it fall upon me by the participation of the sacred Eucharist, which is the precious source of it, and not by the maledictions attached to the despisers of Thy sacraments! In fine, let it fall upon me by influencing my conduct and inducing the practice of good works, and let it not fall upon me for my wanderings, my infidelities, my obstinacy, and my impenitence! This, my brethren, is what we ought to ask today from Jesus Christ crucified. It is with these views that we ought to go to the foot of His cross and catch the blood as it flows. He was the Savior of the Jews as well as of us; but this Savior, says St. Augustine, the Jews have converted into their judge. Avert from us such an evil! May He who died to save us be our Savior! May He be our Savior during all the days of our lives! And may His merits, shed upon us abundantly, lose none of their efficacy in our hands, but be preserved entire by the fruit we produce from them! May He be our Savior in death! And at the last moment, may the cross be our support, and thus may He consummate the work of our salvation which He has begun! May He be our Savior in a blessed eternity, where we shall be as much sharers in His glory as we have been in His sufferings.

JEAN BAPTISTE MASSILLON

Jean Baptiste Massillon was born June 24, 1663, at Hyères in the south of France. He was educated in the school of the Oratorians in his native city, and in 1681 joined the Congregation of the Oratory. He remained connected with this order until in a fit of ascetic enthusiasm he entered the abbey of Septfonds, belonging to the Trappists. He remained here but a short time, for the Cardinal de Noailles, who had perceived his oratorical talents, persuaded him to return to the milder rule of the Oratory. In 1696 he removed to Paris, to take up work as the head of the seminary of St. Magloire, the most important school belonging to his order. He had already attained some distinction as a preacher, and in Paris he was soon employed in preaching in the various churches of the city during Advent and Lent. In 1699 he preached before the King at Versailles with such success that from 1701 to 1704 he preached the Lenten sermons before the court. These sermons were his masterpieces, but on account of the jealousy between the Jesuits and the Oratorians, Massillon received no preferment from the court during the lifetime of Louis XIV. In 1717 he was promoted to the see of Clermont, and in 1718 was appointed preacher before the young King, then but nine years old. The result of this appointment was the famous series of Lenten sermons known as *Le Petit Carême*, the first sermons addressed to a child. In the opinion of many they are of the highest order of merit, though Cardinal Maury considers them the weakest of Massillon's productions. Massillon lived but little in Paris after his appointment to the see of Clermont, and preached there but rarely. His last great sermon was the funeral oration on the dowager Duchess of Orleans. After a blameless administration of his diocese, Massillon died in Clermont September 28, 1742.

Massillon's masterpieces are generally thought to be *Le Petit Carême*, his sermons On the Prodigal Son, On Death, For Christmas Day, On the Small Number of the Elect, and the funeral oration on Louis XIV. By many, among them Voltaire and Maury, he is regarded as the greatest preacher of France, but the relative merits of the great preachers of the age of Louis XIV. can never be settled to the satisfaction of all. Massillon appeals preeminently to the passions, but without the vain declamation that was popular in his time. His style is pure, clear, nervous, and direct He does not attempt to argue, to marshal proofs, or to attack opponents. He assumes principles which are, for the most part, admitted, and then, analyzing them, attempts to show why men do not act upon them. In this is employed to great advantage his wonderful skill in detecting the motives of the heart and in pointing out the various self-deceptions which men practise in quieting their consciences.

The works of Massillon have been very often published. They include, besides his sermons, *Panegyrics on the Saints*, *Ecclesiastical Conferences*, *Paraphrases on the Psalms*, *Synodal Discourses*, and *Episcopal Charges*. The Paris edition of 1810, from which the following selection has been translated, is in fourteen volumes and is useful, containing the analyses of the sermons. Didot, Paris, has also published a good edition. In addition to the various works on French literature, see Blampignon, *La Jeunesse de Massillon*, *L'Episcopat de Massillon*, Paris, 1884; Ingold, *L'Oratoire et le au Temps de Massillon*, Paris, 1880; Theremin, *Demosthenes und Massillon*, Berlin, 1845. Massillon's sermons have been translated into many languages. An English translation appeared in London many years ago, but it was extremely inaccurate.

THE SMALL NUMBER OF THE ELECT

by Jean Baptiste Massillon

The following sermon is generally regarded as the masterpiece of its author in the way of non-eulogistic sermons. It was delivered at Versailles before the King and the court between 1701 and 1704. When Massillon delivered the terrifying passage in which he depicts the last day and then assures his hearers that few, perhaps none, of them would be saved, it is said that the audience rose with a shudder and a cry of horror, as if to escape from the doom that threatened them. Massillon's intensely vivid style was rendered all the more effective by the wonderfully dramatic manner in which he delivered his sermons. He wrote and rewrote them many times, and the passages which proved most effective were often most carefully elaborated. There is an interesting criticism on the passage above referred to in the Edinburgh Review for December, 1826, in which another version thereof is given and commented upon.

"And many lepers were in Israel in the time of Eliseus the prophet; and none of them was cleansed , saving Naaman the Syrian."—Luke 4:27.

EVERY day, my brethren, you ask us whether the road to heaven is really so difficult, and the number of the saved really so small as we represent. To a question so often proposed, and still oftener resolved, our Savior answers you today, that there were many widows in Israel afflicted with famine, but the widow of Sarepta alone was found worthy the succor of the prophet Elias; that the number of lepers was great in Israel in the time of the prophet Eliseus, and that Naaman alone was cured by the man of God. . . .

My intention is, therefore, today, to search in our morals for the cause of this small number. As every one flatters himself he will not be excluded, it is of importance to examine if his confidence be well founded. I wish, in pointing out to you the causes which render salvation so rare, not to make you generally conclude that few will be saved, but to bring you to ask yourselves if, living as you live, you can hope to be saved; to ask: Who am I? what am I doing for heaven? and what can be my hopes in eternity?

I propose no other order in a matter of such importance. What are the causes which render salvation so rare? I mean to point out three principal causes, which is the only arrangement of this discourse. Art, and far-sought reasonings, would here be ill-timed. Oh, attend, therefore, be ye whom ye may! No subject can be more worthy your attention, since its aim is to inform you what may be the hopes of your eternal destiny.

Few are saved, because in that number we can only comprehend two descriptions of persons: either those who have been so happy as to preserve their innocence pure and undefiled, or those who, after having lost their innocence, have regained it by penitence. This is the first cause. There are only these two ways of salvation: heaven is only open to the innocent or to the penitent. Now of which party are you? Are you innocent? Are you penitent? Nothing unclean will enter the kingdom of God. We must consequently carry there either an innocence unsullied or an innocence regained. Now, to die innocent is a grace to which few souls can aspire; and to live penitent is a mercy which the relaxed state of our morals renders equally rare.

Who, indeed, will pretend to salvation by the claim of innocence? Where are the pure souls in whom sin has never dwelt, and who have preserved to the end the sacred treasure of the first grace which the Church has confided to them in baptism, and which our Savior will demand back at the awful day of punishment?

In those happy days when the whole Church was still but an assembly of saints, it was very uncommon to find an instance of a believer who, after having received the gifts of the Holy Spirit and acknowledged Jesus Christ in the sacrament which regenerates us, fell back to his former irregularities of life. Ananias and Sapphira were the only prevaricators in the Church of Jerusalem; the Church of Corinth had only one incestuous sinner. Church-penitence was then a remedy almost unknown; and scarcely was there found among these true Israelites one single leper whom they were obliged to drive from the holy altar, and separate from communion with his brethren.

But since that time faith has grown weak in spreading, the number of the upright diminishes in proportion as that of believers increases, the progress of the Gospel, it would seem, has stopped the advance of piety, and the world, having become almost generally Christian, has brought with it into the Church its corruptions and its maxims. Alas I we all go astray, almost from our mothers' breast! The first use which we make of our heart is a crime; our first desires are passions; and our reason only expands and increases on the wrecks of our innocence. The earth, says a prophet, is infected by the corruption of those who inhabit it: all have violated the laws, changed the ordinances, and broken the alliance which should have endured forever; all commit sin, and there is scarcely one to be found who does the work of the Lord. . . .

Behold, then, one path of salvation shut to the generality of men. All have erred. Be ye whom you may who listen to me now, the time has been when sin reigned over you. Age may perhaps have calmed your passions; but what was your youth? Long and habitual infirmities may, perhaps, have disgusted you with the world; but what use did you formerly make of health? A sudden inspiration of grace may have turned your heart; but do you not most fervently entreat that every previous moment may be effaced from the remembrance of the Lord?

But with what am I taking up time? We are all sinners, O my God! and Thou knowest our hearts! What we know of our errors, is, perhaps, in Thy sight, the most pardonable; and we all allow that only because of innocence we have no claim to salvation. There remains, therefore, only one resource, which is penitence. After our shipwreck, say the saints, it is the timely plank which alone can conduct us into port; there is no other means of salvation for us. Whoever you may be, prince or subject, high or low, penitence alone can save you.

Now permit me to ask—Where are the penitent among us? Where are they? Do they form in the Church a large number? You will find more, says a holy father, who have never fallen, than who, after their fall, have raised them-selves by true repentance. This saying is terrible. But do not let us carry things too far; the truth is sufficiently dreadful without adding new terrors to it by vain declamation. Let us only examine as to whether the majority of us have a right, through penitence, to salvation.

What is a penitent? According to Tertullian, a penitent is a believer who feels every moment his former unhappiness in forsaking and losing his God. He is one who has his guilt incessantly before his eyes; who finds everywhere the traces and remembrance of it. A penitent is a man entrusted with the interests of divine justice against himself; one who refuses himself the most innocent pleasures because he had formerly indulged in those that were criminal; one who tolerates the most necessary gratification only with pain; one who regards his body as an enemy whom it is necessary to conquer, as a rebel he must chastise, as a guilty person to whom nearly everything must be refused, as an unclean vessel which must be purified, as an unfaithful debtor of whom it is proper to exact the last farthing; a penitent, that is, a criminal, regards himself condemned to death because he no longer deserves to live. As a consequence his manners, his attire, even his pleasures ought to be of a certain sad and austere character, and he ought to live only to suffer. In the loss of riches or health, a penitent sees only a withdrawal of favors that he had formerly abused; in the humiliations which happen to him, only the pains of his guilt; in the agonies with which he is racked, only the commencement of those punishments he has justly merited. Such is a penitent. But I again ask you—Where among us, are penitents of this description? Now look around you. Oh! the age of our fathers that saw them still at the doors of the churches! Then sinners, without doubt less sinful than we, of every rank and condition, lay prostrate before the churches, covered with dust and ashes, beseeching their brethren who were entering the house of the Lord to obtain from Him pardon for their faults; shut out from participation at the altar and even from being present at the sacred mysteries; passing whole years in exercises of fasting, scourging, and praying, and in trials so laborious that the most guilty would not endure them at the present time for even a single day; deprived not only of public amusements, but even of the pleasures of social intercourse, of association with their brethren, of the common joys of the holy seasons; living under an anathema; shut out from the holy assembly; stripped for a season of even the customary marks of distinction; and having no other consolation than tears and penitence. Such once were penitents in the Church.

Look now around you. I do not ask you to judge your brethren, but to examine what are the manners and morals of those who surround you. I do not speak of those open and avowed sinners who have thrown off the yoke, and who observe no limits to their crimes. I speak only of those who, like yourselves, live as most live, and whose lives reveal nothing scandalous or notorious. They are sinners and they admit it; you are not innocent, and you confess it. Now are they penitent? or are you? Age, avocation, more serious employments, may perhaps have checked the sallies of early youth. Even the bitterness, perhaps, which the goodness of God has been pleased to make attendant on your passions; the deceits, the treacheries of the world, an injured fortune with ruined constitution, may have cooled the ardor and confined the irregular desires of your hearts. Crimes may have disgusted you even with sin itself, for passions gradually extinguish themselves.

Age, disgust, and establishment for life, fix the heart, and even reconcile it to the sacred mysteries and withdraw it from debauchery; but where are those who are converted? Where are those who expiate their crimes by tears of sorrow and true repentance? Where are those who, having begun as sinners, end as penitents? Show me, in your manner of living, the smallest trace of penitence! Are your graspings at wealth and power, your anxieties to attain the favor of the great (and by these means an increase of employments and influence)—are these proofs of it? Would you wish to reckon even your crimes as virtues?—that God should take account of those labors which you have not undergone for Him?—that the sufferings of your ambition, pride, and avarice, should discharge you from an obligation which they themselves have imposed? You are a penitent of the world, but you are not a penitent of Jesus Christ. The infirmities with which God afflicts you, the enemies He raises up against you, the disgraces and losses with which He tries you—do you receive these strokes of chastisement with submission? or, rather, far from finding in them occasions of penitence, do you not turn them into the objects of new crimes? It is the duty of an innocent soul to receive with submission the chastisements God lays upon him; to discharge with courage the painful duties of the station allotted to him; and to be faithful to the laws of the Church—but do you who are sinners owe nothing beyond this? And yet you pretend to salvation! Upon what claim? Should you say that you are innocent before God, your own consciences would witness against you. Should you endeavor to persuade us that you are penitent, you dare not; and you would condemn yourselves by your own mouth. Upon what, then, dost thou depend, O man I who thus livest so tranquilly?

And what renders it still more dreadful is, that in this you only follow the current; your morals are the morals of well-nigh all men. You may, perhaps, be acquainted with some still more guilty (for I suppose that some sentiments of religion, and regard for your salvation, remain in you), but do you know any real penitents? One would have to search the cloisters and solitudes for .them. You may possibly mention among persons of your rank and station a small number whose morals, more austere than those of the majority, attract the attention, and very likely the censure, of the public. But all the rest walk in the uniform path. I see that every one assures himself by the example of his neighbor; that, in that point, children succeed to the false security of their fathers; that none live innocent, that none die penitent: I see it, and I cry, O God! if Thou hast not deceived us; if all Thou hast told us with regard to the road to eternal life shall be strictly fulfilled, if the number of those who must perish shall not influence Thee to abate from the severity of Thy laws—what will become of that immense multitude of creatures which every hour disappears from before our eyes? Where are our friends, our relations, our masters, our servants, who have gone before us? and what is their lot in the eternal regions of the dead? What shall we ourselves one day become?

When formerly a prophet complained to the Lord that all in Israel had forsaken His covenant, He replied that seven thousand still remained who had not bowed the knee to Baal. That is the number of pure and faithful souls which a whole kingdom then contained! But couldst Thou still, O my God I comfort the anguish of Thy servants today by the same assurance? I know that Thine eye still discerns some upright among us; that the priesthood has still its Phineas; the magistracy its Samuel; the sword its Joshua; the court its Daniel, its Esther, and its David: for the world only exists for Thine elect, and all would perish were the number accomplished. But those happy remnants of the children of Israel who shall be saved—what are they compared to the grains of sand in the sea: I mean, to that number of sinners who are damned?

After this, my brethren, will you inquire if it be true that few shall be saved? Thou hast said it, O my God! and hence it is a truth which shall endure forever. But, even admitting that the Almighty had not spoken thus, I would wish, in the second place, to review for an instant what passes among men: the laws by which they are governed, the maxims which have become the rules of the multitude: this is the second cause of the small number of the elect; and, properly speaking, this is only a development of the first—the force of habit and customs.

Few people are saved, because the maxims most universally received in all countries, and upon which depend the morals of the multitude, are maxims incompatible with salvation. The rules laid down, approved, and authorized by the world with regard to the application of wealth, the love of glory, Christian moderation, and the duties of offices and conditions are directly opposed to those of the Gospel, and consequently can lead only to death.

I shall not at present enter into a detailed account, too extended for a discourse and too little serious perhaps for the Christian pulpit. I need not tell you that it is an established custom in the world, that one may proportion one's expenses to his rank and wealth; and provided it is a patrimony we inherit from our ancestors, we may distinguish ourselves by the use of it, without restraint to our luxury, or without regard, in our profusion, to anything but our pride and caprice. . . .

Now, permit me to ask you here, who confirms you in these ways? By what rules are they justified to your mind? Who authorizes you in this dissipation, which is neither agreeable to the title you have received by baptism, nor perhaps to those you hold from your ancestors? Who authorizes those public pleasures, which you think innocent only because your soul, already too familiar with sin, feels no longer the dangerous impressions? Who authorizes that unending play which has become the most important occupation of your life? Who authorizes you to dispense with all the laws of the Church? Who authorizes you to lead an effeminate and sensual life, without virtue, sufferance, or any disagreeable exercises of religion?—to live like a stranger in the midst of your own family, disdaining to inform yourselves with regard to the morals of those dependent upon you?—through an affected state, to be ignorant whether they believe in the God whom you adore; whether they fulfil the duties of the religion you profess? Who authorizes you to adopt maxims so little Christian? Is it the Gospel of Jesus Christ? Is it the doctrine of the saints? Is it the laws of the Church? For surely some rule is necessary to assure us that we are in safety. What is yours? "Custom:" that is the only reply you can make I "One sees no one around him who does not conduct himself according to these rules. Entering into the world, we find the manners already established: our fathers lived thus, and from them we copy our customs: the wisest conform to them; an individual cannot be wiser than the whole world: one must keep to that which is generally practised and not wish to make himself singular."

Such, my brethren, are your only comforters against all the terrors of religion! None act up to the law. The public example is the only guaranty of our morals. We never reflect that, as the Holy Scripture says, the laws of the people are vain; that Jesus Christ has left us rules, in which neither times, ages, nor customs, can ever authorize the smallest change; that the heavens and the earth shall pass away, that customs and manners shall change, but that the divine laws will be everlastingly the same.

The general mode of living cannot be that of the Christian life. In all ages, the holy have been remarkable and singular men. Their manners were always different from those of the world; and they have only been saints because their lives had no similarity to those of the rest of mankind. In the time of Esdras, in spite of the interdiction thereof, the custom prevailed of intermarrying with strange women: this abuse became general; the priests and the people no longer made any scruple of it. But what did this holy restorer of the law? Did he follow the example of his brethren? Did he believe that guilt, in becoming general, became more legitimate? No; he recalled the people to a sense of the abuse. He took the book of the law in his hand, and explained it to the affrighted people—corrected the custom by the truth. . . .

Trace, from age to age, the history of the just, and see if Lot conformed himself to the habits of Sodom, or if nothing distinguished him from the other inhabitants; if Abraham lived like the rest of his age; if Job resembled the other princes of his nation; if Esther conducted herself in the court of Ahasuerus like the other women of that prince; if many women in Bethulia in Israel resembled Judith; if among the children of the captivity, it is not said of Tobias alone that he copied not the conduct of his brethren, and that he even fled from the danger of their society and intercourse. See if in those happy ages, when Christians were still saints, they did not shine like stars in the midst of the corrupted nations; and if they served not as a spectacle to angels and men, by the singularity of their morals. See if the pagans did not reproach them for their retirement and shunning of ail public theatres, places, and pleasures; if they did not complain that the Christians affected to distinguish themselves in everything from their fellow-citizens; to form a separate people in the midst of the people; to have their particular laws and customs; and if a man from their side embraced the party of the Christians, if they did not consider him as forever lost to their pleasures, assemblies, and customs. In a word, see if in all ages the saints whose lives and actions have been transmitted down to us have resembled the rest of mankind.

You will perhaps tell us that all these are singularities and exceptions, rather than rules which the world is obliged to follow. They are exceptions, it is true: but the reason is, that the general rule is to perish; that a religious and pious soul in the midst of the world is always a singularity approaching to a miracle. The whole world, you say, is not obliged to follow these examples. But is not piety alike the duty of all believers? To be saved, must we not be holy? Must heaven be gained by some with much difficulty, and by others with none? Have you any other Gospel to follow, any other duties to fulfil, any other promises to hope for, than those of the saints? Ah! since there was another way more easy to arrive at salvation, wherefore, ye pious Christians, who at this moment enjoy the kingdom gained with toil and at the expense of your blood, did ye leave us examples so dangerous and so useless? Wherefore have ye opened for us a road, rugged, disagreeable, and calculated to repress our ardor, seeing there was another you could have pointed out, more easy and smooth, and more likely to attract us by facilitating our progress? Great God! how little does mankind consult reason in the point of eternal salvation! . . .

So few are saved, because the maxims most universally adopted are maxims of sin. So few are saved, because the maxims and duties most universally unknown, or rejected, are those most indispensable to salvation. This is the last reflection, which is indeed nothing more than the proof and the development of the former ones.

What are the engagements of the holy vocation to which we have all been called, the solemn promises of baptism? What have we promised at baptism.? Was it not to renounce the world, the flesh, and the devil? These are our vows. This is the state of the Christian. These are the essential conditions of our covenant with God, by which eternal life has been promised to us. These truths appear familiar and suited to the common people; but it is a mistake. Nothing can be more sublime; and nothing is more generally unknown! It is in the courts of kings, and to the princes of the earth, that, without ceasing, we ought to announce them. Alas! they are well instructed in all the affairs of the world, while the first principles of Christian morality are frequently more unknown to them than to humble and simple hearts! They have need of milk, and they demand of us solid food, and that we should speak the language of wisdom as if we were speaking among the perfect.

At your baptism, then, you have renounced the world. It is a promise you have made to God, before the holy altar; the Church has been the guarantee and depository of it; and you have only been admitted into the number of believers, and marked with the indelible seal of salvation, upon the faith that you have sworn to the Lord, to love neither the world nor what the world loves. Had you then answered at the holy font, what you now repeat every day, that you find not the world so black and pernicious as we say; that, after all, it may innocently be loved, and that we only decry it so much in the pulpit because we do not know it; and that since you are to live in the world you wish to live like those who are in it—had you answered thus, the Church would not have received you into her bosom, would not have connected you with the hope of Christians, nor joined you in communion with those who have overcome the world. She would have advised you to go and live with those unbelievers who know not Jesus Christ, and where the prince of this world is adored and it is permitted to love all that appertains to him. And for this reason in the early ages, catechumens who could not yet bring themselves to renounce the world and its pleasures put off their baptism till their death, and did not venture to contract at the foot of the altar in the sacrament of regeneration those engagements of which they knew the meaning and the holiness, and which they did not think that they were in a state to keep. . . .

Where are those who sincerely renounce the pleasures, habits, maxims, and hopes of this world? We find many who complain of it, and accuse it of injustice, ingratitude, and caprice, and speak warmly of its abuses and errors. But in decrying, they continue to love and follow it; they cannot bring themselves to do without it. In complaining of its injustice, they are only piqued at it, they are not undeceived. They feel its hard treatment, but they are unacquainted with its dangers. They censure, but where are those who hate it? And now, my brethren, you may judge if many can have a claim to salvation.

In the second place, you have renounced the flesh at your baptism: that is to say, you are engaged not to live according to the sensual appetites; to regard even indolence and effeminacy as crimes; not to flatter the corrupt desires of the flesh, but to chastise, crush, and crucify it. This is not an acquired perfection; it is a vow; it is the first of all duties, the character most completely inseparable from the Christian faith.

In a word, you have anathematized Satan and all his works. And what are his works? That which composes almost the course and end of your life: pomp, pleasure, luxury, and dissipation; lying, of which he is the father; pride, of which he is the model; jealousy and remorse, of which he is the artisan. But I ask you, where are those who have not withdrawn the anathema they had pronounced against Satan?

Now (to mention it as we go along), behold many of the questions answered! You continually demand of us if theatres and other public places of amusement be innocent recreations for Christians. In return, I have only one question to ask you: Are they the works of Satan or of Jesus Christ? for there can be nothing indifferent in religion. I do not mean to say that there are not many recreations and amusements which may be termed indifferent. But the most indifferent pleasures which religion allows and which the weakness of our nature renders even necessary, belong, in one sense, to Jesus Christ, by the facility with which they ought to enable us to apply ourselves to more holy and more serious duties. Everything we do, everything we rejoice or weep at, ought to be of such a nature as to have a connection with Jesus Christ and to be done for His glory. . . .

My brethren, these are the vows of our baptism, as I have already told you; they are not merely counsels and pious practices, they are our most essential obligations. It is a question, not of being more or less perfect in neglecting or observing them, but of being a Christian or not being a Christian. But who fulfils them? Who even knows them? Alas, my brethren, if you but knew how far the title you bear of a Christian engages you; if you could but comprehend the sanctity of your state; the detachment from all creatures which it requires of you; the hatred of the world, of yourself, and of everything which is not of God, that it enjoins; that life of faith, that constant watching, that guard over the senses; in a word, that conformity with Jesus Christ crucified, which it exacts of you; if you could but comprehend that, if you could bear in mind that, as you are sworn to the love of God with all your heart and all your strength, a single desire that has not connection with Him defiles you; if you could but comprehend that, you would appear a monster in your own sight. How, would you not exclaim, duties so holy, and morals so profane! a vigilance so continual, and a life so careless and dissipated! a love of God so pure, so complete, so universal, and a heart the constant prey of a thousand impulses, either foreign or criminal! If thus it is, who, O my God! can be saved? Few, indeed, my dear hearer! At least it will not be you (unless a change takes place), nor those who resemble you; it will not be the multitude!

Who can be saved? Do you wish to know? Those who work out their salvation with fear and trembling; who live in the world, but do not live according to the world. Who can be saved? That Christian woman, who, shut up in the circle of her domestic duties, rears up her children in faith and piety; who leaves to the Lord the control of their future; divides her heart only be-tween Jesus Christ and her husband; is adorned with decency and modesty; sits not down in the assemblies of vanity; makes not a law of the senseless customs of the world, but regulates those customs by the law of God; and by her rank and her example makes virtue appear more amiable.

Who shall be saved? That believer who, in the laxity of modem times, imitates the manners of the first Christians—who has clean hands and a pure heart; who is watchful: who has not lifted up his mind to vanity, but who, in the midst of the dangers of the great world, continually applies himself to purify it: who is just: who has not sworn to deceive his neighbor, nor is indebted to doubtful ways for the aggrandizement of his fortune: who is generous: who repays with benefits the enemy who sought his ruin, and harms his competitor only by his own merit: who is sincere: who does not sacrifice the truth to a vile interest, and cannot render himself agreeable by betraying his conscience: who is charitable: who makes his house and interest the refuge of his brethren, himself the consolation of the afflicted, and his wealth the property of the poor: who is humble in affliction: a Christian under injuries, and penitent even in prosperity.

Who can be saved? You, my dear hearer, if you will follow these examples; for such are they who will be saved. Now these assuredly do not form the greatest number. But so long as you continue to live like the multitude, it is evident that you disregard your salvation. For if so living you could be saved, nearly everybody would be saved, since with the exception of a small number of impious persons who have given themselves to monstrous vices, all other men do as you do. Now that all men will be saved, is a proposition that the Christian faith forbids us to believe. It is therefore evident that you ought not to make any pretences to salvation, so long as you cannot be saved if the majority cannot be saved.

These, my brethren, are truths that should make us tremble! Nor are they those vague truths which are told to all men and which no one takes as applying to himself. Perhaps there is no one here who may not say of himself, "I live like the majority, like those of my rank, age, and situation; I am lost, should I die in this path." Now, what is there better fitted to alarm a soul in which there remains some care for its salvation? It is the multitude, nevertheless, who tremble not. There is only a small number of the just, who alone work out their salvation with fear. All the rest are tranquil. They know that on the whole the majority will be damned, but after having lived with the multitude, they flatter themselves they shall be distinguished from their fellows at death. Every one vainly imagines that he shall be an exception. Every one augurs favorably for himself.

On this account it is, my brethren, that I confine myself to you who are here assembled. I do not speak of the rest of men; but I consider you as if you were alone on the earth, and this is the idea which fills and terrifies me. I picture to myself that it is now your last hour and the end of the world; that the heavens are about to open above your heads, that Jesus Christ, in all His glory, is about to appear in the midst of His temple, and that you have been assembled here only to await His coming, as trembling criminals, to whom is to be pronounced either the sentence of grace, or a decree of everlasting death I for it is vain to flatter yourselves that you shall die more innocent than you are at this hour. All those desires of change with which you are amused will continue to amuse you till your death-bed. The experience of all ages proves it. The only difference you have to expect will most likely be only a somewhat larger account against you than that for which you would now have to answer; and from what would be your destiny, were you to be judged at this moment, you may almost deter-mine what it will be at death.

Now I ask you, and I am smitten with horror as I ask it, in this respect not separating my fate from yours but putting myself in the same situation in which I suppose you are: I ask, then, were Jesus Christ to appear in this temple, in the midst of this assembly, the most august in the world, to judge us, to make the awful separation between the sheep and the goats, do you believe that the most of us would be placed at His right hand? Do you believe that the number would at least be equal? Do you believe that there would even be found ten upright, when the Lord could not at one time find that number in five cities? I ask you! You know not! I know not! Thou alone, O God! knowest who belong to Thee. But if we know not who belong to Him, at least we know that sinners do not. Now, who are the just and faithful assembled here? Titles and dignities avail nothing; you are stripped of all these in the presence of your Savior! Who are they? Many sinners who do not wish to be converted; many more who wish, but put off their conversion; many others who are converted only to fall back; finally, a great number who flatter themselves they have no need of conversion,—this is the party of the reprobate! Cut off from this assembly these four classes of sinners, for they will be cut off at the great day! And now stand forth, ye righteous: remnants of Israel, pass to the right; wheat of Jesus Christ, separate yourself from the chaff destined for the fire. O God, where are Thine elect? What remains as Thy portion?

My brethren, our ruin is almost certain! Yet we think not of it! If in this terrible separation, which will one day take place, there should be but one sinner in this assembly on the side of the reprobate, and a voice should come from heaven to assure us of it, without naming him, who of us would not tremble, lest he be the wretched being? Who of us would not immediately turn to his conscience, to examine if its crimes merited not this punishment? Who of us, seized with dread, would not demand of Jesus Christ, as once did the Apostles, crying out, "Lord, is it I?" And should a small respite be allowed, who of us would not use every effort, by tears, supplication, and sincere repentance, to avert the misfortune?

JACQUES SAURIN

Jacques Saurin was born at Nimes, France, January 6, 1677. His father was a distinguished lawyer, but as he was a Protestant he was forced to leave the country at the revocation of the Edict of Nantes, in 1685. He took refuge in Geneva, which at that time was the residence of perhaps the most intellectual men of Europe. The son thereby acquired educational advantages which he could not have had at his home. The father himself was a man of most superior culture and of the finest literary taste. Saurin continued his studies until his seventeenth year, when, with other refugees, he entered the English army in the war against France. After three years, peace was declared, and young Saurin returned to Geneva and resumed his studies. In 1701 he went to London as one of the pastors of the Walloon Church, but remained there for only four or five years. In 1705 he removed to the Hague, where he became the pastor of the French Church. For the most part his life in Holland was uneventful, though the closing years were embittered by controversy. His reputation constantly increased, and he enjoyed the favor of the highest ranks. The royal family of England were among his patrons, and he dedicated many of his sermons to the king and queen, as a recognition of their many acts of kindness. Saurin was so popular as a preacher that seats were frequently engaged long before when he was announced to preach, and listeners clustered about the windows on ladders in order to hear him.

Saurin was probably the greatest of Protestant preachers. He combined in the happiest manner the merits of various schools and styles. By birth and temperament he was a Frenchman. His theology was a moderate Calvinism, which restrained by its cold logic the exuberance of the French manner. He was acquainted with the preachers of the English school, but he far surpassed them in that he aimed not merely to expound and discuss a theme, but to stir the religious emotions by appeals that were directed to the heart. He had the fervor of Massillon and the vigor and weight of Tillotson and Barrow. It may be said of his sermons that they are, as is rarely the case, at once valuable as theology and pleasing as eloquence. He was not a homiletical artist He pleases, but he does not seem to strive to please. While Saurin has produced nothing that equals the splendor of Bossuet, his rank as a preacher—which must be judged not only by the production of masterpieces but by the number and average of his sermons—is but little below Bossuet though as an orator he is without question inferior to the latter.

The works of Saurin have been frequently published, and translations exist in almost all European languages. The fact that he was a Protestant greatly stimulated translation, and he has long enjoyed a popularity in lands other than his own. In Germany he was read and studied, and exercised a marked influence, and in England almost all his best sermons have been accessible in the translation of Robinson, Hunter, and Sutcliffe. The English edition has been very frequently reprinted in America. The translations have some account of the life of Saurin prefixed. See Berthault, *Saurin et la Prédication Protestante jusqu'a la fin du de Louis XIV.*, Paris, 1875.

SERMON ON THE SPEECH OF PAUL BEFORE FELIX AND DRUSILLA

by Jacques Saurin

The following sermon is regarded by many as the masterpiece of its distinguished author. It is perhaps somewhat less argumentative than many by Saurin, and appeals more to the feelings and the conscience. But the careful division springing out of the text and the simple manner in which the parts are developed, everywhere lucid and impressive, render it a model of pastoral preaching as opposed to the occasional oratory of the pulpit. It is such a sermon as would be effective in the course of the routine preaching of the Protestant pastor. The power to hold men year after year solely by the force of effective preaching, as was certainly the case with Saurin, is manifested in every line of the sermon. It appeals at once to the intellect, the emotions, and the will.

"And after certain days, when Felix came with his wife Drusilla, which was a Jewess, he sent for Paul, and heard him concerning the faith in Christ. And as he reasoned of righteousness, temperance, and judgment to come, Felix trembled, and answered, Go thy way for this time; when I have a convenient season, I will call for thee."—Acts 24:24, 25.

MY brethren, though the kingdom of the righteous be not of this world, they present, however, amidst their meanness, marks of dignity and power. They resemble Jesus Christ. He humbled Himself so far as to take the form of a servant, but frequently exercised the rights of a sovereign. From the abyss of humiliation to which He condescended, emanations of the Godhead were seen to proceed. Lord of nature, He commanded the winds and seas. He bade the storm and tempest subside. He restored health to the sick, and life to the dead. He imposed silence on the Rabbins; He embarrassed Pilate on the throne; and disposed of Paradise, at the moment He Himself was pierced with the nails, and fixed on the cross. Behold the portrait of believers! "They are dead. Their life is hid with Christ in God." (Col. 3:3) "If they had hope only in this life, they were of all men most miserable." (1 Cor. 15:19) Nevertheless, they show I know not what superiority of birth. Their glory is not so concealed, but we sometimes perceive its lustre; just as the children of a king, when unknown and in a distant province, betray in their conversation and carriage indications of illustrious descent.

We might illustrate this truth by numerous instances. Let us attend to that in our text. There we shall discover that association of humility and grandeur, of reproach and glory, which constitutes the condition of the faithful while on earth. Behold St. Paul, a Christian, an apostle, a saint. See him hurried from tribunal to tribunal, from province to province; sometimes before the Romans, sometimes before the Jews, sometimes before the high-priest of the synagogue, and sometimes before the procurator of Caesar. See him conducted from Jerusalem to Caesarea, and summoned to appear before Felix. In all these traits, do you not recognize the Christian walking in the narrow way, the way of tribulation, marked by his Master's feet? But consider him nearer still. Examine his discourse, look at his countenance; there you will see a fortitude, a courage, and a dignity which constrains you to acknowledge that there was something really grand in the person of St. Paul. He preached Jesus Christ, at the very moment he was persecuted for having preached Him. He preached even when in chains. He did more; he attacked his judge on the throne. He reasoned, he enforced, he thundered. He seemed already to exercise the function of judging the world, which God has reserved for His saints. He made Felix tremble. Felix felt himself borne away by a superior force. Unable to hear St. Paul any longer without appalling fears, he sent him away.

"After certain days, when Felix came with his wife Drusilla, he sent for Paul, and heard him concerning the faith in Christ," etc.

We find here three considerations which claim our attention. An enlightened preacher, who discovers a very peculiar discernment in the selection of his subject. A conscience appalled and confounded on the recollection of its crimes and of that awful judgment where they must be weighed. We find, in fact, a sinner alarmed, but not converted; a sinner who desires to be saved, but delays his conversion: a case, alas I of but too common occurrence.

You perceive already, my brethren, the subject of this discourse: first, that St. Paul reasoned before Felix and Drusilla of righteousness, temperance, and judgment to come; second, that Felix trembled; third, that he sent the Apostle away: three considerations which shall divide this discourse. May it produce on your hearts, on the hearts of Christians, the same effects St Paul produced on the soul of this heathen; but may it have a happier influence on your lives. Amen.

Paul preached before Felix and Drusilla, "on righteousness, temperance, and judgment to come." This is the first object of discussion. Before, however, we proceed farther with our remarks, we must first sketch the character of this Felix and this Drusilla, which will serve as a basis to the first proposition.

After the sceptre was departed from Judah, and the Jewish nation subjugated by Pompey, the Roman emperors governed the country by procurators. Claudius filled the imperial throne while St Paul was at Caesarea. This emperor had received a servile education from his grandmother Lucia, and from his mother Antonia; and having been brought up in obsequious meanness, evinced, on his elevation to the empire, marks of the inadequate care which had been bestowed on his infancy. He had neither courage nor dignity of mind. He who was raised to sway the Roman sceptre, and consequently to govern the civilized world, abandoned his judgment to his freedmen, and gave them a complete ascendancy over his mind. Felix was one of those freedmen. "He exercised in Judea the imperial functions with a mercenary soul." Voluptuousness and avarice were the predominant vices of his heart. We have a proof of his avarice immediately after our text, where it is said he sent for Paul,—not to hear him concerning the truth of the Gospel which this Apostle had preached with so much power; not to inquire whether this religion, against which the Jews had raised the standard, was contrary to the interest of the State; but because he hoped to have received money for his liberation. Here is the effect of avarice.

Josephus recites an instance of his voluptuousness. It is his marriage with Drusilla. She was a Jewess, as is remarked in our text. King Azizus, her former husband, was a heathen; and in order to gain her affections, he had conformed to the most rigorous ceremonies of Judaism. Felix saw her, and became enamored of her beauty. He conceived for her a violent passion; and in defiance of the sacred ties which had united her to her husband, he resolved to become master of her person. His addresses were received. Drusilla violated her former engagements, preferring to contract with Felix an illegitimate marriage, to an adherence to the chaste ties which united her to Azizus. Felix the Roman, Felix the procurator of Judea and the favorite of Caesar, appeared to her a noble acquisition. It is indeed a truth, we may here observe, that grandeur and fortune are charms which mortals find the greatest difficulty to resist, and against which the purest virtue has need to be armed with all its constancy. Recollect those two characters of Felix and Drusilla. St. Paul, before those two personages, treated concerning "the faith in Christ"; that is, concerning the Christian religion, of which Jesus Christ is the sum and substance, the author and the end: and from the numerous doctrines of Christianity, he selected "righteousness, temperance, and judgment to come."

Here is, my brethren, an admirable text; but a text selected with discretion. Fully to comprehend it, recollect the character we have given of Felix. He was covetous, luxurious, and governor of Judea. St. Paul selected three subjects, correspondent to the characteristics. Addressing an avaricious man, he treated of righteousness. Addressing the governor of Judea, one of those persons who think themselves independent and responsible to none but themselves for Paul before Felix and Drusilla 335 their conduct, he treated of "judgment to come."

But who can here supply the brevity of the historian, and report the whole of what the Apostle said to Felix on these important points? It seems to me, that I hear him enforcing those important truths he has left us in his works, and placing in the fullest lustre those divine maxims interspersed in our Scriptures. "He reasoned of righteousness." There he maintained the rights of the widow and the orphan. There he demonstrated, that kings and magistrates are established to maintain the rights of the people, and not to indulge their own caprice; that the design of the supreme authority is to make the whole happy by the vigilance of one, and not to gratify one at the expense of all; that it is meanness of mind to oppress the wretched, who have no defence but cries and tears; and that nothing is so unworthy of an enlightened man as that ferocity with which some are inspired by dignity, and which obstructs their respect for human nature, when undisguised by worldly pomp; that nothing is so noble as goodness and grandeur, associated in the same character; that this is the highest felicity; that in some sort it transforms the soul into the image of God; who, from the high abodes of majesty in which He dwells surrounded with angels and cherubim, deigns to look down on this mean world which we inhabit, and "leaves not Himself without witness, doing good to all."

"He reasoned of temperance." There he would paint the licentious effects of voluptuousness. There he would demonstrate how opposite is this propensity to the spirit of the Gospel; which everywhere enjoins retirement, mortification, and self-denial. He would show how it degrades the finest characters who have suffered it to predominate. Intemperance renders the mind incapable of reflection. It debases the courage. It debilitates the mind. It softens the soul. He would demonstrate the meanness of a man called to preside over a great people, who exposes his foibles to public view: not having resolution to conceal, much less to vanquish, them. With Drusilla, he would make human motives supply the defects of divine; with Felix, he would make divine motives supply the defects of human. He would make this impudent woman feel that nothing on earth is more odious than a woman destitute of honor, that modesty is an attribute of the sex; that an attachment, uncemented by virtue, cannot long subsist; that those who receive illicit favors, are the first, according to the fine remark of a sacred historian, to detest the indulgence: "The hatred where with Amnon, the son of David, hated his sister, after the gratification of his brutal passion, was greater than the love wherewith he had loved her" (2 Sam. 13:15). He would make Felix perceive, that however the depravity of the age might seem to tolerate a criminal intercourse with persons of the other sex, with God, who has called us all to equal purity, the crime was not less heinous.

"He reasoned," in short, "of judgment to come." And here he would magnify his ministry. When our discourses are regarded as connected only with the present period, their force, I grant, is of no avail. We speak for a Master, who has left us clothed with infirmities, which discover no illustrious marks of Him, by whom we are sent. We have only our voice, only our exhortations, only our entreaties. Nature is not inverted at our pleasure. The visitations of Heaven do not descend at our command to punish your indolence and revolts: that power was very limited, even to the Apostle. The idea of a future state, the solemnities of a general judgment, supply our weakness, and St. Paul enforced this motive; he proved its reality, he delineated its lustre, he displayed its pomp. He resounded in the ears of Felix the noise, the voices, the trumpets. He showed him the small and the great, the rich man and Lazarus, Felix the favorite of Caesar, and Paul the captive of Felix, awoke by that awful voice: "Arise, ye dead, and come to judgment."

But not to be precipitate in commending the Apostle's preaching. Its encomiums will best appear by attending to its effects on the mind of Felix. St. Jerome wished, concerning a preacher of his time, that the tears of his audience might compose the eulogy of his sermons. We shall find in the tears of Felix occasion to applaud the eloquence of our Apostle. We shall find that his discourses were thunder and lightning in the congregation, as the Greeks used to say concerning one of their orators. While St. Paul preached, Felix felt I know not what agitations in his mind. The recollection of his past life; the sight of his present sins; Drusilla, the object of his passion and subject of his crime; the courage of St. Paul all terrified him. His "heart burned," while that disciple of Jesus Christ expounded the Scriptures. The word of God was quick and powerful. The Apostle, armed with the two-edged sword, dividing the soul, the joints, and the marrow, carried conviction to the heart. Felix trembled, adds our historian, Felix trembled! The fears of Felix are our second reflection.

What a surprising scene, my brethren, is here presented to your views? The governor trembled, and the captive spoke without dismay. The captive made the governor tremble. The governor shivered in presence of the captive. It would not be surprising, brethren, if we should make an impression on your hearts (and we shall do so indeed, if our ministry is not, as usual, a sound of empty words): it would not be surprising if we should make some impression on the hearts of our hearers. This sanctuary, these solemnities, these groans, this silence, these arguments, these efforts,—all aid our ministry, and unite to convince and persuade you. But here is an orator destitute of these extraneous aids: behold him without any ornament but the truth he preached. What do I say? that he was destitute of extraneous aids? See him in a situation quite the reverse,—a captive, loaded with irons, standing before his judge. Yet he made Felix tremble. Felix trembled! Whence proceeded this fear, and this confusion? Nothing is more worthy of your inquiry. Here we must stop for a moment: follow us while we trace this fear to its source. We shall consider the character of Felix under different views: as a heathen, imperfectly acquainted with a future judgment, and the life to come; as a prince, or governor, accustomed to see every one humble at his feet; as an avaricious magistrate, loaded with extortions and crimes; in short, as a voluptuous man, who had never restricted the gratification of his senses. These are so many reasons of Felix's fears.

First, we shall consider Felix as a heathen, imperfectly acquainted with a future judgment, and the life to come: I say, imperfectly acquainted, and not as wholly ignorant, the heathens having the "work of the law written in their hearts" (Rom. 2:15). The force of habit had corrupted nature, but had not effaced its laws. They acknowledged a judgment to come, but their notions were confused concerning its nature.

Such were the principles of Felix, or rather, such were the imperfections of his principles, when he heard this discourse of St. Paul. You may infer his fears from his character. Figure to yourselves a man hearing for the first time the maxims of equity and righteousness inculcated in the Gospel. Figure to yourselves a man who heard corrected the immorality of pagan theology; what was doubtful, illustrated; and what was right, enforced. See a man, who knew of no other God but the incestuous Jupiter, the lascivious Venus, taught that he must appear before Him, in whose presence the seraphim veil their faces, and the heavens are not clean. Behold a man, whose notions were confused concerning the state of souls after death, apprised that God shall judge the world in righteousness. See a man, who saw described the smoke, the fire, the chains of darkness, the outer darkness, the lake of fire and brimstone; and who saw them delineated by one animated by the Spirit of God. What consternation must have been excited by these terrific truths!

This we are incapable adequately to comprehend. We must surmount the insensibility acquired by custom. It is but too true that our hearts,—instead of being impressed by these truths, in proportion to their discussion—our hearts are the more obdurate. We hear them without alarm, having so frequently heard them before. But if, like Felix, we had been brought up in the darkness of paganism, and if another Paul had come and opened our eyes, and unveiled those sacred terrors, how exceedingly should we have feared! This was the case with Felix. He perceived the bandage which conceals the sight of futurity drop in a moment. He heard St. Paul, that herald of grace and ambassador to the Gentiles, he heard him reason on temperance and a judgment to come. His soul was amazed; his heart trembled; his knees smote one against another.

Amazing effects, my brethren, of conscience! evident argument of the vanity of those gods, whom idolatry adorns, after it has given them form! Jupiter and Mercury, it is true, had their altars in the temples of the heathens; but the God of heaven and earth has His tribunal in the heart: and, while idolatry presents its incense to sacrilegious and incestuous deities, the God of heaven and earth reveals His terrors to the conscience, and there loudly condemns both incest and sacrilege.

Secondly, consider Felix as a prince; and you will find in this second office a second cause of his fear. When we perceive the great men of the earth devoid of every principle of religion, and even ridiculing those very truths which are the objects of our faith, we feel that faith to waver. They excite a certain suspicion in the mind that our sentiments are only prejudices, which have become rooted in man, brought up in the obscurity of humble life. Here is the apology of religion. The Caligulas, the Neros, those potentates of the universe, have trembled in their turn as well as the meanest of their subjects. This independence of mind, so conspicuous among libertines, is consequently an art,—not of disengaging themselves from prejudices, but of shutting their eyes against the light, and of extinguishing the purest sentiments of the heart. Felix, educated in a court, fraught with the maxims of the great, instantly ridicules the Apostle's preaching. St. Paul, undismayed, attacks him, and finds a conscience concealed in his bosom: the very dignity of Felix is constrained to aid our Apostle, by adding weight to his ministry. He demolishes the edifice of Felix's pride. He shows that if a great nation was dependent on his pleasure, he himself was dependent on a Sovereign in whose presence the kings of the earth are as nothing. He proves that dignities are so very far from exempting men from the judgment of God, that, for this very reason, their account becomes the more weighty, riches being a trust which Heaven has committed to the great: and "where much is given, much is required." He makes him feel this awful truth, that princes are responsible, not only for their own souls, but also for those of their subjects; their good or bad example influencing, for the most part, the people committed to their care.

See then Felix in one moment deprived of his tribunal. The judge became a party. He saw himself rich and in need of nothing; and yet he was "blind, and naked, and poor." He heard a voice from the God of the whole earth, saying unto him, "Thou profane and wicked prince, remove the diadem, and take off the crown. I will overturn, overturn, overturn it, and it shall be no more" (Ezekiel 21:25, 26). "Though thou exalt thyself as the eagle, and though thou set thy nest among the stars, thence will I bring thee down, saith the Lord" (Obadiah 4). Neither the dignity of governor, nor the favor of Caesar, nor all the glory of empire shall deliver thee out of My hand.

Thirdly, I restrict myself, my brethren, as much as possible, in order to execute without exceeding my limits, the plan I have conceived; and proceed to consider Felix as an avaricious man: to find in this disposition a further cause of his fear. Felix was avaricious, and St. Paul instantly transported him into a world in which avarice shall receive its appropriate and most severe punishment. For you know that the grand test by which we shall be judged is charity. "I was hungry, and ye gave me meat"; and of all the obstructions of charity, covetousness is the most obstinate and insurmountable.

This unhappy propensity renders us insensible of our neighbor's necessities. It magnifies the estimate of our wants: it diminishes the wants of others. It persuades us that we have need of all, that others have need of nothing. Felix began to perceive the iniquity of this passion, and to feel that he was guilty of double idolatry: idolatry in morality, idolatry in religion; idolatry in having offered incense to gods, who were not the makers of heaven and earth; idolatry in having offered incense to mammon. For the Scriptures teach, and experience confirms, that "covetousness is idolatry." The covetous man is not a worshipper of the true God. Gold and silver are the divinities he adores. His heart is with his treasure. Here then is the portrait of Felix: a portrait drawn by St. Paul in the presence of Felix, and which reminded this prince of innumerable prohibitions, innumerable frauds, innumerable extortions; of the widow and the orphan he oppressed. Here is the cause of Felix's fears. According to an expression of St. James, the "rust of his gold and silver began to witness against him, and to eat his flesh as with fire" (James 5:3).

Fourthly, consider Felix as a voluptuous man. Here is the final cause of his fear. Without repeating all we have said on the depravity of this passion, let one remark suffice, that, if the torments of hell are terrible at all, they must especially be so to the voluptuous. The voluptuous man never restricts his sensual gratification; his soul dies on the slightest approach of pain. What a terrific impression must not the thought of judgment make on such a character! Shall I, accustomed to indulgence and pleasure, become a prey to the worm that dieth not, and fuel to the fire which is not quenched? Shall I, who avoid pain with so much caution, be condemned to eternal torments? Shall I have neither delicious meats, nor voluptuous delights? This body, my idol, which I habituate to so much delicacy, shall it be "cast into the lake of fire and brimstone, whose smoke ascendeth up forever and ever?" And this effeminate habit I have of refining on pleasure, will it render me only the more sensible of my destruction and anguish?

Such are the traits of Felix's character; such are the causes of Felix's fear. Happy, if his fear had produced that "godly sorrow, and that repentance unto salvation not to be repented of." Happy, if the fear of hell had induced him to avoid its torments. But, ah no! he feared, and yet persisted in the causes of his fear. He trembled, yet said to St. Paul, "Go thy way for this time." This is our last reflection.

How preposterous, my brethren, is the sinner! What absurdities does he cherish in his heart! For, in short, had the doctrines St. Paul preached to Felix been the productions of his brain:—had the thought of a future judgment been a chimera, whence proceeded the fears of Felix? Why was he so weak as to admit this panic of terror? If, on the contrary, Paul had truth and argument on his side, why did Felix send him away? Such are the contradictions of the sinner. He wishes; he revolts; he denies; he grants; he trembles; and says, "Go thy way for this time." Speak to him concerning the truths of religion, open hell to his view, and you will see him affected, devout, and appalled:

follow him in life, and you will find that these truths have no influence whatever on his conduct.

But are we not mistaken concerning Felix? Did not the speech of St. Paul make a deeper impression upon him than we seem to allow? He sent the Apostle away, it is true, but it was "for this time" only. And who can censure this delay? We cannot be always recollected and retired. The infirmities of human nature require relaxation and repose. Felix could afterward recall him. "Go thy way for this time; when I have a convenient season, I will send for thee."

It pains me, I confess, my brethren, in entering on this head of my discourse, that I should exhibit to you in the person of Felix, the portrait of whom? Of wicked men? Alas! of nearly the whole of this assembly; most of whom seem to us living in negligence and vice, running with the children of this world "to the same excess of riot." One would suppose that they had already made their choice, having embraced one or the other of these notions: either that religion is a phantom, or that, all things considered, it is better to endure the torments pf hell, than to be restricted to the practice of virtue. Oh no! that is not their notion. Ask the worse among them. Ask whether they have renounced their salvation. You will not find an individual who will say that he has renounced it. Ask them again, whether they think it attainable by following this way of life. They will answer, No. Ask them afterward, how they reconcile things so opposite as their life and their hopes. They will answer that they are resolved to reform, and by and bye they will enter on the work. They will say, as Felix said to St. Paul, "Go thy way for this time; when I have a convenient season, I will call for thee." Nothing is less wise than this delay. At a future period I will reform! But who has assured me that at a future period I shall have opportunities of conversion? Who has assured me that God will continue to call me, and that another Paul shall thunder in my ears?

I will reform at a future period! But who has told me that God at a future period will accompany His word with the powerful aids of grace? While Paul may plant and Apollos may water, is it not God who gives the increase? How then can I flatter myself that the Holy Spirit will continue to knock at the door of my heart, after I shall have so frequently obstructed His admission?

I will reform in future! But who has told me that I shall ever desire to be converted? Do not habits become confirmed in proportion as they are indulged? And is not an inveterate evil very difficult to cure? If I cannot bear the excision of a slight gangrene, how shall I sustain the operation when the wound is deep?

I will reform in future! But who has told me that I shall live to a future period? Does not death advance every moment with gigantic strides? Does he not assail the prince in his palace, and the peasant in his cottage? Does he not send before him monitors and messengers: acute pains, which wholly absorb the soul; deliriums, which render reason of no avail; deadly stupors, which benumb the brightest and most piercing geniuses? And what is still more awful, does he not daily come without either warning or messenger? Does he not snatch away this man without allowing him time to be acquainted with the essentials of religion; and that man, without the restitution of riches ill-acquired; and the other, before he is reconciled to his enemy?

Instead of saying, "Go thy way for this time," we should say, Stay for this time. Stay, while the Holy Spirit is knocking at the door of my heart; stay, while my conscience is alarmed; stay, while I yet live; "while it is called today." The arguments confounded my conscience: no matter. "Thy hand is heavy upon me": no matter still. Cut, strike, consume; provided it procure my salvation.

But, however criminal this delay may be, we seem desirous to excuse it. "Go thy way for this time; when I have a convenient season, I will call for thee." It was Felix's business then which induced him to put off the Apostle. Unhappy business! Awful occupation! It seems an enviable situation, my brethren, to be placed at the head of a province; to speak in the language of majesty; to decide on the fortunes of a numerous people; and in all cases to be the ultimate judge. But those situations, so happy and so dazzling in appearance, are in the main dangerous to the conscience! Those innumerable concerns, this noise and bustle, entirely dissipate the soul. While so much engaged on earth, we cannot be mindful of heaven. When we have no leisure, we say to St. Paul, "Go thy way for this time; when I have a convenient season, I will call for thee."

Happy he, who, amid the tumult of the most active life, has hours consecrated to reflection, to the examination of his conscience, and to ensure the "one thing needful"! Or rather, happy he, who, in the repose of the middle classes of society,—placed between indigence and affluence, far from the courts of the great, having neither poverty nor riches according to Agur's wish,—can in retirement and quietness see life sweetly glide away, and make salvation, if not the sole, yet his principal, concern!

Felix not only preferred his business to his salvation, but he mentions it with evasive disdain. "When I have a convenient season, I will call for thee." "When I have a convenient season!" Might we not thence infer that the truths discussed by St. Paul were not of serious importance? Might we not infer that the soul of Felix was created for the government of Judea; and that the grand doctrines of righteousness, temperance, and a judgment to come, ought to serve at most but to pass away the time, or merely to engross one's leisure—"when I have a convenient season?" . . .

Yes, Christians, this is the only moment on which we can reckon. It is, perhaps, the only acceptable time. It is, perhaps, the last day of our visitation. Let us improve a period so precious. Let us no longer say, by and bye—at another time; but let us say today—this moment—even now. Let the pastor say: I have been insipid in my sermons, and remiss in my conduct; having been more solicitous, during the exercise of my ministry, to advance my family, than to build up the Lord's house. I will preach hereafter with fervor and zeal. I will be vigilant, sober, rigorous, and disinterested. Let the miser say: I have riches ill-acquired. I will purge my house of illicit wealth. I will overturn the altar of mammon, and erect another to the Supreme Jehovah. Let the prodigal say: I will extinguish the unhappy fires by which I am consumed, and kindle in my bosom the flame of divine love. Ah, unhappy passions, which war against my soul: sordid attachments; irregular propensities; emotions of concupiscence; law in the members,—! will know you no more. I will make with you an eternal divorce, I will from this moment open my heart to the Eternal Wisdom, who condescends to ask it.

If we are in this happy disposition, if we thus become regenerate, we shall enjoy from this moment foretastes of the glory, which God has prepared. From this moment the truths of religion, so far from casting discouragement and terror on the soul, shall heighten its consolation and joy; from this moment, heaven shall open to this audience, paradise shall descend into your hearts, and the Holy Spirit shall come and dwell there. He will bring that peace, and those joys, which pass all understanding. And, commencing our felicity on earth, He will give us the earnest of His consummation. God grant us the grace! To Him, the Father, Son, and Holy Spirit, be honor and glory, now and ever. Amen.

ANTONIO VIEYRA

Antonio Vieyra was born at Lisbon, February 6, 1608. At the age of six he was taken by his parents to Brazil, where he was educated. He entered the Jesuit order in 1623, and made his profession in 1644. As a young man he was so proficient in his studies, and had attained such a reputation for learning and elegance of style, that at the age of seventeen he was commissioned to write the annual letter from the province of Brazil. He very early became famous as a preacher and in 1640 was sent to Portugal as chaplain to the embassy. Here he was employed in political negotiations at Amsterdam, Paris, and Rome. In Rome he preached with great success in Italian. He returned, however, to Brazil in the fulfilment of a vow that he would devote himself to missions among the Indians. He soon saw that nothing could be done until they were enfranchised, and to effect this he returned to Portugal, where, by his unaided solicitations, he was successful. He once more took up the work with the greatest success. In 1670 he was again in Portugal and Rome, and on his return he was put at the head of all the Jesuit missions in Brazil. His last years were spent in Bahia, where he died July 18, 1697. "He may surely be considered one of the most remarkable characters that Europe ever produced, when, in the three utterly different characters of an eloquent preacher, an able negotiator, and a devoted missionary, he obtained a first-rate reputation in two continents." (Neale.)

Vieyra has been compared to the mediaeval preachers, and for that reason Neale includes him in his work on mediaeval preaching. The same reasons that rendered St. Francis de Sales in many respects an echo of the great mediaeval preachers were operative in the case of Vieyra. He was at his best in satire, and was terrible in threatening the divine vengeance against sinners. For this reason his Advent sermons are fearfully sublime. He was weaker in pathetic passages.

The sermons of Vieyra were first published in Madrid under the author's direction in thirteen volumes, 1679-1690. Two other volumes appeared in 1710 and 1748, respectively. They have since been reprinted. A French translation of a number of his sermons has been published, and is easily obtainable. An account of Vieyra may be found in Hoefer, *Nouvelle Biographic Génératе*.

SERMON ON THE GREAT EVIL OF SIN

by Antonio Vieyra

The text of the following sermon by Vieyra is "Go and sin no more" (St. John 8:11). It was first preached at Bahia, Brazil, on the fourth Sunday in Lent, 1640. It seems to have been a favorite with the author, for he introduces it with the following preface: "The author entreats those who may take this book into their hands, that, for the love of God and themselves, they would read this sermon of the sinner resolute to sin no more, with the attention and patience which the matter requires."

GOD, in His Divine Mind, has appointed a certain measure to the sins of every man, which, while it is not yet full, may be consistent with the hope of pardon; but after it has once been fulfilled, there is no longer any remedy. The first time that God revealed this secret of His providence and justice, was with respect to the sins of kingdoms, republics, and cities. He had promised Abraham that to him and to his seed He would give the land of the Amorites; but not at once; there must be an interval of many years. In the fourth generation they shall come hither again, for the iniquity of the Amorites is not yet full. And this was one of the reasons why the children of Israel journeyed for so long a time in the wilderness, before they crossed the river Jordan; in order that, in the meanwhile, the measure of the sins of the Amorites might be filled up. This also was the sense in which Christ our Lord spoke to the scribes and to the Pharisees: "Fill ye up, then, the measure of your fathers!" because in political bodies such as our States, which endure through many lives, the sins of fathers, children, and grandchildren all concur to fill up the measure. . . .

God most manifestly teaches and declares, says Augustine, that to each man He has appointed a certain amount or number of sins; that, while it is not yet full and consummated, He waits, that we may be converted; but, as soon as the measure is full, and the number has reached its limit, then God waits no longer, and condemnation, without remedy, follows. . . .

Nor is there any difficulty in the consideration that this measure of sin is greater for one man and less for another; for this very fact, which to our weak understanding might appear injustice, in the wise decrees of the Divine Providence is the highest justice. If not, answer me this: God also sets a certain measure to the days of each man's life. Whence David says: "Behold, Thou hast made my days as it were a span long." And this measure is so certain and determined, that, when its last day is come, there is no further escape. As Job speaks: "Thou hast set them their bounds; which they cannot pass." Since, then, no one thinks it strange, or complains that the measure of one man's days is so much less than that of another's, much less should it seem strange that the measure of sin should also be unequal, especially when we consider that one, and that the very first, sin is enough to cause God, if He judged us according to strict justice, to cast us into hell. The reason is the supreme dominion of God, who is equally the Author of grace and of nature; and thus, since, so far as He is the Author of nature, He can limit life to a certain number of days, without injustice to the individual man, so, without injustice to the same man, can He limit His pardon to a certain number of sins. Whence it follows, as that day which fills up the number of all our days is necessarily the last, and when it has arrived, die you must—so, in like manner, that sin which has filled up the number of your sins is also the last; and, once committed, it leaves you no escape from the condemnation, because there is no longer any place for pardon.

Hear what God says by the mouth of the Prophet Amos: "Thus saith the Lord, For three trangressions of Judah, and for four, I will not turn away the punishment thereof; for three transgressions of Israel, and for four, I will not turn away the punishment thereof." It is as if He said: They committed the first sin, and I pardoned them; they committed the second, and I pardoned them; they committed the third, and I also pardoned them; but because they committed the fourth, I will pardon them no more. What! does God, whose mercies are infinite, forgive no more than three sins? Surely He does. He forgives three hundred, He forgives three thousand; and, if the sinner repents with all his heart, He will forgive three million. But in these texts a certain is put for an uncertain number, in order that, by particular example, the meaning may be made more clear. Taking four, therefore, as the final measure of sin, God says that He will pardon the first time, the second time, and the third time; but that, after the fourth sin, there is no more place for conversion or for pardon; because the fourth sin is in this case that which fills up the measure, and the sin which fills up the measure is without remedy and without forgiveness.

Hence we may easily understand a most difficult passage in the First Epistle of St. John; and it is a proof of that which I assert. The words of the holy Apostle, called above all others the Divine, are these: "If any man sees his brother sin a sin which is not unto death, he shall ask, and He shall give him life for them that sin not unto death. There is a sin unto death: I do not say that he shall pray for it." The difficulty of this text is so great, that expositors and theologians are divided into more than fifteen opinions as to what this sin is which is called to death; and for which we are not to pray, as being incapable of pardon, irremissible, remediless. Some say that it is the sin of murder; others, that of adultery; and St. Augustine and Bede do not hesitate to affirm that it is that of envy. But because these offences do not seem so enormously great, others, ascending higher, say that it is the sin of blasphemy; others, that of infidelity; others, that of apostasy; others, that of obstinacy; and others, without defining the species, say in general that it is any prodigious crime. But, against all these opinions, it is to be held for certain that there is no sin, howsoever most grievous it may be, that God does not pardon. It is no particular crime, nothing of its own nature more enormous than any mortal sin,—nay, and it may be of far lighter dye than some of the above named: it is the last; it is that which fills up the measure appointed to every man; and St. John, therefore, with propriety, calls it a sin unto death,—a sin which, without remedy, delivers the soul to eternal destruction. For although every mortal sin slays the soul, it may be raised up again, and restored to life, subsequently to others, but not subsequently to this.

Having laid down, then, this so certain truth, and this proceeding of Providence and Divine justice, so many times revealed by God Himself, see, now, if there be any motive for each of us, more efficacious, more powerful, and more terrible, why a man who has common sense, and a Christian who has faith, should not only more firmly resolve against sin, but should not even be able to dare to think of its commission. Go, and sin no more. Other motives leave some hope after sin: this uproots it and cuts it off so completely, that only he who is resolved on damnation and determined to go to hell, can again dare to sin. For if I know that God has appointed me a certain number, and marked me out a certain measure, of sins; and if I know that, the number completed and the measure filled, there is no more place for repentance, who can assure me that the sin which I am now meditating may not be the last, and that which alone is wanting to make my measure complete? You will say that as it may be, so it may also not be, the last. What then? What then! As if I had intended to finish my sermon here, and to dismiss you with this question! You shall hear, to impress you more, what God does at that very point of time in which a man, by his last sin, fills up his number.

That which God then does is either to slay the sinner at once, or to leave him and forsake him forever. See how each alternative is equally terrible: either to go to hell at once, or to go some time hence; but to go infallibly. As to the first: that God instantly deprives the sinner of his life, it is the express declaration of St. Augustine. . . . Thus it happened to King Belshazzar, whose sentence of death appeared to him written on the wall while he was at the banquet. The first word was, "He hath numbered"; for God had counted up the sins of Belshazzar; and, as in that night, and in that hour, he committed the last sin which accomplished the number which God had determined to allow him, in that very hour came forth the fingers of a man's hand, and wrote; and in that night was Belshazzar, King of the Chaldeans, slain.

How many times this is seen, though not understood around us! This very night such an one has been murdered, going from such a place to such another place; and how many nights had he gone and returned in safety? Many. Why, then, was he not slain then, but now? His offences against God and his sins against man were the same, and equally open; why, then, did God bear with them—why did not man avenge them—till this day and till this hour? Because his antecedent sins went on filling up his measure; that of this day and this hour made it absolutely complete. The same thing happens in sudden death and unexpected accidents, though they may appear natural, and in other disasters which seem fortuitous; they, for the most part, are the effect and execution of the last sin, which, joining itself to the others, and heaped up upon them, accomplishes the measure. ... Job says that the sinner shall die before he fulfils his day; and the cause is no other but this, that he accomplishes all his sins before he has accomplished all his years. And who, then, can assure you, who at this day and at this hour are living and in health, that the first sin which you determine to commit shall not also be your last? That Israelite and that Midianitish woman, whom the zeal of Phineas slew in actual sin, very little thought that in that act their life would end, as has happened to many others. But as that sin alone was wanting to fill the measure of both, life and sin and all were concluded together; to the end that all may fear and tremble to sin again, not knowing whether that sin may not be their last.

But suppose that life is not ended at the same moment in which the last sin is committed,—which was the other alternative,—those who have filled up their measure are in no whit better a condition; because, seeing that they are left by God, the days which remain to them serve no other purpose but to increase their damnation. "Woe to them when I depart from them," says God by the Prophet Hosea. Oh, if men could understand the full meaning of a woe pronounced by God! What a high, what a deep woe it is! so high, that it reaches to heaven, whence the sinner is cast out, and of which he is disinherited forever; so deep, that it penetrates even to the abysses of hell, where the sinner will be thrown and reserved under chains, to burn as long as God is God. To this woe infinite woes will reply through all eternity; but woes of grief without repentance, woes of torment without alleviation, woes of despair without remedy. Before this, one woe of true contrition would have sufficed, and God would have pardoned every sin; but after the measure is full, and the soul is left by God, these woes shall no longer have any place, or shall be without fruit, because no one can be converted to God without God. How can the soul return to God, if He has already left it? . . . St. Isidore says: "When God, by His secret and just judgments, leaves a soul, immediately the devil takes possession of it for its eternal perdition; because, to say that God leaves it, is to say that it is delivered to Satan." . . .

This is that most miserable estate of final impenitence, consummated in the next life, but commenced in this. Oh, how many condemned men are still living and walking among us, not absolutely because they could not, but because they will not, be converted! They are bound by the sins of which they have filled up the measure. They think that they shall loose themselves from the last, as perhaps they have loosed themselves from others; but they are deceived by their own fancy, as Samson was. Three times Samson broke the fetters with which the Philistines sought to bind him; but when the fourth time came, and his hair had been cut off, Scripture notes that he awoke and said, "I will go out as at other times before, and shake myself"; and he wist not that the Lord was departed from him. Because God had left Samson, he loosed himself no more; the Philistines took him, and put out his eyes, and made him grind in the prison. The same thing happens to the soul when left by God: the devils seize it and take possession of it; they put out its eyes, so that it remains blind, obstinate, and impenitent; and they take it to grind in the mill of hell. . . .

Oh, would to the Divine Majesty and mercy that this heavenly lesson might be so imprinted on—might so penetrate into—our souls, that from this hour, from this moment, we might most constantly resolve never to sin again, neither for advantage, nor pleasure, nor fear, nor any accident or event of life or death! See who it is that tells you to sin, and who it is that tells you not to sin. That which tells you to sin may be the world, may be the devil, may be the flesh; three capital enemies, who only desire and contrive your eternal condemnation. And He that tells you not to sin is that same God who, after giving you your existence, made Himself Man for love of you,—is that God and Man who, only that He might save you and make you eternally blessed, shrank not from suffering so many torments and insults, and from dying, nailed upon a cross. This so mighty Lord, this so wise Counsellor, this so true and so faithful friend—He it is who tells you not to sin: *Iam amplius noli peccare.*

Consider well these words of the most loving Jesus, that they are not only sufficient to persuade, but also to soften any man that has a heart: *Iam amplius*: no more. Let it suffice, O Christian, redeemed with My own blood, let it suffice that thou hast already sinned so much; let it suffice that thou hast lived without Lord, without reason, without conscience, without soul. Let that suffice in which thou hast already offended Me; let that suffice in which thou hast already despised Me; let that suffice in which thou hast already crucified Me. If thou hast no compassion on Me, at least have compassion on thyself; I say it out of love to thee. If it is not enough that I command thee to sin no more, I entreat thee, I beseech thee, I set forth to thee not only My will, but I invoke all the powers of thine own: *Noli, noli peccare.* In thy hand, in thy power, in thy will, rests thine own salvation, if thou desirest it; that thou may'st see what, blindness, what folly, what unhappiness, what misery, what eternal confusion, what irremediable grief will be thine, if, by thine own choice, and for the sake of not resisting a sin, thou condemnest thyself. If thou wert already in hell, whither thou art so furiously running, and where thou wouldst now be burning if I had not restrained My justice, what would be thy condition now? And' if at this very hour I were to offer thee deliverance from hell, and the kingdom of heaven, only on the condition that thou wouldst never sin again, what wouldst thou do, and what thanks wouldst thou render? If, then, through My mercy and loving-kindness, thou art still in life, why not, in all earnestness and forever, take the same resolution? Why not deliver thyself from eternal evil, and secure eternal good? Why not gain the crown and the kingdom of heaven, and make thyself forever blessed? And all this by having a determination so excellent, so useful, yea, and so delightful, as that of never sinning again. Put an end, put an end to being thine own enemy; put an end to offending Him who loves thee so dearly; put an end to choosing hell without Me, rather than glory with Me: *lam ampltus noli peccare.*

22388298R00140

Printed in Great Britain
by Amazon